Now We Read, We See, We Speak

Portrait of Literacy Development in an Adult Freirean-Based Class

Now We Read, We See, We Speak

Portrait of Literacy Development in an Adult Freirean-Based Class

Victoria Purcell-Gates
Michigan State University

Robin A. Waterman
*Adams County School District 14,
Commerce City, Colorado*

LAWRENCE ERLBAUM ASSOCIATES, PUBLISHERS
2000   Mahwah, New Jersey   London

Lawrence Erlbaum Associates, Inc., Publishers
10 Industrial Avenue
Mahwah, NJ 07430

Cover design by Kathryn Houghtaling Lacey

Cover photos:
Left: Deonicia and Francisca working together on a text in the
literacy class.
Right: Margarita and Chunga thinking and writing during one
of the literacy classes held inside the artesan workshop—the
classroom space during the rainy season.
(Photos by Robin A. Waterman)

Library of Congress Cataloging-in-Publication Data

Purcell-Gates, Victoria.
Now we read, we see, we speak : portrait of literacy development in
   an adult Freirean-based class / Victoria Purcell-Gates, Robin
   Waterman.
      p. cm.
Includes bibliographical references and index.
ISBN 0-8058-3469-9 (cloth : alk. paper) — ISBN 0-8058-3470-2 (pbk. :
   alk. paper)
1. Functional literacy—El Salvador—Case studies. 2. Literacy programs
   —El Salvador—Case studies. 3. Critical pedagogy—El Salvador
   —Case studies. 4. Freire, Paulo, 1921-1997.   I. Waterman, Robin.
   II. Title.

LC155.S22 P87   2000
302.2'244 —dc21   99-058535
                                                         CIP

Books published by Lawrence Erlbaum Associates
are printed on acid-free paper, and their bindings are
chosen for strength and durability.

Printed in the United States of America
10   9   8   7   6   5   4   3

*To the Women
of the Papaturro Literacy Class*

Contents

Preface

GOALS AND CONTRIBUTIONS

This is a book for teachers, teacher educators, and researchers who are interested in, and curious about, Freirean literacy instruction. It focuses on adult literacy and adult literacy issues, but we believe that many of the resulting insights and highlighted principles are relevant to literacy learners of all ages, as well as their teachers. While it is most definitely not a "how to" book, it does provide a detailed and lively portrait of one teacher's implementation of principles gleaned from Freire and process-based literacy theory in an adult women's literacy class in the *campo* (rural area) of El Salvador. Up-close studies of teaching and learning in process, such as this one, provide important concrete examples for teachers who are on their own journeys of development and change, and it is our desire that this book make such a contribution.

For those educators and theorists already quite familiar with Freire's theories and with critical literacy practice, this book provides a slightly different lens for your consideration. This is the lens of sociopsycholinguistic literacy development, a lens that has been for the most part employed outside of a critical theoretical arena. It is our contention that this fact does not make the sociopsycholinguistic lens noncritical, per se. Rather, our stance is that it is possible, and theoretically informative, to synthesize this lens with that of a Freirean one to explain literacy development in ways that incorporate cognitive, linguistic, and social perspectives along with, or within, Freirean critical perspectives.

No book can do everything, and this is certainly true about this one. It is important to note, particularly for Freirean theorists and educators who are currently active in further exploration and development of Freirean theory and practice, that the analysis in this book is not intended to push the theoretical envelope. Neither of us, as authors, are prepared for or interested in such an undertaking. Rather, our contribution is to explore Freirean-influenced practice from a sociopsycholinguistic lens and to provide a detailed description of one Freirean-influenced literacy class for those who are still trying to understand what such a class could look like in action.

The 18-month ethnographic study of a women's literacy class in rural El Salvador, from which this book results, was a research collaboration between the university-based researcher, Victoria Purcell-Gates, and Robin Waterman, the on-site teacher of the class and director of the regional literacy program, *El Moviemento de las Mujeres de Cuscatlán*. Our intention was to carefully document, reflect on, and analyze the Freirean-based methodology Robin utilized, in order to arrive at a deeper understanding of the methodological implications of Freirean theory. We wanted to gain telling insights into how people learn to read and write in a program that focuses on achieving awareness and knowledge of the nature of one's own oppression and ways to act to achieve liberation and social justice. In other words, using what we know about how people learn to read and write—cognitively, linguistically, socially, and developmentally—what relationships can we see between the developmental processes involved in becoming literate and the essential aspects of Freirean-inspired curriculum.

To our knowledge, no one before has studied in-depth, with systematic data collection, a Freirean-based literacy program through a sociopsycholinguistic literacy development lens. We sought to see and understand for ourselves how these adult learners learned to read and write as they transacted with the Freirean curriculum: What happens? How does literacy development occur? What are the relationships between the Freirean components of the program and the literacy development of the learners? We strongly believe that educators need access to data-based insights such as these in order to most effectively inform the fashioning of Freirean programs addressing literacy problems in the United States.

There are several descriptions of Freirean literacy programs available, but none of them focus primarily on the literacy development that takes place within them. Most of these accounts are focused on the need for such programs for marginalized populations, and they view education and educational issues within a sociopolitical frame. Literacy development is defined as the ability to think critically, and reading and writing are seen as reading and writing one's world.

The development of the cognitive and linguistic abilities to read and write within this frame is yet to be explored and explained. This leaves educators who are not primarily critical theorists, or are primarily literacy development researchers–practitioners, unclear about what critical pedagogy says to them or ways in which critical pedagogy can be relevant to their work.

For teachers who consider themselves critical educators, a close look at the cognitive aspects of learning to read and write within a critical frame can also be informative and, we believe, crucial to the mission of critical literacy education. If students are to claim their own agency and act in such ways that the power imbalance between themselves and the current powerholders is erased, they must, in today's society, learn to read and write. Many teachers who are sympathetic to critical literacy principles and committed to social change have little understanding of how learners actually go about learning to read and to write. Nor do they have a clear understanding of what they, as teachers, can do to help their students do this. We believe that this study will contribute to this need.

Literacy is, as always, a "hot" issue. Given issues of increased marginalization, impoverishment, and alienation between social classes in the world, as well as politicization of literacy and literacy instruction, we feel that this report is highly significant at this time and will be a welcome contribution to the field of education and literacy.

ETHNOGRAPHIC APPROACH

An ethnographic design is best suited for inquiries such as this one because it allows the researchers to examine an intact phenomenon—in this case a Freirean-based literacy class—within all of the relevant contexts. The goal of an ethnography is to construct a description of a total cultural phenomenon from the insider's perspective and to examine all of the interrelationships of factors as they occur naturally within the phenomenon (Goetz & LeCompte, 1984; Spradley & McCurdy, 1972).

Because ethnography as a scientific discipline admits the subjective biases and perceptions of the researcher (Goetz & LeCompte, 1984), we believe that any report of an ethnography must provide the reader with a clear statement of who the researchers are, particularly in regards to areas that would affect their theoretical lens, their motivations, their collection of data, and their interpretations. In this way, the reader is better prepared to make sense of the study as conducted and accommodate the researchers' final interpretations into the results of other studies. Ultimately, a study such as this is one of interpretation; thus, it is essential that the reader "know" the interpreters as much as possible. For this purpose, in Appendix A, we each share our own history and stance in relation to the study. We urge the reader to read this description and the following Appendix B on Methodology before beginning chapter 1 to forestall questions that will inevitably arise during the course of reading about such a complex and complicated study.

While ethnography precludes conclusions of a causal nature, it provides the kind of detail and depth of understanding that may eventually lead to experimental designs, if and when that becomes a significant goal. However, our interest at this point was not to decide whether literacy programs that reflect Freirean tenets are better than, or more effective than, those that do not. We did, however, want to understand just what is a Freirean-based program; what are some of its characteristic methodologies? One conclusion we came to early in the study is that we can only describe what could be a Freirean- based literacy program; there is no single, true Freirean literacy program. Freire presented multilayered philosophies of education that inherently preclude the possibility of one singular methodology; there can only be individual instantiations of Freirean precepts, contextualized by different settings, players, histories, and purposes. Thus, what the reader will find herein is our description and analysis of one Freirean-based literacy program, situated, studied, and analyzed in multilayered contexts and through a literacy development lens. We then apply our findings from this study to a U.S. context (and, at times, a world-based context) to speculate upon ways in which our resultant insights might inform adult literacy issues more generally.

INSIGHTS FOR ADULT EDUCATION

An especially useful feature of this book, we believe, is the connection we draw between our interpretations of the data from this one case study of a Freirean-based literacy class and larger issues and conundrums facing the field of adult literacy in the United States and elsewhere. The reader will find chapter–by–chapter discussions of adult education issues as well as a concluding chapter devoted to this purpose. In the presentation of the results of our analysis, following the chapters devoted to contextualizing the research site, we structure each chapter around final themes. Following our portrayal of each of the themes that emerge from the El Salvador data, we apply the theme to the more general field of adult education to conclude each of these chapters. We pull this all together in chapter 9 and muse further on the ways in which insights gleaned from this study can help stimulate ideas for improving adult literacy education and thus begin to truly provide transformative and liberative opportunities for adult students.

ORGANIZATION OF CHAPTERS

The content in this book is structured to reflect methodological requirements of an ethnography, situating the data source—the literacy class—within its many layers of context before reporting on the results of our analyses.

Part I: Contexts

Chapter 1: "Adult Literacy and Paulo Freire: A Lens for Hope"   In this chapter, we present an overview of adult literacy concerns and issues as well as the data that demonstrates the intransigent relationship between literacy achievement and social and political empowerment, oppression, and marginalization. We also present a summary of Freire's theory and work in the area of literacy and liberation in developing countries as well as applications people have made between his work and current conditions and issues in developed countries such as the United States. Finally, we present the rationale and focus for our research.

Chapter 2: "Revolutionary Struggle and Literacy: Historical Context"
In this chapter we present the historical context for the study. We describe the roots of the poverty and oppression suffered by the participants in the study, the resulting civil war and the atrocities they experienced, and the ways in which literacy and literacy acquisition became both a political and a personal quest during this time. We take the reader from the time before the war up to the recent establishment of the community where the literacy class was held. Within this, we describe the social and political make-up of the community.

Chapter 3: "A Literacy Class Takes Shape: Eight Women's Literacy Histories and Motivations"   This chapter details the establishment of the literacy class and introduces the main characters: the eight women who were our primary informants. This introduction includes their literacy histories and their motivations for participating in the basic literacy class. All of the women were essentially nonliterate at the beginning of the study. We end with the first "Insights" section, commenting on how issues that arose in the establishment of the class reflect similar issues in adult education in other countries and other settings.

Part II: The Literacy Class

Chapter 4: "The Literacy Class: Engaging With Social Reality and Print to Effect Change"   We begin with a typical literacy class session and then illustrate and motivate each of the elements of the class. Throughout this chapter and the following ones, we describe and illustrate the ways in which literacy instruction and learning transact with Freirean theory and principles. We employ the voices and the writings of the women and of Robin, reporting from the site, as much as possible. We conclude with the "Insights" section, commenting on issues of curriculum and process. We relate our findings to current issues in literacy such as balanced instruction, learner-centered curriculum, and whole–part–whole literacy learning. We also discuss the issue of dialogical relationships between teachers and students, bringing in some of the latest research in the adult education field on this topic.

Chapter 5: "Learning Through Dialogue: Reading and Writing the World" This chapter presents our primary conclusion: the success of the students in learning to read and write can be explained by their heightened engagement by and in the entire process. Primarily this involves their increased motivation to read and write due to their involvement in discussing and coming to understand their sociopolitical realities, but it also includes their involvement in a kind of process reading and writing which furthered their thinking and expression on these issues. To illustrate how this happened in the class, we present several selected oral dialogues and their subsequent written counterparts. In the "Insights" section, we call on Engagement Theory as it applies to literacy development to explain our conclusion.

Chapter 6: "The Language of the People: Issues of Language and Power" In this chapter we focus on issues of language and power. We describe how Robin used the language of her students as the base of her instruction. We defend our conclusion that such pedagogy is necessary to ensure (a) that learners understand the connection between language and print, and (b) that learners engage with print to the degree needed for further literacy development. We also address the need to progress beyond one's personal language knowledge to being able to read and write the language of others, albeit critically. As an illustration for teachers, we describe the ways in which Robin facilitated this. In the "Insights" section, we discuss how this issue of language and power plays out in the ways we think about programs for adults and in curricular choices that teachers must make.

Chapter 7: "Dialogic Practice: The Teacher as Student and the Student as Teacher"   This chapter focuses on the issue of power relations between teachers and students. We describe the ways in which Robin came to know her students, learning from them and about them. We also describe the impact this knowledge had on her instruction and on her responses to her students' attempts to read and write. We also address issues that have been raised by critical theorists who object to liberal educators' interpretation of Freire as recommending a laissez-faire facilitator role and abdicating the role of teacher. We demonstrate how Robin maintained her role as 'teacher' and brought it to the dialogical relationship with her students. In the "Insights" section, we further explore this issue, bringing in recent research and theory related to it. We also explore the concept of *community-based education* and discuss why it appears so promising but so difficult to implement in the world of adult education.

Chapter 8: "¿Quién fui, Quién soy, Quién puedo ser?" Who Was I, Who Am I, Who Can I Be?   In this chapter, we chronicle the individual reading and writing successes for each of our eight informants. We take a realistic look at each woman's abilities at the end of the data collection period and speculate on the relationship between their impressive growth and specific features of the class. To help us in this, we compare the success of the women and of the class to that of the other classes in the program, also directed by Robin but not taught by her. In the "Insights" section, we discuss issues of significance for the field of adult education world-wide, for example, assessment, teacher training, access to appropriate materials, the need for community-based programs, and student retention.

Part III: Insights for Adult Literacy Education

Chapter 9: "Literacy Development and Freirean-Based Pedagogy"   In this chapter we pull together our thinking as presented in all of the "Insights" sections. We re-present our conclusions regarding the relationships between Freirean-inspired pedagogy and literacy development and explore related issues as they apply to adult education in general.

Appendices: Researchers and Methodology

Researchers' Histories and Stances   Because ethnographies acknowledge the researcher's presence and influence on phenomena under study, and because ethnographies are essentially interpretation, we each locate ourselves in relation to this study, describing our professional and academic histories and evolutions as educators. We also detail how these histories led each of us to this study and the entering stances we both had toward its topic, procedures, and processes.

Methodology   In this section, we carefully describe the ways in which we collected the data for this study, analyzed it, and arrived at our conclusions. We detail the processes of our collaboration, our division of duties, evolving research decisions, data collection procedures, coding, recoding, and writing. We provide examples of field notes and codes to exemplify our process.

ACKNOWLEDGMENTS

This book could not have been conceived of or written without the collaboration and help of numerous individuals. First of all, the women of the literacy class and the people of the community of Papaturro, with their limitless commitment to getting their stories "out there," are the cornerstone of this project. It obviously, and literally, could not have been done without them.

Robin's many supporters, both financial and emotional, must also be thanked for their belief in her work and willingness to dig one more time into their pockets to provide her with necessary living expenses, as well as some support for the literacy class. Particular appreciation is extended to Jay Kenny and the Jay Kenny Foundation for his tremendous generosity. Relatedly, the Capital Heights Presbyterian Church in Denver played a crucial role in coordinating the donations and providing institutional support for Robin's work in El Salvador.

The Harvard Graduate School of Education provided the only funding we could obtain for this research project, and for this we are deeply grateful. For 2 years, they granted Vicki funds from the Faculty Research and Innovation Fund, which allowed us to purchase the laptop computer for Robin; pay for copying texts and writing samples from the different literacy classes in the program; pay for mailing, computer disks, and batteries; pay research assistants; provide travel money for Vicki to go to El Salvador and for Robin to visit Boston for periods of analysis, and provide some salary for Robin to work on the analysis and writing of the findings.

We also thank the Wellesley Hills First Congregational Church in Wellesley Hills, Massachusetts for their gift of Bibles and songbooks to all members of the community of Papaturro. Orchestrated by Vicki, this was viewed as a partial repayment for their participation in this study.

We would also like to thank the following individuals for their support and advice during various stages of the project: Patty Lawless for helping to raise money for the literacy program, for providing information on the history of the community, and acting as courier for such items as permissions forms and literacy materials; Mary Hupp for her tremendous generosity in coordinating Robin's support and all donations to the community, and for her constant caring and emotional support; Walt Clarke for doing all of the accounting work necessary for Robin's financial support; Amy Weigand for helping collect taped literacy histories; Chris Mannion for carrying the new laptop to Robin and helping her set it up one Christmas vacation; Jennifer Abel for field-note preparation and for translation of written artifacts; Faith Harvey for field-note preparation and organization of incoming data; Natalia Casco and Eliáne Rubinstein-Ávila for audiotape translation of the literacy histories of the women, data entry, and initial data analysis of literacy histories; Erik Jacobson for his consultation on the field of semiotics; Sophie Degener and Marta Soler for their insightful responses to different drafts of the book; Kevin Murray for sharing his expertise on El Salvador as well as his advice on writing about it; Christopher Clark for helping to think about a compelling and, at the same time, telling title; and Joel Milgram for again providing limitless reading and discussion time as well as ongoing emotional support.

We also thank Erlbaum editor Naomi Silverman for her patient and firm belief in this book and its topic. Without her encouragement and persistence in finding reviewers, the publication of this book would have been a much more involved and lengthy process. Finally, the reviewers of the manuscript provided us with much to think about, and their suggestions went a long way toward making this final product a better one.

PART I
CONTEXTS

1

Adult Literacy and Paulo Freire: A Lens for Hope

Eight women bent over their notebooks in a tiny, one-room hut in the steamy countryside of El Salvador. Tightly clutching their pencils, lost in concentration, they each struggled with what they intended to write about the day's topic. Celia gazed over the heads of her classmates as she silently ordered her thoughts before committing the next sentence to paper. Deonicia reviewed her brief writing, searching for the breaks between "words," trying to make sure that she had "left spaces." Chunga wrote steadily, remembering the horrors of the war as her pencil moved across the page. Margarita's pencil pressed relentlessly into her paper, and her voice could just be heard above the background clamor of farm animals and children playing as she struggled to hear the sounds in her words, trying to match those sounds to newly learned letters.

Eight women, ages 23 to 66, were learning to read and write for the first time in their lives. Eight women—only a few of the more than 885 million adults worldwide who are functionally illiterate and unable to participate as fully as they would like in their communities.[1] But, nonetheless, eight women who, against all odds and predictions, were becoming fully literate through their participation in an adult literacy program that was structured and run according to the precepts of Paulo Freire, as interpreted by the director of the program, Robin Waterman, a U.S.-trained literacy teacher. This book is dedicated to the telling of the story of these women's journey toward full literacy, the conditions that contextualized their previous illiteracy, and our analysis of the ways in which Robin implemented an adult literacy program based on the teaching of Freire, an educator who has been the inspiration of many throughout the world who strive to overcome the educational injustices suffered by marginalized people.

ADULT LITERACY AND SOCIOECONOMIC STATUS

Adult literacy–illiteracy has been a topic of concern since the invention of the printing press. With mass availability of printed materials and broadening functions for print use (Kaestle, Damon-Moore, Stedman, Tinsley, & Trollinger, 1991) came the increasingly widespread belief that the ability to read and write is a desirable social, religious, political, and economic goal. It is now believed that literacy is central to basic survival in an increasingly technical society. Whereas once it may have been possible, given the agrarian nature of the U.S. and world economies, to provide food and shelter for oneself and one's family without being able to "cipher," many illiterate and low literate adults today struggle to get by in a world of complex, print-based, information networks. Even the most low-level service jobs require reading and writing capabilities that are beyond those of many adults. As developing countries join the world economy, the disparity in literacy levels among subgroups in their populations has also increasingly become an international concern.

Recently, educational and governmental agencies have attempted to quantify and describe the problem through surveys and analyses of existing data. Examining the results of these studies, many of us are uncomfortable with the implications of some very basic facts (Kirsch, Jungeblut, Jenkins, & Kolstad, 1993; National Center on Adult Literacy, 1995; UNESCO, 1997):

1. Worldwide, more than 885 million men and women still cannot read or write at a basic, functional level.[2]
2. Of this number, 98% reside in developing countries.
3. Of the total populations in developing countries, slightly more than 38% are illiterate women and 21% are illiterate men.
4. In developed countries, up to 29 million people are considered to be functionally illiterate.
5. In the United States, where a commitment to universal literacy by the year 2000 has been declared, 25% of adults with an average of 10 years of schooling cannot read above the fourth-grade level.
6. Nearly half of all adults in the United States scored at levels that the National Educational Goals Panel asserts are well below what adults in the United States need to compete in a global economy.
7. Ethnic minorities are overrepresented in these figures.

8. In urban areas, fewer than 50% of minority children complete 10 grades of school.

Marginalized and Low Literate: Cause or Effect?

The relationship between socioeconomic status (SES) and literacy achievement is clear worldwide. Most often, the poorer you are, the lower the social status assigned to you by the dominant culture. Simultaneously, the higher the degree to which you are marginalized politically, the lower your literacy level (Kaestle et al., 1991).[3] This relationship can be interpreted and understood from two different directions. The most commonly held interpretation is a causal relationship between low literacy and poverty and low sociopolitical status. According to this interpretation, people who have difficulty reading and writing cannot qualify for and/or hold jobs that pay a decent wage because of the increasing demands for high levels of literacy abilities in the workplace. As a result, the low literacy of this population constrains them as wage earners. Consequently, this group remains outside of the mainstream, powerholding group, their low literacy constraining them sociopolitically as well.

The other way of looking at the relationship between literacy level and SES is from the other end: one's SES and sociopolitical status constrains one's literacy level potential or attainment. Several different factors suggest themselves as operative in this type of relationship, factors that are identified with poverty and could result in either failure to participate in literacy instruction or impaired abilities to learn from instruction: ill health resulting from poor nutrition, lack of access to health care, or both; inability to buy literacy materials for literacy practice and use such as books, papers, pencils; and, particularly in developing countries where universal education is an as-yet-unachieved goal, lack of access to schooling.[4]

Purcell-Gates (1995), in a case study of a nonliterate, poor, urban Appalachian family, described and illustrated the factor of exclusion/marginalization, citing it as primary in this status/literacy relationship. She described the family's experience of the literate middle class as a foreign place, populated by those who did not recognize her and her family nor include them. Purcell-Gates saw the family as living in another world, a world without print. The world of print was for "other people," and only "other peoples" words made up the print that they copied and tried to read. This world was impenetrable to Jenny, the mother, her husband, and their two young children.

While Jenny experienced the world of print as a place for others, different from herself, Purcell-Gates concluded that those with sociopolitical power who inhabited that world agreed with Jenny: the world of print could not include her. In other words, Jenny and her family were excluded from learning to read and write by the literate, middle-class socioeconomic groups that controlled school policy and curriculum. This denial of access to literacy resulted from a confluence of factors emanating from negative stereotypes of urban Appalachian people and a refusal to take them seriously as potential learners. Urban Appalachians were (and are) believed to be mentally and morally deficient, dirty and slothful, and unfit, ineffective parents (Adams, 1971; Benjamin, Graham, & Phillips, 1978; Borman, 1991; Borman & Obermiller, 1993). A particular area of difficulty for the middle-class powerholders was that of language. The urban Appalachian dialect is a distinctive marker for all of the negative stereotypes held of its speakers. "Hillbilly talk" is still used by comics and the media to signify lack of sophistication, lack of education, incestuousness, drunkenness, and brutality. Speakers of this dialect in urban schools told of being ridiculed and forced to read without using their own pronunciation and to write without using their own words. They were literally shut out of the process by the ethnocentricity of the middle-class powerholders and their assumptions of moral and intellectual superiority.

Looking at the statistics on adult literacy, again, we can view the link between low sociopolitical status and literacy level from this vantage point. In many countries in the world, including the United States, the groups with the highest levels of illiteracy and low literacy are marginalized by the dominant culture; they are considered "low status" and kept from positions of sociopolitical power.[5] In most countries, the educated, middle-class powerholders view these groups as inherently inferior in some basic way: ethnically, intellectually, morally, and/or linguistically. Often, the language spoken by these marginalized groups is a completely different one from that spoken by the sociopolitical group in power[6] or of the language of instruction. When this is not the case, the low-literate group often speaks a dialect perceived by those in power as critically different, and as a marker of their low SES.

Policy Effects of Attitudes Toward Marginalized

Reflecting this disdain for people marginalized by dominant cultures, governmental resources for adult literacy programs have historically been scarce and unstable. In the United States, 15 times the government funds (federal and state) spent on education went to K–12 endeavors as compared to adult education.[7] The United Nations, tackling the issue in its member countries, funds literacy programs through UNESCO, and these programs do include adult literacy programs. However, in all countries, including the United States, the lion's share of funding and attention go to K–12 programs. The majority of adult literacy programs in developed and developing countries operate on the proverbial shoestring. They are, for the most part, conceived and directed by volunteers who often do not possess professional knowledge of literacy development, teaching, or learning, and who must devote undue time and energy to obtaining a continuous flow of funds to maintain their programs. Usually the teachers in these programs are also concerned volunteers who are desperately in need of basic teacher training to render them minimally prepared to handle the many serious and complex issues they will undoubtedly encounter while working with adult learners at a basic literacy level. Materials appropriate for adult basic literacy students are scarce and many teachers and students must make do with discarded books and workbooks, materials that have often been designed for young children and reflect cultures other than those of the students.[8]

On the one hand, the general public seems to have the attitude that those in need of adult literacy programs had their chance when they were in school (K–12). Thus, they believe, the public should no longer be responsible for their continuing failure to learn. On the other hand, we can question the effectiveness of K–12 programs and argue for increased attention to adult programs by pointing out that, disproportionately, children from sociopolitically marginalized populations are the primary clients of adult literacy programs (when they become adults). Thus, it appears as if public funds for universal literacy have been misdirected and misapplied. So, one could argue, if the public fails the children in K–12 classrooms, then it must work to make up for this when these children become adults.

ADULT NON/LOW LITERACY: IMPACT ON CHILDREN'S LITERACY DEVELOPMENT

We have become increasingly aware of one of the consequences of adult non/low literacy as it relates to families and children's literacy development. After almost 20 years of research into emergent literacy, we can now recognize and document the many critical ways in which young children learn about reading and writing, before beginning formal instruction, by virtue of participating in a literate home environment where people read and write for many different reasons (Clay, 1975, 1991; Dyson, 1982; Harste, Woodward, & Burke, 1984; Heath, 1983; Morrow, 1993; Neuman & Roskos, 1993; Purcell-Gates, 1988, 1995, 1996c; Taylor, D. 1983; Taylor & Dorsey-Gaines, 1988; Teale & Sulzby, 1986).

Foundational Emergent Literacy Concepts

In homes where children observe and experiment with print use, such as using the *TV Guide* for program selection, coupons for shopping, written recipes for food preparation, printed instructions for game playing, magazine and book reading for information and entertainment, young children acquire and build concepts about print that are foundational for later success with formal literacy instruction (Purcell-Gates, 1995, 1996c). These concepts include (a) the knowledge that print signifies, conveys linguistic meaning, and is used for various life purposes; (b) print conventions such as directionality, concepts of word and letter, and so on; (c) implicit knowledge of semantic and syntactic features of written, as compared to oral, discourse; and (d) the knowledge that written English codes language at the phoneme level, often referred to as the Alphabetic Principle.

Impact Continues Into School Years

In a 2-year study that followed 35 low SES children, randomly selected from three public schools, from the time they entered kindergarten through their first-grade year, Purcell-Gates and Dahl (1991) found that those children who possessed fuller knowledge of these basic concepts at school entry were better readers and writers at the end of first grade, as measured by standardized tests, teacher observation, and informal literacy measurements. This was particularly true regarding a concept known as Intentionality—written language signifies, or means, linguistically and is used for a variety of real-life functions. Referring to this knowledge as The Big Picture, the researchers concluded that it was this concept that best predicted the degree of success that these children from minority, low-SES homes would later have with literacy acquisition in school.[9]

Examining this issue from the obverse side, Purcell-Gates (1995) concluded from her 2-year case study of the nonliterate urban Appalachian family that the young children in the family did not possess The Big Picture beyond a critically narrow level ("print is for writing your name"), and that this lack of knowledge accounted to a significant degree for young Donny's (Jenny's son) failure to benefit in any real way from formal literacy instruction. Phenomenologically, print for Donny was linguistically and semiotically insignificant, much like the patterns of branches in trees or of wallpaper on walls. This was because, Purcell-Gates concluded, no one in his home ever used print for any purpose. With parents who could neither read nor write beyond signing their names, Donny began school conceptually eons behind his classmates who had experienced print in use before they began school. Unaware of the significance of this emergent literacy knowledge (or lack thereof), Donny's teachers could only watch in frustration, unable to help, as he failed to learn to read and write in school.

Thus, the impact of adult non/low literacy extends well beyond the individual and his or her quality of life. It impacts directly on upcoming generations of children who will face undue odds when transacting with formal literacy instruction as children—the arena where the bulk of educational funding and focus is presently situated. By refusing to take adult literacy issues seriously and by not appropriating funds to adequately address those issues, we are in fact significantly reducing the chances of success for generations of children in our schools. We are helping to guarantee the next generation of adult low/nonliterates and, in essence, wasting a great deal of public funds targeted to K–12 programs.

RECENT POLICY RESPONSES TO NEED

Recently, the U.S. public has become increasingly aware of adult literacy as a significant issue for the social/economic well-being of the United States. Consequently, the U.S. government has provided support for several initiatives designed to investigate the adult literacy picture and to begin to address perceived needs. From the beginning, these initiatives have included an awareness of the relationships between adult literacy, family literacy, and the future success of young children in learning to read and write in school.

National Literacy Act

In 1991, the passage of the National Literacy Act in Congress resulted in several focused moves toward the eventual establishment of a separate national adult basic education system (Draft Summit Document, 1997). The U.S. Department of Education established the National Center on Adult Literacy (NCAL) as a way to explore, research, and advance knowledge in the area of adult literacy, as well as find ways to improve adult literacy programs and services in the nation. Its stated mission was to address three primary challenges: (a) Enhance the knowledge base about adult literacy, (b) improve the quality of research and development in the field, and (c) ensure a strong, two-way relationship between research and practice. Over its 5 years as a federally financed research center, NCAL addressed such topics as (a) literacy testing, (b) staff development in adult literacy education, (c) workplace literacy programs, (d) technology in adult literacy programs, (e) prison literacy, and (f) literacy skills of GED graduates.

Federal funding for this center, renamed National Center for the Study of Adult Learning and Literacy (NCSALL), moved in 1996 to the Harvard Graduate School of Education. Research topics for this consortium of researchers include issues of practice, learner persistence, literacy and health care, learning disabilities among adult learners, English as a second language (ESL) issues in adult learning programs, and relationships between types of adult programs, functional uses of literacy by learners, and family literacy with impact on young children's literacy success. A central goal of the center is to create effective communication links between the center and practitioners so as to affect and be informed by practice to the highest degree possible.

National Institute for Literacy[10]

On another front, the National Institute for Literacy (NIFL), established in 1991 by The National Literacy Act, began funding research, evaluation, and development of new adult or family literacy program models across the country in 1992. In its first year of funding, NIFL supported such varied projects as (a) the feasibility and effect of embedding cognitive skills instruction in Adult Basic Education (ABE) and ESL courses; (b) the teaching of native-language literacy skills to Hmong adult immigrants; (c) the identification of effective structures, strategies, and approaches of community-based family literacy programs; (d) the use of new curriculum approaches and the "inquiry-based" evaluation method for collaborative family literacy programs; (e) the development of an instructional guide and video to help Native American parents be better teachers of their children; (f) the creation of a family literacy program for homeless single mothers; (g) an investigation of the frequency and type of literacy events in low-SES homes and their relation to the emergent literacy knowledge of the children in the homes; and (h) the development of a center to research literacy needs and model programs and to provide materials and training for educators in jails and correctional facilities (National Institute for Literacy, 1995).[11]

Failure to Solve Link of SES, Power, Marginalization and Literacy

Clearly, an increased effort on the part of the government and research institutions to address the needs of adult learners is underway. Examining the topics of the funded projects, the socioeconomic/political nature of the issue is highlighted. Marginalized populations in the United States are at the center of each project. At the time of this writing, none of the projects had demonstrated success with these populations with sufficient data to suggest a clear solution to the problem of the link between low literacy and low-SES/low sociopolitical power and value.

PAULO FREIRE AND HIS PEDAGOGY OF THE OPPRESSED

Freire, a Brazilian educator, theorist, and political reformer, elucidated a theory for the education of marginalized peoples more than 30 years ago[12]. Influenced by such theorists and activists as Sartre, Fromm, Ortega y Gasset, Mao, King, Jr., and Guevara, Freire developed a theoretical methodology for the poor and marginalized peasants of Latin America (Shaull, 1993). Freire's methodology was considered such a threat to the existing order that, following a military coup in 1964, he was exiled from Brazil for 24 years. His influence grew during this time as he took his theories about the education of marginalized populations to literacy campaigns in Nicaragua, Cuba, Portugal, Chile, Angola, Tanzania, and Guinea-Bissau. During this time, he worked with UNESCO on adult education programs, consulted at the Harvard Graduate School of Education, and served as Special Consultant to the Office of Education of the World Council of Churches in Geneva.

Many educational reformers view Freire's pedagogy as a viable response to adult illiteracy/low literacy throughout the world (Auerbach, 1995, 1996; Giroux, 1985; Lankshear, 1993). Henry Giroux (1985), for example, specifically stated that a Freirean approach to education "can no longer be dismissed as irrelevant to a North American context" (p. xviii). He explained that Freire drew from an understanding of developing countries that is ideological and political, rather than geographical. Consequently, a critical understanding of both Freire and individual student populations could guide U.S. educators towards creating a more effective and vital pedagogy.

Literacy and Liberation Are Inextricable

Freire believed that the attainment of literacy can be, and should be, intricately tied to personal, social, and political liberation. He posited a pedagogy based on a belief that the true purpose of education, and particularly literacy education, should be to liberate people so that they can achieve their full potential—their true humanity (Freire, 1993; McLaren & Leonard, 1993). He situated the educational event—curriculum, process, and product—within the lives and culture of the people attaining literacy. Literacy attainment, he believed, is a result of a dynamic, mutual exchange between educator and students; the content and goals are guided by this exchange. Ultimately, one of the most primary of these objectives is personal and social transformation, toward greater power and freedom for oppressed peoples.

One of Freire's most essential presuppositions is that there are tremendous social, political, economic, and educational inequities in the world, and that particular forms of education either perpetuate these inequities, or work toward transforming them so as to allow for greater equality and liberation for all. One of the root causes of these inequities, Freire believed, is that people in power view poor, marginalized people as objects, not fully human. Those in power oppress and control those who are marginalized in order to maintain their monopoly on privilege, and this stance dehumanizes the oppressors as much as it does the oppressed. For these reasons, one cannot trust the education that is imposed on people by those with social-political power. According to Freire, this type of education is designed such that poor, marginalized populations never develop critical thinking skills, and in this way, never question or challenge the belief that they are incapable of learning and thus deserve their poverty and lack of sociopolitical power.

The "Banking" Quality of Traditional Education

Freire (1993) characterized the kind of education imposed by the dominant, mainstream culture as a "banking concept" of education. He explained that traditional education treats adult learners as "undernourished" and "empty," in need of being fed by the teachers who are "full" of knowledge. This form of education situates the learners as passive recipients of information, chosen by the ruling class, and the teachers as those who pour this information into the heads of the learners. This pedagogy implies a one-way teacher-student relationship characterized by domination and control.

This type of practice fails to acknowledge the humanity of people, Freire asserted, and their inherent ability for assessing their personal situations and transforming these situations as they determine valuable. It fails to recognize the knowledge that learners already possess, and the reciprocal learning relationship that occurs between teacher and student. Freire proposed, therefore, that educators need to lead all students to recognize that they already have a tremendous amount of knowledge and capabilities, and that the educational experience simply serves to bring that to the surface, reinforcing and developing it (Freire, 1993).

Alternative to Banking is Dialogue and Critique

A central Freirean goal has also been to foster education that engenders critical thinking and critical awareness among oppressed, marginalized people. Educators should lead all students to critically understand their social-political situations as well as their potentials as full humans to alter these situations toward creating a more just and equal social and political world. This, he asserted, is achieved primarily through dialogue between teachers and students. Authentic dialogue, Freire said, must take place between learners and educators as equally knowing subjects. In this way, he explained, knowledge emerges as a result of true collaboration between and among teachers and students. This form of education, therefore, requires a reconciliation of the teacher–student contradiction so that both are simultaneously teachers and students. Liberating education, he said, consists in acts of cognition, not transferrals of information; to study is not to consume ideas, but to create and re-create them (Freire & Macedo, 1987).

A significant purpose for the use of dialogue, Freire believed, is that it leads students to begin to read both the world and the word. Reading the world, he said, always precedes reading the word, and reading the world implies continually reading the word (Freire & Macedo, 1987). Words are "pregnant with the meaning of the world"; they contain many layers of social and political significance which influences our thought and behavior. We must all be vigilant about thinking critically about all words, and concepts contained within, thus working to be able to "de-construct" these layers of social-political meaning. It is this that allows us to be able to re-construct new meanings that can contribute toward the transformation of the structural bases of an unjust society. According to Freire, the learning process is only valid when the learner begins to recognize this relationship between language and thought, and the relationship it has to his or her own transformation (Freire, 1985). The aim of a class would be, therefore, to bring the learners to the point where they can view themselves from without as historical humans in a people-created sociocultural context, that is, one which they have the power and possibility to transform to their liking.

Personal and Social Transformation

Equally essential to the educational process, also facilitated and guided by dialogue, is an emphasis on personal and social transformation. All dialogue, and subsequent class instruction, should ultimately lead students toward determining what it is that they can do to co-create the kind of personal and social transformation that they would like to see. Within this pedagogy, education leads students to clarify these desires and goals, as well as recognize that they can be the protagonists in bringing about this change. Freire described this as leading students toward not only "reading the word and the world" but also "writing" the word and the world. In Freirean pedagogy, therefore, reading, writing, and social transformation, as co-created between students and educators, are all inextricable. There should never be one without the other; they are all vehicles toward making each component more potent and effective.

Teachers Must Be Learners

Educators, those assuming the teacher role in adult education, must conform to certain prerequisites to authentically participate in a Freirean-type of program. Teachers must develop a critical awareness of the learner's world, through the learners' eyes. This must be done carefully over time, with the goal of critically understanding what they see. Educators must never approach the learners from a superior position with the goal of keeping them passive, "for their own good." Rather, educators should work at being with the people, with the goal of developing the students' capabilities to think critically, as well as increasing their awareness of their inherent control over their own lives. While teachers must always remain aware of their role as teacher (Freire & Macedo, 1995), they must also remain as student, aware that they are constantly learning about and from their students so that both teacher and student learn and are transformed through the act of dialogue and critical reflection. According to Lankshear (1993), "This whole approach establishes literacy as a medium for expressing one's own intentions, creative potency, and (emerging) critical perspective rather than serving as a vehicle for absorbing directives and myths imposed from without" (p. 114).

Literacy Education Through Generative Themes and Words

Literacy education is an integral part of this pedagogy and proceeds within it. Participants are convinced of the absolute necessity to attain literacy as part of dialogue, reflection and subsequent personal and social transformation. Freire (1985) described a process wherein educators choose "generative" themes/words, selected from the learners' own vocabulary, words that embody the challenges that the learners confront every day, with the potential to spark viable discussion around the core issues (p. 22). These words should also be composed of sufficient syllable combinations such that learners can eventually generate almost any word they may wish to use (Freire, 1993).[13] Criteria, therefore, for selection of these generative words include phonemic richness, phonetic difficulty, and the embodiment of the learners' social, political, and cultural reality.

The chosen words are often accompanied by visual presentations, such as a photo or a drawing, which Freire referred to as "codes." These codes, which represent significant aspects of the historical, cultural, social and/or political life of the students, focus the dialogue and learning. For example, one codification could be a picture of a group of peasants tilling a field of corn with the accompanying word *tierra* (land). The dialogue would draw from the learners' experiences, opinions and feelings, as well as an analysis of current related issues, such as their experience of working the land, their hardships related to working for wealthy land owners, their continued struggles for a fair wage for their agricultural products, and ultimately, their ideas about how to work toward improving these situations. Using generative words and focusing on the student's historical, present-day, and future reality allows the educational process to be vital and engaging, which, according to Freire, is a necessary characteristic of effective education.

Following the critical discussions of themes related to a generative word, the learners are directed to a syllabic family, that of a syllable contained in the generative word. The students then study the syllabic family, eventually also studying words that contain syllables from that family (Lankshear, 1993). This component of class instruction often involves a list of words contained in a student workbook, and/or words suggested by the students. These word lists are created by educators who are familiar with the subculture of the students, and they represent an attempt to select words that are also generative words, that is, words that contain components of the syllabic family being studied, while reflecting important aspects of the social-political reality of the students. The educator writes these words on the board, leading the students to read them aloud, discuss them, and ultimately copy them into their individual student notebooks. Because the generative word and the word lists subsequently studied come from the world of the student, the students experience powerful motivation to learn to read and write these particular words. This, Freire explained, engenders further motivation to read and write, as well as a desire for dialogue, reflection, and subsequent transformative action.

Application of Freire in U.S. Context

Freire's work has recently sparked tremendous interest in the United States as it has been interpreted and applied by critical theorists like Giroux, Peter McLaren, Donaldo Macedo, and bell hooks. This body of theory and interpretation currently coincides with the increased attention given to adult literacy and learning. As a result, mainstream adult literacy programs in the United States are coming under increased attack by Freirean theorists for perpetuating an educational model that aims to "incorporate (marginal) adults into established economic and social values and practices" (Lankshear, 1993, p. 91) rather than facilitating their emergence as aware, empowered people who recognize their ability to transform their sociopolitical worlds. According to these critiques, family literacy programs for adults, as well as those incorporating whole families, reflect the banking model of education rather than a dialogical one (Auerbach, 1995; Lankshear, 1993).

For the most part, this discussion has taken place among educational theorists. Many researchers and most practitioners who struggle to understand effective ways to teach children and adults to read and write in the classroom have little familiarity with and/or depth of understanding of Freire's philosophy and pedagogy. At the same time, many critical theorists who advocate such radical educational change have little knowledge of the basic cognitive and linguistic aspects of learning to read and write. This study was designed to begin to remedy this situation. The adult literacy gap between the "haves" and the "have nots" is real. Equally real is the persistence of this gap, with no clear solution in sight. Looking at the issue from a cultural–sociopolitical–Freirean perspective is worth our time and effort. This study was designed and carried out with this impetus in mind, its goal being to achieve an in-depth understanding of the literacy development process, that is, how people learn to read and write, and what it looks like within a Freirean-based pedagogy . The related goal was to reflect on ways that these data-based insights could offer hope toward closing the literacy gap between high- and low-level learners in a context such as exists right now in the United States.

ENDNOTES

1. As of 1995, according to the *UNESCO Statistical Yearbook 1997,* this figure represents 22.6% of the world population, 16.4% of whom are male and 28.8% of whom are female.
2. Numerous problems abound around the definition of *literate*. As Wagner (1992) pointed out, the use of the term *functional* before the term, while acknowledging the cultural aspect of literacy and the ways in which it is used by different cultural groups, is problematic in that it is hard to think of any kind of literacy which is totally nonfunctional. The statistics published by UNESCO of literacy rates in countries around the world reflect, for the most part, individual countries' definitions of literacy and thus are not reflective of any type of uniform level or definition of what is "literate." What is clear, according to Wagner, is the widespread acceptance of the belief that the concept of literacy reflects a continuum and not a simple yes/no state. See Wagner (1992), particularly chapters 1 and 2 for a more in-depth discussion of this and of the problems inherent in the UNESCO statistics.
3. A few politically marginalized communities do have a history of providing literacy education for their children, for example, the Jews in Eastern European countries and the Chinese in places such as Malaysia and Indonesia (we thank Brian Morgan for this reminder). Rather than pose a challenge to our reading of this issue, this seeming contradiction is informed, we suggest, by our discussion of the role and effect of community-based literacy programs in chapters 8 and 9.
4. For an interesting and informed discussion of the relationships between literacy and economic development and well-being, see Wagner (1992).
5. Note, though, that in many developing countries, particularly those that have recently gained independence, there exist powerful individuals with low literacy. It is also true that in these countries that the first-generation educated middle class often hold tremendous respect for the wisdom of their uneducated parents and grandparents (we thank Penelope Bender of the World Bank for this note).

6. In the United States and other developed countries, immigrants often arrive without knowledge of the language of the host country. Furthermore, in many formerly colonized countries such as Mexico and those of Central and South America, indigenous languages are spoken by many who are poor and without formal education. It is not uncommon to have up to 70 different languages spoken by the indigenous people in a country where the language of schooling, commerce, and power is that of the former, or present, colonial power. See D. Archer & P. Costello (1990) for a discussion of this issue concerning Central and South American indigenous people.

7. The NCAL report (1995, May) cites R. L. Venezky & D. A. Wagner (1994) in stating that the per-pupil cost in 1991 in the United States was estimated at $3,000, compared to $200 per adult student.

8. The *Draft Summit Document* (Dec, 1997), collaboratively produced by the Division of Adult Education and Literacy (DAEL), the NIL, and the NCSALL, addressed all of these issues. Under the section "The Charter for Change," the document lists eight points around which to focus the efforts of the adult literacy community:

   1. We must establish our field as an essential and integral part of a national emphasis on lifewide and lifelong learning, wherein adult learners are perceived as valuable resources who deserve support and respect.

   2. We must establish a learner-centered emphasis, in all its implications, through our policy and practice. This emphasis will broaden our mission to include learning goals associated with all adult roles while basing learner progress and program accountability on realistic time-frames and fair measures of gain.

   3. Local, state, and national structures must be designed to reflect our learner-centered emphasis. Restructuring will entail stabilizing individual learning programs, combining resources, and establishing ABE state and national government offices in positions of authority and power.

   4. We must provide our learners with a professional level of service. From one-to-one tutoring through large state-supported public education systems, the preparation of ABE educators for teaching, administration, and research must be raised to a professional level.

   5. We must demand and justify much higher levels of federal, state, and local funding. Beginning with a baseline federal funding target, the field needs significant levels of funding to support both the work of practitioners and improvements in service.

   6. We should exploit recent advances in communications and electronic technology. New developments and capabilities, along with lower costs, have combined to offer our field a new opportunity to improve and expand services, share information, and unify the field.

   7. We must plan and conduct an ambitious array of research projects. Addressing the gaps we have identified in our field's knowledge base will insure that our present and future actions will be well informed while helping us to make our case to funders and policymakers.

8. We must take the initiative in our field's development by exploiting promising projects and initiatives that are currently under way. By coordinating and supporting these efforts, in tandem with the Summit Document process, we will move toward change in a more focused and effective way.

9. One third of the sample of children were white, urban-Appalachian and two thirds were African American. This ratio reflected the low-SES population of the midwestern city in which this study was conducted.

10. Harvard Graduate School of Education and World Education, Inc. (Jan. 12, 1996). *The National Research and Development Center for Improving Adult Learning and Literacy*. Grant proposal submitted to Office of Educational Research and Improvement, Washington, D.C.

11. Other efforts include the publication of the National Adult Literacy Survey in 1992 and the formation within the U.S. Department of Education of the DAEL.

12. Freire began writing and theorizing about education and implications regarding illiterate adults in the Third World in his native country of Brazil. His philosophy of education was first expressed in writing in his doctoral dissertation in 1959 at the University of Recife where he later became Professor of the History and Philosophy of Education. Drawing on this and his experiences teaching illiterate adults, he first published the influential *Pedagogy of the Oppressed* in 1970. See "Foreword" by Richard Shaull in the reissue of *Pedagogy of the Oppressed* by Continuum, 1993.

13. Freire developed his pedagogy in countries like Brazil and Mexico; languages like Spanish and Portuguese are phonetically regular to a much greater degree than languages like English and therefore more often lend themselves to word-building out of syllables.

2

Revolutionary Struggle and Literacy: Historical Context

I t was the rainy season and the relentless pounding on the tin roof of the small, one-room mud and stick home threatened to overwhelm the tape recorder set out between us on the small wooden table. At 7 p.m. it was already dark, with the light of a single candle illuminating only the faces of Robin and the individual speaker, while everyone else sat back from the table in shadow. It was a Friday evening and Lino, José Angel, and Celia had fulfilled their promise to come to Robin's house in order to share their stories with Vicki about their lives as Salvadoran *campesinos* before and during the recent civil war. Lino and José Angel were both exhausted from working in the fields since daybreak, and Celia was suffering from a serious chest cold that had prevented her full participation in the literacy class earlier that afternoon. They all, though, were committed to taking the time to respond to Robin's request that they share their story. They understood that speaking with Vicki was a way to get their stories about their experiences, and their understanding of the underlying issues—poverty, resistance, the brutality of war, and the strength of solidarity—out to the rest of the world.[1] The topic of literacy wove itself throughout.

Lino began. The candlelight highlighted his multilined, nut-brown face, and his dark eyes shone alternately with anger, reverence, hurt, and remembered pleasures and rewards as he recalled his experience as an adult literacy teacher in the refugee camps.

> I'm going to tell you a part of the story of our life. We can say that when we talk about the life story of a *campesino*, we are talking about the lives of all *campesinos* in El Salvador. Before the war, we lived in extreme poverty, a time when the things that one produced were valued very cheaply. I remember being 15 and 20 years old and never having any money; what we produced was what we needed for survival.

> I was my father's eldest son and so I had to help him support the whole family. I was only in school for two years because of this. I had to dedicate my time to working the land. During those years, I'd walk on the trail for close to 4 kilometers to get to the school. The closest health clinic was 4 hours of walking. The only way to take a sick person there was to carry them on our shoulders, in a sling made of tree branches and a hammock. I remember having gone various times with a patient. We'd leave at around 7 p.m., and we'd get there at 2 or 3 a.m. as the dawn was breaking.

> There was very little food. Most of the *campesinos* in El Salvador ate only corn (tortillas) and beans. Some didn't even have that.

Lino went on to explain the beginnings of the war, starting with a description of the campesinos' early attempts to organize nonviolent demonstrations as a way to protest the lack of many basic human rights and needs. These demonstrations were influenced, to a large degree, by the Liberation Theology movement that spread throughout Central and South America in the 1970s and 1980s. Liberation Theology had begun to inspire new ways of reading the Bible, through critiques and discussions led by priests, nuns and lay persons, leading people to draw from Biblical text as they critically analyzed their own sociopolitical reality, all through a social justice lens.

> Before the war, you could say that we were not very organized. But because of the same situation of our *miseria*, our extreme poverty, and through the light of the Gospels, we began to discover the great importance of unity. At this time, we began to organize our communities. Drawing from the light of the Gospels, we began to recognize that there was a great situation of injustice in our country. Because of this, leaders began to surface, those who worked as catechists. At the same time, through the light of the Gospels, we all came to understand the political reality that we were living in the country.

> I remember going to a demonstration in the center of San Salvador, September 14, in the year 1980. It was a nonviolent demonstration—peaceful, with no arms. As soon as we began to march around Cuscatlán Park, I heard what I thought were fireworks that they were going to set off at the march. But I then became aware that it was bombs that the Army was throwing. I remember that

there was 1 person dead, and around 22 wounded. We had to leave, all of us lost, scattered, all around the capital.

Many times, during demonstrations when the people were demanding their rights, that is how the Armed Forces would respond, with bullets and bombs. At that time, Archbishop Romero also made demands of the government, and they blamed him for being involved in politics. But he was only defending the life of the *campesinos*, defending our basic rights.

Armed Struggle Begins

At Robin's invitation, José Angel replaced Lino at the table, ready to share other important aspects of the history of the Salvadoran *campesino* people. José Angel began by describing how the previously peaceful protests evaporated, escalating into an armed struggle. He explained the Salvadoran military's violent response as the organized leftist movement grew.

As Lino mentioned, when we began to organize, we began to feel the oppression (from the military) even more strongly. The military began these large *operativas*, large-scale invasions. We oriented ourselves and began to dig some very deep tunnels under the ground for refuge. When the military invaded, many protected themselves in these deep tunnels. There were mothers who would stay in the tunnels with their children, remaining hidden. Sometimes the fathers of these children would remain above, observing, during the military invasion. During these military invasions, the soldiers would capture people, women and men, taking them away and assassinating them. Some, they would hang them from trees. Others, they would tie their hands and legs, put them on a pile of wood, and then burn them alive. When they captured pregnant women, they'd cut open their stomachs, and throw the fetus to the dogs. Sometimes they would grab young children, throw them up in the air and then catch them with a bayonet. This was the situation. The people felt very frightened when they said, "The soldiers are coming"; "The army is coming."

As the conflict intensified between the Army and the leftist *Frente Farabundo Marti para la Liberación Nacional* (FMLN)[2] combatants, José Angel explained, with the *campesinos* who lived in the conflicted zones caught in the middle, many rural communities organized a mass exodus, known as a *guinda*. The plan was to travel by night toward the Honduran border, cross the river, and take refuge in Honduras.

The Flight From Home

At this point, Robin invited Celia to share aspects of the women's experience of *campesino* history. Celia moved to a seat at the table, the candlelight now illuminating her worn face. The strength of her spirit and character became clear, however, as she began to speak.

We women suffered very much because we always needed to stay alone in the house. The men of our families couldn't stay with us. They were fearful and would hide in the hills. The army was always after them. They'd follow them, and if found at home, they'd kill them, man or boy. That was a war strategy. The army had no respect for the *campesinos*. It was very painful. We were left without the support of our children who were murdered.

The years of 1980 and 1981 were the most difficult because we had nothing, barely any food even. Neither the women nor men could leave to go to other communities. We couldn't bring salt or sugar—nothing. We couldn't even go attend Mass in the town. Anybody who went to town was captured, assassinated, and then cut to pieces. The Army went to all the villages (the communities) and burned the houses. When we finally left (for Honduras), there were few houses left. They also burned all the grain. The majority of the people had nothing to eat.

Because of all this, we had to flee for Honduras. We left in 1981. The Army launched continual invasions, every day further reducing the space through which we could escape. During this time, we began to organize, getting people from the hills and out of the underground tunnels. Others went to get those that were hiding in caves. So, after 3 days, when the Army was in control of the entire zone, we had to leave for the Lempa River,[3] the only way we could escape (El Salvador and seek refuge in Honduras). We walked all night, carrying the sick on our shoulders. Some pregnant women had to give birth on the way, and then keep walking. We arrived at the edge of the Lempa River around six in the morning. It was a very sad day. It was a day of weeping, a day of lamentation, because all we expected was death. But that is where we saw a clear miracle.

Carnage at the Border

José Angel then described the confluence of forces facing the refugees when they reached the Lempa River.

We were 7,000 people. The Army oriented themselves, knowing that we were fleeing to Honduras, so they were there at the Lempa River. They had helicopters and they started shooting at the people who were at one side and the other. The Honduran Army joined in as well.

Celia continued:

There was shooting and bombing from both sides, El Salvador and Honduras. When they dropped the first bombs, people began to cry and cry, call out, and pray. People got lost in the hills. Some children were lost, others drowned, and others were killed by soldiers firing from helicopters. Sometimes, they would shoot a child held in a mother's arms, and the child would fall, dead, and the mother had to keep on walking. Yes, the passage was hard, very hard. It's the largest river in El Salvador. They had the idea to get people across by tying a rope on the rocks from one side to the other, and the people hung onto the rope.

That's how some got to the other side, but the tide was so strong that it took some people. They drowned. The people who arrived to the other side of the river had no clothes on because their clothing remained on the other side. That's how we all walked forward—without shirts or shoes. At around 11 that night, the Honduran Army arrived. They killed many people, all of those that were arriving. They also captured many men, and took them away to kill them. They killed almost 50 men in one part of the road. The poor women, we were left with only our children. And this is the way that we arrived, arriving to a place where we were almost completely surrounded by the military.

International Solidarity and Intervention

Lino and José Angel then spoke about the intervention of international solidarity volunteers and priests, an event that prevented a full-scale massacre. During the fighting, a group of refugees reached the community of Los Hernández and informed the authorities that many *campesinos* were trapped by the armies at the river. Several international volunteers and priests left to join the fight, carrying white flags. Lino explained:

> By the time the international volunteers and priests arrived, they had already bombed and killed many; something like 250 adults and children died there. And others drowned in the middle of all the confusion and shooting, or died from inhaling the fumes of the bombs. And from there, there were some that arrived to Los Hernández (in Honduras), and others that returned to El Salvador because they were so lost in all of the bombing.

> Upon arriving at Los Hernández, we spent 8 days. The local people, they helped us, giving us some clothing and food—tortillas, tamales, whatever they had. Everyone collaborated, helping us. We remember this very well, because the people of Los Hernández are poor just as we are. We remember this very well, one person helping another, the poor sharing with the poor. And from there we were taken to the refugee camp in La Virtud, Honduras.

Literacy Linked to Social Justice

A new form of literacy education, one inextricably linked to social justice, was born in the midst of this carnage. Lino explained:

> When we first got to Honduras, we were right by the border, by La Virtud. That is where the idea came about, with the participation of the church, together with our own ideas, that we had to teach people to read and write. I remember when a community meeting was organized for all of the people in the camp, asking if people were willing to study, to learn to read and write. The people responded that they were very much in agreement. A census was conducted which told us that 60% of the people did not know how to read. So one of the international solidarity organizations, primarily Caridad, showed support to-

ward this. They asked that some of us participate as literacy teachers, and gave us some training. I remember I went through a training for 2 weeks, and with those 2 weeks of training, I was able to work. And people responded. I remember we had something like 12 literacy classes there in La Virtud. But we were not there for more than a year. From there we were relocated to Mesa Grande, and there, there were seven camps and people were even more organized and united. There was a great deal of work. I remember that after working for 6 months as a teacher, I was asked to be part of the Education Coordinating Team.

The nature of the education classes reflected the input of Freirean-influenced educators who had come from many other countries as part of a international solidarity effort. As such, the classes reflected ongoing dialogues between the *campesinos* and the international volunteers, as Lino explained:

> On the education team, I was working alongside some international volunteers, all of us working together to develop new materials and train new teachers. Although we were in consultation with some international volunteers, the ideas and the line of education was ours—what we were going to teach the people. They would give us support, giving us more training as literacy teachers—we had a very low level of (formal) education, and we needed to learn more mathematics, more spelling, etc. But we created the literacy materials ourselves. First, we had a community meeting with all of the teachers. We always said that the content of adult literacy should teach us to "learn to read our reality, the one we are living, and learn to write history, to form our future." So, at the meeting, we elaborated some principal questions, our own questions: "Who are we?" "Where are we?" and "What do we have to do?" From these three questions, there were different responses, and from this we created a student workbook. There were 12 lessons, and each one had a generative word, as we call them. The first word was *refugee*. The word *refugee (refugiado)* contains the five vowels. The second word was *Salvadoreña*. Another word was *campesino, campesina*. We also used phrases, like "We need work." "We are poor peasants." Each of these lessons had many parts, where we studied the syllables and learned to form new words and sentences.

Lino recalled his 6 years as an adult teacher with great fondness and appreciation. He loved being a teacher and felt that he had learned much more than he would ever have learned if he had stayed in El Salvador.[4]

Women and Literacy in the Refugee Camps

Celia, however, had a different experience with the adult classes in the camps, one that reflected the experiences of many of the women Robin encountered in Papaturro, as well as the other communities in which she established basic literacy classes.

I was one of those who tried to go to literacy classes in the refugee camps. I had a great deal of interest and enthusiasm for learning. But after I started studying, I found out my son was murdered. My capacity for learning was gone! That is the hardest thing, when you are told your son is dead. I didn't even have the opportunity to see him or bury him. As the years went by, I lost my will to do anything. But later, I tried again (to attend the literacy class). I was just starting when I heard that another one of my sons was gone, he had "disappeared" is what they call it. That is how I could not study in Honduras—on account of the bad news and sorrow. It is like a stabbing into your heart! For us mothers, every child they kill causes us great injury to our hearts. We mothers still feel these wounds as if it just happened. We'll never forget our dear sons and our family members who died in the war. That is how the tragedy went. We are thousands of mothers who were left without our sons.

The candlelight was burning low, and everyone was tired, wrung out by the memories and stories that had been shared. Lino, José Angel and Celia each took up their flashlights, said goodnight, and walked out along the muddy paths, making their way to their respective homes.

THE ROAD TO PAPATURRO

It's not easy to get to Papaturro. You must first board an old, marginally safe, Blue Bird (former school) bus, a bus that no longer meets U.S. standards and has been passed on to El Salvador. You board the bus at a chaotic crossroads in San Salvador, find a seat among the Salvadorans traveling between the crowded, smoggy capital city and the quiet, lush green countryside, and bounce and jounce along as the bus makes its way up one of the few paved roads in the country, headed for its destination town of Suchitoto, a centrally located town that functions as a hub for many of the political, economic, social, and cultural nongovernmental organizations (NGOs) of the region.[5] After about 45 minutes, as the bus rounds a long curve, it slows at one of its regular stops where a dirt road emerges shyly from the overgrown vegetation hugging the edges of the concrete strip. A few *campesinos* are waiting patiently on the side of the road to ride into Suchitoto. You get off the bus at this point, and enter the side road through a break in the trees and bushes.

Papaturro lies about 1 hour walking down this rocky, rutted, and often muddy road that crosses two rivers, forded either by balancing on rocks or simply wading through. Three different "repopulation" communities lie along this road and its branches, Papaturro being one. The residents of these communities are all returned refugees from the recent war in El Salvador, and the communities are all new, built on a former single-family plantation. As part of the land reform initiatives begun under the Christian Democrats in 1979, this land was subdivided and sold to the banks, who were directed to loan money at low interest rates so that poor Salvadorans could become owners of the land (Murray, 1995).

This part of El Salvador, the Suchitoto region of the Department (state) of Cuscatlán, is one of the former "conflictive zones," a mountainous region where much of the fighting between government troops and the guerrilla armies took place only a few years before. This region is still heavily influenced by the FMLN, the umbrella opposition party that rose to power during the civil war. The people of Papaturro celebrated their sixth year as a repopulated community in 1996. Its residents had moved to the site and built their homes, their schools, and their clinic and prepared brush-covered land for cultivation after an initial attempt to repopulate where they had formally lived, the Department of *Cabañas*. All of the adults and young people over the age of 4 were returnees from the refugee camp of Mesa Grande in Honduras. They were all still coping with the lingering traumas of the brutal civil war that had cost them so much and had resulted in so few tangible gains.

THE WAR IN EL SALVADOR

Conditions Leading Up to the War

El Salvador is a small Central American country about the size of Massachusetts. It is the smallest and most densely populated country on the American continent (Hammond, 1998; Murray, 1995). From its inception as a Spanish colonized country in the 16th century, El Salvador has experienced extreme economic and class disparities, with a small group of the politically powerful controlling all of the land and, thus, the great majority of the resources of the country. Central to this economic and political picture was the availability of cheap human labor, provided by rural *campesinos*.

Poverty. According to the people of Papaturro, others that Robin worked with, and verified by published accounts (Hammond, 1998; Murray, 1995), before the war, the Salvadoran *campesinos* lived isolated lives, marked by extreme poverty. They were highly marginalized by the upper and middle classes of the country. The *campesinos* worked the land in serf-like arrangements, paying the land owner for the right to farm, and giving over almost all of their produce to the land owner. They survived, if strong and lucky, on tortillas and beans day in and day out. Families worked as a unit to survive, children working alongside parents from a very young age. Coffee, corn, sugar cane, and, at times, cotton were the main crops produced by the *campesinos* for the country.

The poverty of the people defined their realities. Tomasa, a woman in her 30s described it this way:

> When I was born, we were very poor. Our house was very small. My father died soon after I was born and my mother was always looking for even small amounts of corn so we could eat (there were six children). We ate tortillas with salt. Sometimes when she was able to get a bit of beans, we would eat beans. Sometimes she couldn't even find corn, so we didn't even have tortillas; we just endured the hunger. It was very sad, the poverty we lived with before.

> The closest (health) clinic was very far from the house. We would leave at 4 o'clock in the morning to get to it at 8 o'clock. If we had to go to the hospital, we had to leave at 3 o'clock in the morning. And we always had to walk, because there was no transportation, not even streets, just narrow dirt paths. Sometimes when a child was very sick, there wasn't even time to take him to the hospital. He would die along the road because the hospital was so far.

Lack of Health Care. There was virtually no accessible health care available to *campesino* people; disease and malnutrition were rampant, and many children did not survive to age 5. Celia, a literacy student in her early 50s, describes the fate of several of her children, a characteristic portrayal of this lack of health care and the results of extreme poverty:

> I was 17 years old when I had my first child. We were very poor. When I was pregnant, all we had were tortillas and beans. No milk, nothing more! I was very malnourished. After my baby was born—when he was two months old—I developed a fever. For 2 days I had an incredible, very high fever. So they took me to the nearest clinic, the men of the community having to walk 4 hours just to get there, carrying me in a hammock over their shoulders. I had to leave my baby with my mother-in-law. I stayed in the hospital for a month. My fever was high and would not go away.

Celia's eyes, large in her thin, high-cheekboned face, shone with tears and desperation as she remembered:

> My baby, he died 8 days after I left for the hospital, dying of the same fever that I had. But my husband, he didn't have the strength, or capacity, to tell me. He came every week to visit me, always telling me that the baby was fine. "The baby is fat, very healthy," he would tell me. But he was deceiving me. I cried every day in the hospital, crying for my baby. My milk was coming, and I kept forcing it out so that when I returned I could feed my baby. But he was already dead.

Celia fell silent, bowing her head as she sank back into this memory. Taking a deep breath, she continued:

> In the hospital, I was very malnourished. All my hair fell out! But I was desperate. I wanted to leave; I wanted to see my baby. And so, Arturo, my husband, he came to get me and we walked home. And still, even on the way home, he did not have the strength to tell me that my baby was dead. I did not find out until I arrived home. When I arrived and they told me, I laid down on the bed and wept! All I could do was lie in bed and cry.

She looked up at Robin at this point and uttered her reflection on the larger issue, *"La vida de pobreza es muy dura"* (The life of poverty is very hard).

Celia's second and third children, both sons, lived to young adulthood, only to die later during the violence of the war. Her fourth, however, lived for only 10 years, again weakened to the point of death due to illness brought on by poor nutrition and disease-ridden water.

> My fourth child was a girl. When she was 3 years old, she became quite sick, suffering from severe vomiting and diarrhea. We had no money for medicine, but I went searching in the hills for a special kind of plant bark. They said this would be good for her. But for the next 7 years, she remained very weak. She was very malnourished, but we had nothing to give to her except beans and tortillas. She died when she was 10 years old.

During Celia's fifth pregnancy, she experienced frightening symptoms of the severe anemia and malnutrition that would continue to plague her through the time we knew her.

> When I was 5 months pregnant with my fifth child, I became very sick. I couldn't see in the nighttime. In the daylight I was ok, but after 6 p.m. I couldn't even see the light of a candle, nothing! I couldn't see the stars, the moon, I could not see anything. But I could not go to the clinic because we did not have any money. I also did not go because I didn't even know where I could go. I had never left the community when I was a child, and I simply did not even know where I could go to get help. And so I endured this sickness for my entire pregnancy. When I was 8 months pregnant, I began to cry every night. "How was I going to see my child?" I thought. I cried and I cried. My husband told me that I should stop crying, but I could only think, "How will this be if my child is born and I can't see?" I continued to cry. My child was born 1 month later, with eyes that were yellow. After he was born, my own sight returned and I could see again just like I could before.[6] But my child, he died when he was only 7 days old. We never knew why.

Stories of children and adults dying for want of access to any type of decent health care before the war were prevalent in our interviews. A trip to the health clinic, never mind a hospital, always meant at least a 3- to 4-hour walk along rutted, muddy paths. This trip would usually involve the labor of several men of the community carrying the sick person on their shoulders in a sling made of branches and a home-made hammock.

The health care available in the capital city, San Salvador, was often out of reach for rural *campesinos* as well, both physically, because of distance, and economically because of cost. Most *campesinos* lived in extremely remote areas, without transportation or adequate access roads. Moreover, they survived, barely, on a subsistence income, eating that which they grew, without any disposable income that they could use to pay for hospital costs. The *campesinos* who were able to access hospital care were relegated to poorly equipped hospitals with minimal staffing; the care that they received at these hospitals was significantly distinct from the care given to wealthy Salvadorans, and adequate attention and recovery was not guaranteed (Murray, 1995).

Little Access to Education.   Within this poverty, there was a 90% illiteracy rate among the present Papaturro residents.[7] Schools were few and far between. It often took hours to walk along the dirt roads and paths to reach a school, and this was viewed by many as time taken away from the daily work required for family survival. Children did not have clothes or shoes to wear to school, nor could they afford the pencils and paper required to participate. Moreover, the schools that did exist usually went only as far as the third or fourth grade, and their functioning depended on capricious funding and the inconsistent availability of teachers. It was hard to get to a school; it was hard, if not impossible, for parents to provide the clothes, shoes, and school supplies that their children needed for school; it was hard for parents to excuse their children from the labor needed for family survival; and it was hard to really learn anything in school to warrant all of these sacrifices. Chunga, a 66-year-old student in Robin's basic literacy class, explained some of the reasons:

> All five students that were there (in school) didn't learn anything. So, there was no reason to go. And it was too far from where we lived. It was really far; we had to cross the trails, and there was a ravine that got so full in the rainy season, we couldn't get through.

Within this general lack of access to education, women, in particular, were denied opportunities to learn to read and write. *Campesina* women lived, and still do, in a male-dominated culture where their significance was seen as bounded by home and children and where all believed that women are born to be controlled and dominated by men. As a function of this gender-related marginalization, whenever parents would and could send any children to school, they prioritized male children. The girls, particularly the older ones, were seen as needed around the home to help with the daily tasks of collecting wood, making the tortillas, cooking, washing dishes, caring for the younger children, and so on. Celia remembered:

> I was 8 years old when I wanted to go to school. The nearest school was in San Felipe, 45 minutes from San Rafael were we lived. A teacher from the school came to visit my father, saying that his children should be in school. My mother told me, "Hide yourself so that they don't know you're here! You will NOT be going to school." And so I hid behind the door so that they would not see me. But I wanted to go to the school. I begged my mother, asking to be able to go. But because I was the oldest, she told me that I needed to stay home and care for the younger children and help her do all the daily work of the house. I had three brothers, one just 4 months old and the others 5 and 3 years old. My mother was sick and unable to do it all. But I told her that I HAD to go to school, that I wanted to learn to read and write. But again she told me no. She said that I had to care for my father, bring him his lunch each day. And so I did, walking 2 hours each day, carrying his lunch in a basket on my head. I felt depressed. And I cried, many times.

The government provided very few schools, prioritizing those that were located in the capital or other larger towns. There were some schools located in rural areas, but they were few, and access was difficult. Students would need to walk long distances on rugged terrain (that required adequate footwear), thus making access prohibitive to those who could not afford to dedicate the necessary time or purchase the necessary footwear.

Trained teachers were scarce, and all teachers were seriously underpaid. Compounding this, most teachers did not live in the rural communities where the schools were located and thus needed to travel long distances to reach the schools, often on foot, along rugged, often muddy, terrain. This created the problem of sporadic teacher attendance, with only the most committed making the sacrifices to be consistent. Therefore, children who made the effort to get to a school were often faced with a locked door and/or an absent teacher. Among other problems, this gave rise to high student attrition as students themselves determined that their sacrifices were not worthwhile. Of those children who managed to obtain schooling in the rural areas, virtually none of them went beyond the basic level (primary through sixth grade), with the vast majority of them finishing only two or three grades.

Solidarity and Liberation Theology

Lack of Social Organization.   Lino, a *campesino* in his late 50s, described the lack of social organization before the war: "Before the war we were very poor, but we were not organized. We all struggled to survive on our own, but we did not know to help ourselves by organizing and working as communities."

This lack of community organization existed as a result of and in response to the 1932 massacre, known as *La Matanza* (the slaughter). This was a large-scale, brutal massacre, committed by the Salvadoran military and directed at rural and urban groups who had organized, demanding changes in the social and economic structures that were causing extreme polarization between the classes. This type of organized opposition to government policy and existing social structures virtually ended after this event, as many opposition leaders had been killed, and most people who survived were severely traumatized by the brutality of the massacre. Organized opposition did not arise again until the 1960s, when newly formed rural cooperatives and sectors of the urban middle class joined to demand social change (Hammond, 1998; Murray, 1995).

A New Religious Lens.   At the same time, many religious leaders and church workers in Latin America began to reconsider their roles in response to the poverty and suffering they saw around them. In the context of several large gatherings of Latin American Catholic bishops (Medellin, 1968, Puebla, 1979, Santa Domingo, 1992), church leaders decided that they needed to acknowledge the extreme poverty that characterized the lives of the majority, and that they needed to take a decisive role, as a church, toward addressing the issue. Some liberal Protestant denominations, such as the Lutheran church in El Salvador, also began to view their Christian faith differently at this time (Murray, 1995). As a result, a new theology evolved, known as Liberation Theology, and grassroots Bible study groups, known as Base Christian Communities (BCCs), began to form, all of which entailed a new reading of the Bible. A central component of this new reading is what is known as "the preferential option for the poor," a Biblical interpretation (stating) that God has particular concern for the poor, and calls all people to work together to co-create the Reign of God. The Reign of God, in this interpretation, is understood as a world, here on earth, where there is justice, equality, and dignity for all.

Liberation theologians stressed that they were not putting forth a new faith, but rather "the faith of the Apostles, the faith of the church linked to the sufferings and hopes for liberation of the oppressed of this world" (Boff & Boff, 1987, p. 43). The guiding theme of this theological interpretation was Jesus' identification with the poor and the marginalized, stressing that Jesus was born poor and chose to be poor throughout his life.

Liberation Theology highlighted the primacy of Jesus' efforts to speak out against injustice, as well as the ways that he lived his life in accordance with these teachings, in many ways living a life that was counter to that of the dominant culture. Liberation Theology asserted that the institutional Catholic Church had been one of several social/political institutions that perpetuated injustices that oppressed the poor and benefitted the privileged. Therefore, according to the tenets of Liberation

Theology, it was not God's will that the poor should suffer, as the church had indirectly taught for many years. ("Endure your poverty. Look to heaven. There you will live in God's abundance.") Rather, God wanted people to work together to liberate the poor from their suffering, creating the necessary economic, political, and social conditions such that the poor could have the basic means of subsistence and human dignity, such as food, clothing, shelter, basic health care, elementary education, and work. Those who worked and lived in solidarity with the poor to achieve these ends, according to Liberation Theology, were living the Christian life (Berryman, 1987; Boff & Boff, 1987; Gutierrez, 1985, 1994; McAfee, Brown, 1984; Sobrino, 1988).

Viewing the church as an organized human response to Christ's life, liberation theologians asserted that the best way of liberating the poor was to recognize that the poor themselves are the church. All people need to be open to be "evangelized by the poor," as the poor are those who can best identify with Jesus, and therefore are best able to recognize and understand central Christian concepts.

Organization Through Religious Study Groups.   In response to this theological development, thousands of BCCs were established throughout the urban and rural poor communities. A vast network of BCCs arose throughout Latin America, serving to provide the people with ways of connecting with each other and with God in ways that the institutional church had previously not allowed. Priests and nuns trained local *campesinos* to be leaders of these groups, such that many poor *campesinos* became religious leaders of their own communities.

Emergence of Social Justice Demands.   During BCC gatherings, participants would study the Bible, analyzing the ways that it interfaced with their own reality. In particular, through the BCCs, marginalized people began to understand their lives in relation to their oppression/poverty, while always focusing on ways that they could organize themselves in relation to social action projects, such that they could transform the sociopolitical roots of this oppression.

Lino described his participation in BCC meetings, conveying the ways that it awakened a deep desire for social justice.

> As a consequence of our miserable conditions and the illumination of Biblical text, we came to discover that unity is of great importance. That is how we organized into communities. And from there, drawing from the illumination of the Bible, we began to become aware of the enormous injustices that occur in our country. And for that same reason, the catechist leaders arose as they became aware of the political reality that was lived in this country.

The number of BCCs grew rapidly with the ensuing increase in calls for social and economic change. Murray (1995) described the result:

> By the mid-1970s, both urban and rural movements had grown tremendously and had begun to inspire a vibrant political opposition. A unique and explosive relationship began between the urban-based left—undergoing its own process of transformation—and the new popular movements rooted in Christian base community organizing. The predictable response of the oligarchy was violent repression. In both 1972 and 1977 clear electoral victories for the opposition were vetoed by the military and protests drowned in pools of blood. Death squads, which were not a new phenomenon in El Salvador, became the preferred weapon for the elimination of the opposition, and the death toll mounted. (p. 171)

With the systematic murder of priests, nuns, lay leaders, and *campesino* catechists, in the 1970s and 1980s, the BCCs virtually disappeared. In their place arose new opposition movements, now determined to respond to the violence with violence. The 12-year civil war began. It was only recently, with the leadership now including women from the literacy class, that the people of Papaturro began to form another BCC.

The Repression

As the war between the FMLN combatants and the government's army[8] intensified, life became intolerable for the *campesinos* living in the zones[9] where the heaviest fighting took place. As described by Lino, José Angel, and Celia at the beginning of this chapter, the *campesinos* were caught between the leftist FMLN forces and the government soldiers, who were determined to wipe them off the face of the earth. Entire villages were destroyed as the government's military forces implemented a war strategy known as *quitarle el agua al pez* (take the water from the fish). This strategy consisted of military efforts to destroy anyone and anything that would provide support to the members of the FMLN forces, thus justifying the killing of women, children, and elderly family members, as well as burning entire homes, stores of grains, animals, that is, every family member and anything they owned (Danner, 1994). When this effort was not completely successful, the army attempted to at least make life completely intolerable for the *campesinos*. While the men, at least those who had not joined the opposition forces, hid in the hills whenever word came that soldiers were near, women were captured, tortured, raped, and killed as a way to try and force them to reveal their sons' and husbands' hiding places, or simply as a way to carry out the military's desire for complete destruction of *campesino* communities.[10]

As one woman expressed it, "These are the wounds that are engraved on our hearts; we will never forget the moments when we lost those that we love." Approximately 75,000 rural Salvadorans were killed between 1977 and 1983 (Murray, 1995).

The Refugee Camps

The *campesinos* had no choice but to flee their homes and try to reach refuge in Honduras and Nicaragua where international refugee camps were being established. By 1983, one-fifth of the total population of El Salvador—1 million people—had become refugees or displaced persons. The people of Papaturro ended up in the camp of Mesa Grande in Honduras where they lived for 8 to 10 years.

The refugee camps were not safe havens, however. Fighting continued around the camps, as well as above them, with both Honduran and Salvadoran government soldiers shooting, kidnapping, and bombing from above using U.S.-supplied military helicopters and planes. International solidarity/relief groups devoted to helping and protecting the refugees provided some measure of safety in the camps by living there with the refugees. The international presence also illuminated the government repression that had led to the flight from El Salvador and continued to prevent their return.

Learning Social Organization.   In the refugee camps, the people were taught how to live and work as an organized community, learning such skills as how to develop local leadership and governing structures and how to create crafts from local resources. Other refugees learned basic health care techniques in order to work alongside nurses and doctors in the camps and conduct basic health care in their own communities when they returned to El Salvador. The men also worked together to cultivate some basic crops, providing a supplement to the minimal supplies of donated food. Some women worked in daycare centers, thus freeing other women to attend school or to participate in one of the other camp tasks or workshops.

International and Salvadoran priests, nuns, and lay people worked together with *campesino* catechists to conduct weekly *Celebraciones de La Palabra* (Catholic Liturgical Celebrations, literally, "Celebrations of the Word"). These were conducted in the format of the BCCs, again emphasizing active participation on behalf of all who attended, particularly after the reading of the Biblical texts, when the facilitator would encourage reflection and dialogue. The theological underpinnings of these *Celebraciones* emphasized the centrality of Jesus' dedication to denouncing injustices against the poor and marginalized, implying the need for all participants to reflect on Biblical text in light of lived reality, with focus on societal injustice and oppression, and to look toward the future they believe God would like them to co-create. These *Celebraciones* were central to the life at the refugee camps.

Literacy Classes. The Salvadorans and international volunteers also provided opportunities for basic literacy education for both children and adults and teacher training for those adults who already knew how to read and write (Hammond, 1998). As Lino described it for us (see beginning of this chapter), the work of adult literacy in the refugee camps was based largely on Freirean philosophy and pedagogy. Classes were taught by the Salvadoran refugees themselves, and lessons emanated from and revolved around the reality of *campesino* life. The materials and pedagogy reflected a particular emphasis on establishing an awareness of one's ability to change one's sociopolitical reality and developing concrete plans as to how the students themselves could make that happen.

In spite of sincere attempts to train teachers in Freirean pedagogy, however, the legacy of many years of rote methods of recitation and copying seeped its way into the subsequent methodology that the new teachers employed in their instruction. Consequently, much of the teaching that occurred in the refugee camps relied on these traditional (for Latin America, that is) rote methods, such as dictated word lists, copying words from the board, and writing activities aimed solely at improving penmanship. Regardless, many formerly illiterate *campesinos* began to learn to read and write in the refugee camps, and thousands of children, who would have grown up without access to any sort of education if they had remained in El Salvador, also attended school for the first times in their lives.

Papaturro had an adult literacy rate of 73%,[11] according to a census taken a year before Robin's arrival. A majority of those with basic literacy skills indicated that they learned these in the camps.

Different Experience for Women. All of the women in Robin's basic literacy class had also attended classes during their years at Mesa Grande. The women did not, however, attend classes with the same degree of regularity as did the men.

According to Robin's students, several factors intervened to prevent their regular attendance and their learning to read and write in the refugee camp classes. All of the women reported suffering from an array of physical ailments, such as body aches and sudden, intense experiences of emotional sensitivity, sadness, or anxiety, all of which they described as a result of "nerve problems." These ailments, along with the frequent complaints of headaches, backaches, ulcers, and stomachaches, were undoubtedly related to the extreme trauma the women experienced during the war and throughout their time in the refugee camps. In addition, the women battled other health problems as a result of their years of poverty and the lack of adequate nutrition and health care, such as eye strain (from untreated vision problems) and general fatigue and weakness. Many of these symptoms were exacerbated when the women were in the refugee camps because of the fighting around them and the occasional strafing by aircraft flying overhead.

Secondly, the women reported that they did not have as much time to attend the classes as did the men. While both men and women contributed to the functioning of the refugee camps, such as participating in the artisan workshops or the clothing and shoe-making workshop, or participating as health care or pastoral care workers, the men had fewer labor-intensive duties than the women because they had less land to cultivate than they did in El Salvador. The women, however, still had all of their same domestic tasks, such as taking care of the children, washing the clothes, cleaning the house, making the tortillas, and so on.

THE RETURN AND EVENTUAL ESTABLISHMENT OF PAPATURRO

Struggle to Return Home

Although all longed to return home to El Salvador, the journey toward resettlement was long and grueling. Most of those who resettled in Papaturro first returned to the village of Santa Marta, Cabañas, where they had originally lived before fleeing to Honduras. They made this trip with the first *retorno*, October 10, 1987. Life was difficult there, however, because of considerable overcrowding, which impacted the availability of farmable land, adequate living space, and wood for cooking. A group of families began to look for other available land, tapping into underground networks in order to learn about farmable, available land. Three years later, on November 25, 1990, 30 families once again uprooted and traveled to Cuscatlán to begin to resettle in Papaturro.[12]

Travel across El Salvador at this time was still very dangerous. There were frequent military checkpoints, where all men were body-searched and all baskets and belongings of any kind were torn apart and searched. Initially, the families trying to reach Papaturro had to sleep along the road for at least a day, as the military would not allow them beyond a certain point. Moreover, this part of Cuscatlán, near Suchitoto, was considered a "conflict zone," a place of intense, armed conflict. Many people recount that they frequently heard the sound of fighting at that time. The armed conflict and military harassment continued until the signing of the Peace Accords in 1991. At this time, there was no more fighting, but the military checkpoints remained until April, 1992. This meant that even after the people resettled in Papaturro, they were stopped and searched every time they wanted to go in or out of the community, whether to go to the hospital, to purchase food items, or simply to send or receive mail.

Their initial days in Papaturro were extremely difficult. Papaturro was originally the site of a single family plantation of approximately 260 acres. It had been abandoned, however, for more than 11 years by the time the families arrived. It was completely overgrown, with no source of potable water and no housing. The only food they had was what they were able to carry with them from Cabañas. Once again, as in the refugee camps, people suffered from disease, hunger, and severity of the elements.

Rebuilding Lives and Community

In a characteristic spirit of resiliency and unity, however, the people of Papaturro immediately began to rebuild their lives. They had already elected a *directiva* (a governing body) before they left Santa Marta. The *directiva*, together with the support and insight of all of the families, decided that the first, most important project would be building homes. All agreed that this work would be done collectively, with all people working together to build each home. Simultaneously, some people began to look for a source of potable water. Teams of people worked together to create three places where community members could come to collect water. As soon as the homes were built and water sources created, the men began to prepare the land for planting. They planted their first crops in May. People shared whatever resources they had, be that food or skills, working together to create a new community.

Along with the development of the basic necessities of food, shelter, and water, people worked together to build other, essential aspects of community life. In general, under the guidance of the *directiva*, with the input of the entire community, the families worked together to create a social and political infrastructure that could help them work, in an organized, united manner, toward accomplishing the goals that were the essence of the revolutionary struggle. They created an artisan cooperative, where women and girls sewed clothing and crafts for community use and for sale outside of the community.

The *directiva* established an education committee, eventually forming an elementary school for children. Young women from the community volunteered to be the first "popular teachers," offering to draw from whatever knowledge they gained at the schools in the refugee camps in order to teach the younger children. The first school consisted of children sitting on logs under the sprawling, protective branches of the *pepeto* tree. Eventually, when the community received funding, they were able to purchase enough materials to build the first building, a multipurpose building made of cinder blocks, chicken wire, and metal sheeting. This building then served as the school, as well as a meeting place for any other purpose. In a similar spirit, other young people in the community volunteered to work as health promoters, again drawing from what they had learned in the refugee camps, wanting to use that toward the purpose of helping the community reach its shared goals. Several years later, in 1993, there were efforts toward creating adult literacy classes.

PAPATURRO

In the Quiet of the Campo

Walking from the highway into Papaturro, one is struck by the quiet, lush beauty of the countryside. Deep blue skies, with the imminent heavy rain clouds lurking on the horizon, envelop the land, unmarred by any tall trees. Heavy dark green foliage surrounds the walker, broken only by the fields of corn, coffee, and sesame seed that exist near the communities that lie along the road. Up here, there is no view of the impressive volcano that dominates the skyline of San Salvador. Instead, one is surrounded by sky and crops and verdant foliage. Blue grey mountain tops can be glimpsed in the far distance. No traffic noises mar the quiet; absent is the background hubbub of people talking, shopping, or going about their business, another feature of the capital. Instead, if one listens carefully, the gentle sounds of wildlife can be detected: the chittering of birds, a mother duck instructing her young, the scurrying of unseen wildlife through the bushes and undergrowth.

During the rainy season, from November to April, rains fall, sometimes quite heavily, every day, turning the rocky dirt road to slippery mud. When the rains stop, in April and May, the foliage loses its rich and vibrant coloring, and the mud turns to dust, blowing about with every burst of wind or passing vehicle, covering all travelers along the road with a thin layer of dirt.[13]

Within a 30-minute walk from the highway, one approaches the first of the three repopulation communities located in the *Canton de La Bermuda*[14] along the road, Las Americas. Soon after, one veers off on the path to Papaturro, and before long the first dwellings appear, set back from the path that follows a deeply cut rut in the land.

The Homes of Mud and Sticks

The small, one-room houses are virtually camouflaged from their sur-
roundings, being constructed of the same earth, mud, and sticks that sur-
round them. A mud and grass mixture, sometimes in the form of bricks, is
the prime component of all homes. Large tree trunks and branches com-
pose the supporting frame. Most of the homes contain a single, very
small window and a make-shift sort of door for openings and daylight.
Sheets of corrugated tin form the roofs of many of the homes, with an increasing presence, however, of roofs made of clay tiles, the preferred material in El Salvador's tropical climate.

Cooking is done in an attached, three-walled structure often built of
sticks bound together with twine and vines. Inside this structure, a raised
platform constructed of thick branches holds an open fire contained by
large rocks and hardened mud. These provide the base for the pots used to
boil the beans and coffee, and the *comal* (flat skillet) used for cooking the
thick corn tortillas. Many kitchens also include a large cast-iron grinder,
used several times a day to prepare the corn for the tortillas. Plastic water
jugs, tin cups and plates, and plastic tubs for washing dishes hang from
the walls or are wedged between the branches that make up the walls.

In front of each home, there is a canopy of branches and sheets of tin
that hangs above a wooden table, several chairs, and at least one home-
made hammock. This is a central gathering spot for most families, where
they sit to eat, drink coffee, and converse with each other and their neigh-
bors. Inside, the darkness is relieved by a few shafts of sunlight through
the single window or door during the day or by the small, homemade gas
lanterns or wax candles that burn after sunset. Flashlights are used
whenever a particular item is sought from inside the house.

Usually, there is only enough space for beds, which hug the walls and
are shared by family members. Wooden boxes, shoved under the beds,
contain clothing and other family treasures. Very few homes have floors.
Hard-packed earth that turns dusty or somewhat muddy, depending on
the season, serves the purpose. Inevitably, a battery-run radio sits on a table or an upturned box, providing the only regular contact that people
have with life outside of the community.

Tomasa's Home

Licho and Tomasa's home lies along the path at the outskirts of
Papaturro. Tomasa is a regular member of Robin's basic literacy class. So
is Deonicia, Licho's mother and Tomasa's mother-in-law, who lives with
the family, having been widowed during the war. Tomasa has planted a
small flower garden immediately opposite the door; it blooms with a

lovely mixture of colors and brightens the outdoor eating area and Tomasa's daily life. A lover of beauty, Tomasa has added other touches of color to the outside of her home: A red and blue patterned vinyl table-cloth (oilcloth) covers the wooden table where people eat and where the radio resides, colored pages from old magazines and newspapers are pasted up and down the exterior mud wall of the home, and a red and black plaid blanket is positioned with wire along a piece of the corrugated tin wall along the northernmost side of her house.

Near the house, there is a simple water pipe and faucet. Water is now available to all Papaturro residents through these outdoor taps, spaced around the community. A recent donation of international money made this form of running water possible. The people in many other rural communities, however, still rely on river water for their drinking and washing needs. In fact, it was little over a year ago that the people of Papaturro received this water project. Previously, as they had done for all of their lives, they walked to the closest river and carried large buckets of water on their heads to gather enough water for their daily washing tasks. These water faucets, according to community members, are a small, but very significant, step toward an improved existence for all families in the community.

Tomasa and Licho, like many other families in Papaturro, have created an area for washing dishes and clothing, as well as for bathing, around this water source. Tomasa and Deonicia wash all of their family's clothing there, scrubbing each article multiple times against a cement surface, created by placing a flat slab of cement at waist height and propping it up with several large rocks. The women wash the dishes in a large plastic tub placed on the ground close to this water source. This space becomes a bathing area by stringing up a large sheet of black plastic on a frame around the faucet.

During mealtimes, Tomasa's children, and sometimes grandchildren, alternately sit on their parents' laps, on the ground, or balance precariously on a wooden bench as they consume their meal of tortillas and beans. Several small chickens weave in and out of the chairs, pecking up whatever drops to the ground. Competing with them for bits of food are two small cats and an emaciated white dog. No one pays any attention to the animals except to kick them out of the way whenever they approach too close.

It is evident that there is no problem with waste in the community. Whatever is not consumed by the people (e.g., peels, bones, extra tortillas, any leftover beans) is tossed to the ground for one of the dogs, cats, pigs, turkeys, ducks, chickens, cows, or donkeys that wander among the houses.[15]

Into the Center of the Community

Continuing down the road into Papaturro, one nears the confluence of homes where Robin lives. Celia's house sits just down a small incline from Robin's. Celia is also a member of the literacy class, as well as the primary person providing Robin with her meals. Typical of the generosity of most people in Papaturro, Celia is willing and eager to share her family's breakfast, lunch, or dinner. Robin quickly discovered that many people in the community are, in fact, anxious to share their food with her, seeing it as a way to show their appreciation for her work in the community, as well as a simple way to share time and friendship. Robin would often bring gifts of rice or fruit from visits to San Salvador or Suchitoto to Celia and others who shared their meals with her. Whenever visitors ate with families, they would usually pay for their food when they left the community.

The *clinica* is located in the center of the community, across the road from Celia's. It is attached to another building serving as storage space. The clinic is small and dark, and contains a desk, a wooden chair, and a simple canvas cot. Wooden shelves line the walls and hold a sparse collection of antibiotics and other medications and bandages. Boxes that held, or hold, medical supplies are stacked around the room. All of the surfaces are covered with dust and dirt from the crumbling walls and animal droppings from the rodents and the cats that wind their way in and out through the opening near the roof. The initials FMLN are spray painted on one of the outside walls.

The clinic is staffed part time by young women who are members of the community. These women, who have limited formal education, are paid a small stipend by a local NGO, which provides them with ongoing training in basic health care with emphasis on pre- and postnatal care.

Meeting Basic Needs in Papaturro

Between Robin's house and the artisan workshop is the water pipe and faucet where Robin washes her dishes and gets her water. Robin, along with many people in Papaturro, walks to a small stream, however, to bathe. Participating in this aspect of community life, Robin learns all about this daily ritual. Often bathing and washing the family's clothing at the same time, the women enter the stream wearing only half-slips, covering that part of their bodies that they feel needs to be covered. (Similarly, men bathe in the river clad only in their underwear.)[16] Using small plastic tubs as scoops, the women pour river water over their entire bodies. They often wash their hair and bodies with a soap they've made from local seeds which they have boiled for hours in a large pot. Still clothed

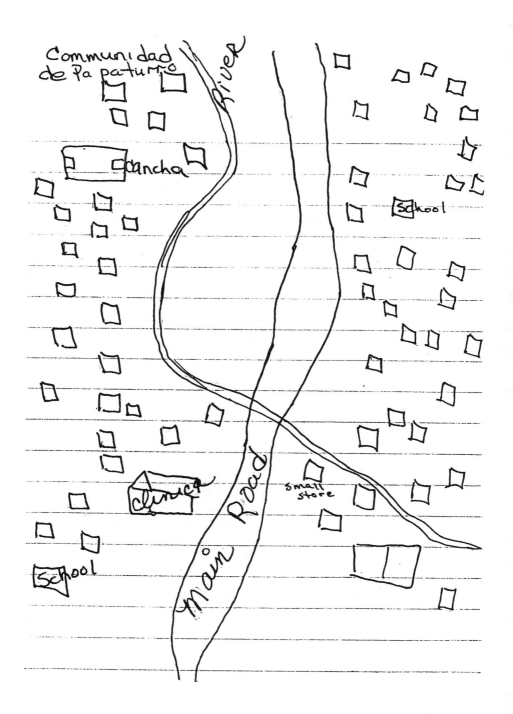

Map of the Papaturro community copied by Vicki into her research notebook from the wall of the *clinica*.

only in their slips, the women then begin to wash their clothes, scrubbing them against the rocks in the stream. When they are finished, the women modestly and carefully replace their wet slips with dry ones, and then dress with the rest of the dry clothing they wore to the river.

With no plumbing, the people of Papaturro rely on outdoor latrines that are privately owned and built. Margarita, a woman in her early 30s who was a member of the literacy class and Robin's neighbor, shared her latrine with Robin. The latrine is a small structure, made of cement blocks. The many families in Papaturro who cannot afford a latrine must make use of the surrounding bushes and undergrowth for their bathroom needs.

Community and Government

The people of Papaturro have worked diligently, in an organized and unified manner, to purchase their land. With all members signing the legal documents in 1995, they are in the process of purchasing the land as a community (rather than proceeding with individual purchases). The community has decided, however, to divide up the land such that each family has an individual plot on which they can cultivate corn and beans for their own family. They have also decided to use the rest of the land to grow coffee, sugar cane, and sesame seed. Community members work together to cultivate and sell these crops, with the earnings dedicated primarily to the benefit of the community as a whole. Designated community leaders oversee the picking of the coffee; other appointees investigate all aspects of the eventual sale of this coffee. All families contribute to picking the coffee, working long and numerous hours during coffee season. Those who work are paid a small percentage of what they produce, with the largest portion of the profits going toward the ultimate purchase of the land. The community has also worked together to raise the money for, and build, two small schools, the clinic, and an artisan workshop.

Most repopulation communities have an internal governing body, *La Directiva*, and regular community meetings to deal with community affairs and issues. Seven elected officials make up *La Directiva*, and in Papaturro these were, at that time, Eliseo, the President, who had the primary responsibility for the coordination of the *directiva*, and ultimately, the coordination of all the activities of the community; Francisco, the Vice President; Alejandro, who was responsible for the agricultural production and related projects; José Angel, who was responsible for the credit committee and for the purchasing and sale of the collective community products; Rodrigo, who was responsible for the control of the finances, working with the credit committee to coordinate expenses, available funds, and the purchasing of items related to collective community projects; Lolo, the Education and Social Coordinator, who coordinated all of the work in the area of education as well as that related to pastoral work, the musical group, and the sports activities; and Juana, who was responsible for projects related to women's issues.

This was the community to which Robin came to live and teach. This was the *directiva* that made her work possible through their support and encouragement of those community members who still needed to acquire basic literacy skills so that they could contribute to the well-being of the community as well as achieve personal goals and needs.

ENDNOTES

1. It is important to note that the conditions in El Salvador during the course of our study were very different from those before, during, and immediately following the war and as related by our informants about those times. The Peace Accords had been in effect for several years by the time Robin arrived in Papaturro and the repression and intimidation had ended. Literacy work was no longer dangerous work and the Salvadoran government was officially committed to literacy development for children and adults. Therefore, it was not only not dangerous for our informants to share their stories with us, but it was viewed by them in a positive and desirous light. All of the people of the community of Papaturro sought opportunities to tell foreigners, particularly those from the United States, about their previous conditions and their experiences during the war. They experienced this as a way to heal, to recover from the trauma inflicted on them as a result of the armed conflict. Robin noted instances when the community members would talk openly about their experiences with complete strangers who would appear in the community as members of delegation. They would do this with no trepidation or insistence on anonymity or secrecy. When Vicki visited the community, Robin explained to the people that she and Vicki were writing a book, primarily for people in the United States, to tell their stories and to describe how they were learning to read and write. They all enthusiastically gave us permission to do this and to use their names and their pictures. This may seem strange given the adversarial role played by the United States in the war. However, a prevalent understanding existed: there can be a very distinct difference between a government and individuals. The Salvadoran people knew this very well, given their own experience of the Salvadoran government. Therefore, most Salvadoran people quickly and clearly acknowledged that they greatly appreciated U.S. visitors and U.S. volunteer workers and did not associate them with the millions of dollars of U.S. aid that supported the Salvadoran government and the war. Further, the Salvadoran people eagerly welcomed any chance to tell the U.S. people the truth about the realities of the war and the conditions of the *campesinos* that led up to the war.

2. The FMLN is a leftist revolutionary movement organized in El Salvador in 1980 in order to participate in an armed struggle against the military-controlled right-wing government. The armed struggle between the two forces continued until 1991.

3. The Lempa River is one of the largest rivers in El Salvador. It forms part of the border with Honduras.

4. Lino named the refugee camps as the place where popular education initially took hold in El Salvador, and this was undoubtedly his experience of it. Hammond (1998), however, described a process in which organized attempts to provide literacy training to *campesinos* who had previously lacked access to schools or had failed to learn to read in schools were initiated as part of the Liberation Theology movement and the attendant BCC meetings, where the ability to read the Bible was considered basic to becoming aware of one's reality and taking action to change it. All of this took place several years before the beginning of armed combat in El Salvador and constituted the base and precursor of the later civil war.

5. All of the NGOs in Suchitoto reflected the politics and values of the leftist movement, such as commitment to literacy development, creation of local government structures, and agrarian development and reform.

6. Celia's experience of blindness may be attributed to a condition called "night blindness," which is caused by a severe deficiency of vitamin A. The most basic symptom of night blindness is a lack of functional vision in the dark. See D. Werner (1992, p. 226).

7. Hammond (1998) cited the following for overall literacy rates among Salvadoran *campesinos:* In 1975, the illiteracy rate was reported to be 48.9% for men and 57.2% for women. In 1978, the illiteracy rate was 62.1% for those who earned their living in agriculture. In 1970, 60% of the rural population over 14 years of age had never attended school. Although statistics of literacy and illiteracy vary widely, depending on who is doing the estimating for whose agenda and which definition of literacy is being applied, it is clear that literacy among the *campesinos* was relatively rare and extremely difficult to come by.

8. Between the years 1983–1994, the U.S. government, in a concerted effort to stabilize the Salvadoran economy and support the Salvadoran government during the civil war, sent over 3.33 billion dollars in economic aid to El Salvador. During these same years, it also provided 911.3 million dollars in military aid (Murray, 1995).

9. A "zone," also know as "a conflict zone," is an area where the FMLN had established influence, and, therefore, was an area that experienced the greatest impact during the war. Established ways of indicating geopolitical boundaries, however, are to refer to *Departamentos* (Departments), which are the largest divisions, and within Departments are cities, towns, and small rural communities.

10. Danner (1994) and Hammond (1998) provided descriptions of the ways in which the government army consisted of conscripted *campesinos* who were forced to fight against their own people.

11. This figure represents a computation wherein everyone who was at least 18 years old with at least 2 years of school, as noted on the census, was considered literate. With this as the definition and baseline, 27% of adults in Papaturro were nonliterate. Of those adults who had completed at least 2 years of schooling, the average grade completed was 3.9, with a range of 2 to 9 years of school.

12. These families constituted a self-chosen unit and shared goals, values, and political ideologies. They had all belonged to the same FMLN party before and during

the war, had lived in the same village before the war, had shared the same experiences during the fighting and the flight from El Salvador, and had lived together in the refugee camps. Thus, there was a great deal of social and political cohesion among the residents of Papaturro during our acquaintance with them.

13. There are many hardships caused by the rainy season. Because most people travel by foot, along rough dirt roads, one must always be careful to return home early enough. Otherwise, one could end up walking home through ankle- or knee-deep water, along uneven, unsure surfaces below. As almost none of the *campesino* people own rain gear, rainy season also impacts their participation in community programs. For example, if it rains, people will not leave home because exposing themselves to heavy rainfall without adequate protection could pose health problems. Early, heavy rainfalls can also impact the crops, in that such rains could wash away seeds that have not yet had time to develop into rooted plants.

14. Historically, a *canton* was the smallest geopolitical form of division, with the largest being the *Departamento*. Currently a *canton* refers to an area that contains smaller villages, or communities. No one lives exclusively in a *canton;* they always live in a community which is identified as being part of a particular *canton.*

15. In poor, rural communities, it is rare that meat is ever consumed at mealtime. The chickens are kept for their eggs, and only at very special holidays, or when a foreigner visits, are they killed and eaten. Cows are used for their milk. Pigs and turkeys are kept primarily to be sold to "rich" people who buy them at special times of the year for their meat.

16. The custom of wearing a slip is one that has been passed on since the colonial days, and the women wear them, throughout the entire day, in spite of the tremendous heat. The custom of wearing slips while bathing in an outdoor stream can also be attributed to the modesty that prevails among the Salvadoran *campesina* women.

3

A Literacy Class Takes Shape: Eight Women's Literacy Histories and Motivations

Recruiting Students

Word was out, passed from house to house, and the people of Papaturro had gathered for the *asamblea*[1] regarding the new literacy classes. The community gathering was held, as always, under the *nisperas* tree, its large, sprawling branches providing some shelter from the burning rays of the tropical sun. Children ran around, noisily playing nearby, drawn to the event as out-of-the-ordinary entertainment. Dogs, chickens, ducks, pigs and cows contributed to the noise and commotion, haphazardly weaving their way through the crowd. Yet what may seem like chaos to an outside observer is apparently familiar and functional, as most all that are gathered are attentive to what Eliseo, the community president, wants to communicate.

The prime reason for the *asamblea* is the announcement of two new literacy classes to be held in Papaturro. There will be a basic level class, Eliseo explains, for those unable to read or write even their name or a simple sentence. There will also be a second-level class, aimed at students who have attained approximately a first-grade level of reading and writing. The teachers will be members of the community, Lita and Sylvia, two young women who are already working as teachers in Papaturro's newly established elementary school. Robin will provide supervision and assistance.

The program will be sponsored by a local NGO, *Fundación 16 de Enero*, Eliseo announces. They will provide a small stipend for the teachers, and notebooks and pencils for the students. Aware that the cost of pencils and notebooks has been prohibitive to their school attendance in the past, potential students murmur in relief. Eliseo discusses the importance of being able to read and write, reminding people that they will also develop their critical thinking skills, and learn information about agricultural work, basic sanitation and health care, and the basic constitutional rights of all Salvadorans. Eliseo reminds people of some of the values that they learned during the war, in the refugee camps, specifically explaining how vital this *popular*[2] form of adult education is. It is important not only to the development of the individual, he explains, but most importantly, this kind of education "will help our development as a community. It is essential that we are knowledgeable," he adds, "and that we have the skills to continue to grow more knowledgeable. It is this that will help us to remain organized, and ultimately be what helps us overcome our poverty." He closes the *asamblea* by indicating that all who are interested should sign up with Lita or Sylvia right after the meeting.

Although many people in the community signed up for the classes, Lita, Sylvia, and Robin spent an entire week visiting each individual who had signed up. Each of these teachers had learned through experience that a personal visit is necessary in order to ensure that people come to class. During their visits, they encountered a great deal of self-doubt and hesitation. *Pues, no me queda nada en esta cabeza. Ya intentaba, y no aprendía nada* (Nothing stays with me, in this head of mine. I already studied, and I didn't learn anything). *Ya estoy muy vieja* (I'm too old). Through the *confianza* (rapport and trust), however, that each of the teachers have with the people of the community, they were able to convince many of the potential students that they could learn and that they should attend class the following week. On the first day of class, a majority of those who had signed up arrived at the schoolroom.

The Class Begins

Beginning with that first day of class, Lita and Sylvia decided to combine the basic-level and the second-level classes. They would conduct the initial discussions together and then break the class up as they worked on specific reading and writing skills development. Fifteen women and five men began the class. Many of the men in the community had acquired basic reading and writing skills in the refugee camps and did not feel that even a second-grade level class was appropriate for them.[3]

The students gathered at 4:00 p.m. in the children's school building. They sat in the only chairs available, chairs designed for children 5 to 10 years old. Lita struggled as she tried to write new words on the board. The blackboard was old, and the black paint no longer served to provide a contrast against the bits of white chalk that remained on the surface. By 5:00 p.m., the sun's light was beginning to fade, and students with poor vision struggled to see even their own writing on the page. Without electricity, all three teachers knew that they needed to end the class early, in spite of their awareness that even 2 hours a day was not as much time as they would like.

The students appeared undaunted, however, and eager to proceed as they discussed their literacy goals and desires. Deonicia and Margarita hoped to learn to write their names. Celia, Antonio, José, and Chunga spoke of hopes to learn to read the Bible and to write letters to family members now living in the United States. Carmelita and Tomasa each spoke of how often they have felt "blind," that is, deceived by store owners or government workers: "I want to learn to read and write so that no one will be able to deceive me anymore," they told their new teachers. The students inspired one another, their contributions reminding each other of the many ways that reading and writing skills would enhance their daily lives.

And so, with this mix of enthusiasm and inspiration, along with the immediate obstacles of lack of adequate materials, the literacy class began. Over time, the physical location of the class shifted from place to place for varying reasons. Within 2 months, the male students, having decided that they could not leave their agricultural work so early in the day (3:30 p.m.), stopped attending the class.[4] At this point, the class became one single class, with Lita and Sylvia deciding to work together. Lita's participation was very sporadic, however, due to her responsibilities caring for a young infant. Within the next month, she completely withdrew her involvement with the class when she gave birth to her second child.

At the time of these changes, the students who remained decided to change the class hour to 2:00 p.m., a time that better allowed them to prepare and serve lunch to their families, as well as return home in time to prepare and serve the evening meal. This meant that the class needed to be moved outside, however, as the children used the school building during the day. To furnish this outdoor classroom, Robin solicited money from her U.S. sponsors toward the purchase of wood, and Lolo donated his skills and time to make three beautiful benches with accompanying platforms for desks.

The remaining 10 women began their outdoor studies under the protection of the expansive branches of the *pepeto* tree. Reading, writing, and reflective dialogue took place among the inevitable children, too young to be in school, playing and, at intervals, staring in curiosity at the sight of their mothers and other women of the community discussing issues, reading aloud, or writing intently in their notebooks. Dogs, too, seemed to gravitate toward this new activity taking place in the open air. All seemed unaware of the students' need for quiet and concentration.

Whereas studying outside was the most functional location during the 6 months of the dry season (approximately November through May), during the 6 months of the rainy season, the women moved the class indoors, into the *artesania* workshop, a small mud hut used by the members of the community's artisan cooperative. During these months, when it is not raining, the tropical sun is particularly strong and the air is steamy with humidity. It became even more difficult for the students to concentrate as the afternoon sun, beating down on the tin roof, generated tremendous heat. Participation in the more demanding class activities was inevitably affected by the resulting fatigue. Regardless, the women faithfully attended class and progressed toward literacy goals, discovering multiple nuances of literacy skills along the way.

Although the literacy class began with 15 women, the number decreased as different women found life's responsibilities too overwhelming for regular attendance. Some students dropped out, only to return after a year to find the class had moved too far along for them to meaningfully participate. These women then formed a second literacy class with a new teacher recruited and trained by Robin. This class then became the basic literacy class, and the original class became the second-level class. Of the original group, there were eight women who formed the core of the class, participating consistently throughout the time of our study. It is this group of eight women who informed our inquiry.

THE WOMEN

Deonicia

Deonicia was always the first to arrive to class, often arriving 15 min early. She would sit quietly, holding onto her plastic bag containing a single notebook and pencil, patiently waiting for the rest of the students to arrive. Regardless of weather or household tasks, Deonicia never missed a class.

Deonicia was the oldest student in Papaturro's literacy class, having turned 68 years old just before the class first began. She is a small and frail woman, worn down by the war and the anguish she suffered in losing three of her sons. Early in her studies she would often say that she didn't have the necessary strength to really learn to read and write, distinguishing herself from others whom she considers to have regained the fortitude that they had lost through their experience of the war. When asked, she explains that she has been weakened by the loss of her children. One day, during an aided writing activity, Deonicia explained further that she had seen the mutilated body of one of her sons, crying as she haltingly told Robin that they had cut her son into many pieces, his body parts strewn about.

Deonicia has five sons who live in Papaturro and who provide her with a great deal of material and emotional support. She lives with one of her sons, Licho, while her other sons are preparing to build for her a small home of her own, just in front of Licho's house. She also has a multitude of grandchildren. During class, Robin would often notice several of Deonicia's grandchildren draw close to her as she was reading or writing. As Robin watched, Deonicia would inevitably reach into one of her apron pockets for a piece of hard candy to slip to each one of them.

Deonicia was 12 years old when she first attended school. "Before that," she explained, "it was much harder to even go to school. The teachers came from far away, and did not always come more than 3 days a week. So, one did not learn anything. And, too, we could not always buy the pencils and notebooks that we needed." Deonicia went for the first 3 months of first grade before her parents decided that she should no longer attend. "I was anemic," she explained. "When I went to school, I always had tremendous headaches. And I was very thin and weak. So my parents decided that it was better that I did not go to school. Going to school required such sacrifice, and I could not have really learned anyway."

Later in her life, in the refugee camps, Deonicia attended literacy classes. "I studied for about 1 year. I was learning, but the afflictions.... One gets so mixed up, it was so hard to concentrate."

Now, 7 years later, Deonicia believes that she has "forgotten everything." During the first days of class, Deonicia could not even write her name without a great deal of help. She was one of the few students who was unable to write out any of her thoughts, even with invented spelling, after the class discussions. Six months later, when Deonicia had gained writing skills that allowed her to express her opinions and feelings, Robin often recalled the first phrase that Deonicia wrote independently after a discussion of land rights: *nido de pajaro* (nest of a bird).

Deonicia.
(All photos courtesy of Robin Waterman
unless otherwise noted.)

Tomasa.

Chunga grinding corn for tortillas.

Francisca reading over her writing in her notebook.

Celia reading intently during class.

Margarita in front of her house.

Carmelita nursing her child while writing her thoughts on the day's generative theme.

Esperanza reading in class while attending her infant.

Deonicia frequently participated in class discussions, particularly when invited. She is a devoutly religious Catholic, often mentioning seeking strength from "God and the Virgin." Deonicia particularly invoked her understanding of the Biblical examples of Mary, the mother of Jesus, seemingly drawing tremendous strength from her understanding of Mary as a woman who also suffered because of the loss of her son.

Deonicia also frequently invoked the concept of "love" during class discussions. In her gentle and kind manner, she would explain, "We must love all equally, mustn't we? We should not have hatred, and we should not look at others as less. We must forgive; we must have love, for all people, equally."

Deonicia offered this as insight regarding attitudes toward the Salvadoran government, attitudes that she wishes the government would have toward poor *campesinos*, as well as attitudes that Papaturrans should have toward one another in the community.

In these same conversations, however, Deonicia revealed the source of some of her insights, expressing the great pain that she has felt because of the way that wealthier people have treated the Salvadoran *campesinos*. In reflecting on the attitudes wealthy people have toward the poor, as well as such things as the cruel behavior of the Salvadoran army, Deonicia was always clear that this is not what God wants, this is not what is right. According to Deonicia, love, equality and compassion should be our guiding values.

Tomasa

Tomasa Recinos, one of Deonicia's daughters-in-law, also faithfully attended the literacy class, arriving with enthusiasm and dedication ever since the first day. Tomasa was 37 years old and the mother of five children. She had a sixth child whom she lost during the war, an infant who died in her arms when she and her family were in flight toward Honduras. Tomasa was one of the most vibrant students of the class, having grown up during the time of the initial formation of the BCCs and of revolutionary thought for the Salvadoran *campesinos*. And although Tomasa expressed the characteristic Salvadoran doubt about her abilities to learn and progress,[5] she was exceptionally focused on her reading and writing goals, exceptionally determined to be committed to the class and to learning.

Tomasa never attended school as a child. Because she was the oldest girl in her family of six children, four of whom were boys, her mother asked that she help her with the survival tasks relegated to females. So Tomasa helped care for younger siblings, helped make the tortillas and prepare the beans, washed the family's clothing, and collected wood for cooking. Tomasa's father died when she was still young, which further increased the need that Tomasa stay home from school and help her mother.

Tomasa also explained that her family did not have enough of a cash income to enable all of the children to attend school. In fact, there was not even enough cash income to purchase pencils and notebooks for the children in her family who were already attending school. Her mother needed to be creative, making homemade notebooks from a very crude form of paper, drawing lines on this paper and then sewing it together to form a notebook.

Consequently, Tomasa's first experience of school was in the refugee camp. "In Mesa Grande," Tomasa told Robin one day, "those who knew even a little taught us what they knew. So, I started to go (to the classes). But I became pregnant, and was very sick. All the time I was sick. But still, I attended class for 1 year."

Due to sickness and the rigors of the camps' collective work, however, Tomasa was not able to attend class every day. "In the refugee camps," she explains, "we worked very hard, always working *en colectivo*, in an organized manner." Tomasa helped to serve the food as well as make the clothing. "For me," she said, "there was very little time to attend class."

Tomasa was able to write her name and a few words in the first days of the class in Papaturro, and through her commitment and determination, progressed rapidly in her acquisition of all critical literacy skills. In part, she attributes some of this to her time in Mesa Grande: "In the year that I did go (to the class in Mesa Grande), I learned many letters that I have not forgotten, and now they are useful to me." She added, "Now, I feel very happy because there are many more letters that I am learning so that now I can write many small words. Yes, I feel very happy because of this."

Francisca

Unlike Deonicia and Tomasa, Francisca Sanchez did not consistently arrive on time for the class, given that she looked to the shadows of the sun to indicate the hour; nevertheless, she was one of the most faithful and committed students. Francisca was single, yet cared for Alex, a young, orphaned boy. When asked, she says that she is "about" 50 years old, explaining that she is not really sure because all of her records were burned in the war. Knowing her exact age did not seem important to Francisca. Regardless, Francisca appeared older than she was, having been worn down by the manual labor necessary for survival and the strain of frequent illnesses. She strained to see, needing to stand right in front of the board in order to read even letters printed in very large print. Francisca frequently remarked that she didn't think that she could really learn to read and write, yet she watched the movement of the sun daily, waiting for that particular shadow that would indicate that it was just about 2:00 p.m. Francisca rarely missed a class.

Francisca was one of the poorest people in Papaturro, surviving almost entirely on beans and corn, without any cash income. She explained to Robin one day that she was just recovering from having been seriously ill, fearing at one point that she would die. "But I have never been to a hospital," she said. "No, I have never even seen the inside of a clinic!" Her bloated stomach gave witness to a chronic condition she believed was due to some kind of intestinal parasite, which caused abdominal pain, fatigue, and headaches. Unable to afford medical care, Francisca looked to local plants for relief of her symptoms.

As a child, Francisca never attended school. She had three brothers and no sisters. As a result, she had to help her mother with all of the household chores, including making all the daily tortillas and walking long distances to carry them to where her father and brothers were working in the fields. In describing her mother, Francisca says, "All she knew was suffering." And pausing for a moment, she adds, "We have all suffered, all of our lives."

While in the refugee camp at Mesa Grande, Francisca attended her first class. She reported that she attended school for about 7 years in the camps but that she didn't feel that she had really learned anything.

> There was a great deal of bombing much of the time, with the soldiers always nearby. At times, the soldiers would come into the camps, and if we were studying, we would have to hide because if they saw we were studying, they would have killed us. We were *aflijidos*, under great affliction, great stress, and we lost our morale, our spirit. There has always been great suffering.

In spite of Francisca's claims that she will never really learn, however, she is progressing in the literacy class in Papaturro. Due to her fragile health, and a spirit that still seems injured by all of the trauma she suffered during the war, Francisca was less vibrant and active in class discussions than most of the others. But when asked to read or write, she was successful, able to slowly sound out new words and, when writing, carefully considering her thoughts, able to determine the letter sounds necessary to encode some of what she wanted to say. She would ultimately form at least one sentence that expressed her own feelings or thoughts regarding the topic of the day's discussion. "I feel happy," she told Robin one day, "happy that I am studying in the class and learning to read, because when one can't read, it is as though she can't see."

Chunga

Ana María Sorto (known in the community as "Chunga") was another student who consistently arrived late, arriving about 30 min after the scheduled start of class. Yet Chunga's commitment to the class was as strong as that of the others. Aged 66, Chunga was widowed during the war. She had taken on the role, therefore, of serving noon-time tortillas to several single men in the community, a task which she attended to for several hours in the morning, up until the time she arrived for class. But although Chunga arrived late, she rarely missed a class.

Chunga is a gentle, quiet woman with a soft, radiant smile and a generous and caring nature. Living close to Robin, and wishing to express her appreciation for Robin's work with the literacy class, Chunga would often arrive at Robin's door with such gifts as a few newly hatched chicken eggs or some raw honey that she had collected.

Like many other woman her age, Chunga attended school only briefly as a girl. "This time period was *tranquilo,* quiet, calm," Chunga explained, comparing this time with the chaos of the war-time years.

> But there were not opportunities for all of us to go to school. And the school was very far from where we lived. Only if you walked a long way, and crossed two roads, with a large stream in between, could you reach the school. The days that I did go to school, I did not have anything to eat. So, instead of becoming sick, my father said, it would be better that I did not go to school. And besides, the teachers did not really spend any time with the girls. The four of us girls that went, we learned nothing. We could read nothing.

Therefore, as with the others, Chunga's first real educational opportunities arose in the refugee camp in Mesa Grande. In spite of the fact that Chunga was in Mesa Grande for almost 11 years, she felt that she had acquired very few reading and writing skills during that time. Her mother was sick, and this meant that Chunga had to care for her, help her with the daily domestic tasks, and care for her own family.

These factors alone were not the most significant, however. "We were worried about all of the *oficios* (domestic work) we had to do, but we were also worried because of the Army, because they announced that they would invade and burn our houses." She described one situation when the Army killed a group of men, cutting them into pieces, simply because they had stepped outside of the boundaries of the camp. "There were also many times when we had very little to eat because we were surrounded by the military and no one could leave (in order to bring in food and medical supplies)." She paused, deep in thought, and concluded quietly, "It was a very hard time."

Despite these many obstacles to her literacy development over the course of her life, Chunga quickly became engaged in the literacy class. When it came time to write out one's thoughts on the generative theme, Chunga would often draw away from the others, sit on whichever log she could find, and become absorbed in her own thoughts and her efforts as she wrote in her small notebook. Chunga would remain on that log, writing, uninterrupted, for a period well beyond that of many other students. She frequently expressed fears that she had many spelling mistakes, yet all of the teachers found that her mistakes were usually few, and often very common errors, characteristic of difficult aspects of particular letter sounds.

Chunga was also a particularly insightful and reflective student. She would often introduce thoughts in class discussion, or in her writing, that brought greater clarity to the political, social, or religious content of the generative theme of the day. When Robin would visit Chunga in her home, Chunga would also discuss the class itself, sharing her thoughts and concerns about such things as teaching methodology and materials.

Celia

Celia Avelar was also among the most insightful and skilled students in the class. After listening to her contributions during class or during a dialogue within a religious service, or simply sharing conversation outside of her home, many visitors were struck by Celia's capacities to articulate, with tremendous social, political, and theological astuteness, her thoughts about the lives of the Salvadoran people.

Celia was 52 years old, and her emotional hardships during the war and subsequent debilitating illnesses show in her face and frail body. She has given birth to eight children, lost three when they were very young, and another two during the war.

Celia never attended school as a young girl, being needed for tasks around the home (see previous description in chapter 3). Therefore, as with the others, Celia's first experience of education was in the refugee camp at Mesa Grande. Celia suffered greatly due to the conditions in the camps, however, and identified this as the reason for her inability to learn to read and write as she deeply desired. Celia told Robin one day:

> The refugee camp at Mesa Grande was like a prison. The entire time that we were there, we could never leave because the military always surrounded us. And we lived in shacks, houses made of sheets of canvas. Later we lived in houses of *lamina* (metal sheeting), but these also caused suffering.

> So I went to literacy classes there, but I never learned anything. My children were always sick. There was so much sickness because of the lack of food and medicine and the bad water! And I was often sick as well. The climate caused me many problems. It was too cold, and our houses did not protect us.[6]

When Celia and her family returned to El Salvador and began to rebuild their lives, Celia became actively involved in many aspects of community life in Papaturro. Together with several other women, she participated in creating and running a cooperatively owned store. This involved all aspects of ownership, including traveling long distances to purchase food items and spending many hours attending the store. This exposed Celia to literacy and basic math activities. Simultaneously, this work also further clarified her recognition of the value that literacy acquisition could have for her life.

Celia also encouraged all of her children to pursue as much education as was available. Eventually, her oldest daughter Lita sought training to become a *maestra popular* ("popular" teacher). Once trained, Lita began to teach elementary school in Papaturro. Celia continued to support Lita in this work by caring for Lita's children when Lita was working. Celia explicitly stated that caring for Lita's children was her way of contributing to the education of the community's children. Celia often spoke of Lita's work and the commitment it involved. She was extremely proud of Lita's work as an educator, always emphasizing the commitment that it represented to contributing to a better future for the community. Celia always explicitly stated that she perceived education to be central to the community's ability to work toward creating a better future for all.

In many ways, Celia is an extremely magnetic and charismatic person in the community. She possesses a particular gift for speaking about the war and all of the political, religious, and social implications involved. For these reasons, she is often asked to serve as a host for visitors who come to Papaturro. On one level, this simply involves offering a meal to visitors. On another level, however, this involves dialogue about multiple aspects of community life in Papaturro as well as the larger reality in El Salvador.

For this reason, Celia was asked to provide meals for Robin when she first arrived. Robin immediately recognized the value of this time with Celia. They spent a great deal of time talking, often talking hours after they had shared a meal. The relationship between the two women became a valuable, mutual exchange: While Robin learned a great deal about the sociopolitical reality in Papaturro and El Salvador, Celia benefitted from the exposure to Robin's commitment to adult literacy. As a result, Celia spent a great deal of time developing her reading and writing skills outside of the class, either at her own home or during visits to Robin's home.

Celia engaged fully with the literacy class. As did Chunga, she often drew away from the class during the time designated to writing, becoming lost in her own thoughts about the theme and in her efforts to determine which letters are necessary to express those thoughts in writing.

Her writing, although containing a number of common spelling errors, often reflected tremendous comprehension and insight into the theme, as well as an ability to write out the words necessary to express those thoughts.

Margarita

Margarita Hernández, a tall, lanky woman with a gentle, shy smile, was 30 years old, with five children, ages 3 to 13 years old. With her husband in the United States working to send money back to the family, Margarita had been raising her children alone for the past 3 years.[7] While Margarita cultivated corn and beans and cared for a cow and her numerous chickens, her two girls, Evelyn and Noeli, aged 9 and 7, took on a great deal of the responsibility of caring for the younger children as well as helping to prepare the tortillas. Her oldest daughter lived with Margarita's mother, now widowed and needing help with domestic tasks, as well as some companionship.

Margarita had a harder time than the other students focusing in the class. She was often tired, worn down by the demands of manual labor performed under the hot sun. She was easily distracted by the children and animals who played near the open air "classroom." She often complained of headaches and eye pain, which also contributed to her difficulty in being able to focus. Learning and remembering her letters was particularly difficult for Margarita, and she progressed more slowly than anyone else in class. Despite this, she was a faithful student, rarely missing a class. The literacy class was important to her, and she made intentional efforts to organize her time and activities such that she (and her children) could get everything done either before or after class.

Margarita never attended school as a young girl. She was the third-oldest child in a family of 11 children. Three of those children died, leaving four boys and seven girls. "Many people did not have the opportunity to study; everyone had to work," Margarita explained. "As one who is poor always needs to work, we worked, doing agricultural work, maintaining and sustaining ourselves. So there were not a lot of opportunities to go to school."

"There were many things that made it difficult," Margarita added, after pausing for a moment. "We were also very poor, and did not have the money to buy the pencils and the notebooks. So some went, and others didn't."

Margarita and her siblings attended school when in the refugee camps at Mesa Grande. Whereas all of her brothers and sisters learned to read, she never did. "I tried to study in the camps; I really did. But I had headaches and great eye pain most of the time. For this reason, I was hardly able to study." Then she adds, "I did not learn, but many others learned a lot. But I could not learn." Margarita believed, however, that she was learning in the class in Papaturro. "Now, I know more than just the letters of the alphabet. Now I can write out many small words."

Carmelita

María del Carmen Gomez, affectionately known as Carmelita, was 26 years old and had five children. Her husband, Francisco, was a member of Papaturro's governing body, the *directiva*, providing leadership for many of the community's locally initiated development activities. Francisco had also been very creative with his own family's cultivation, being the first in the community to experiment with growing peanuts and soybeans.

Carmelita was quiet and shy. She rarely spoke out in any group setting and did not become involved in community development projects. But many people had great love and appreciation for Carmelita, as she was a caring neighbor, quick to attend to anyone who was sick and in need of support.

Carmelita, like Margarita, did not progress as much as the other students in the class. In part, this may have been a result of her class attendance, which was more intermittent than the others. Carmelita often came to class just 2 or 3 days a week, often because of illness, either her own or that of one of her children. She frequently complained of severe headaches and intestinal problems when she did attend class, and her children often suffered from extreme diarrhea, even on the days that they were well enough to come with Carmelita to class. Carmelita also occasionally left Papaturro to care for a sick member of her extended family.

When in class, Carmelita had to deal with the distractions of her two youngest girls whom she needed to bring along. She could often be observed reading or writing while breast feeding, easily holding her tiny daughter against her with one hand while holding the pencil or booklet with the other.

Carmelita never attended school until she was in the refugee camp at Mesa Grande, explaining that the only school available to her family was too far away and "there was a large stream, and you couldn't cross it (during the 6 months of the rainy season)." Carmelita added that "It was hard, too, because my mother had to raise us alone, four boys and four girls, without my father, and she did not have the money (to send us to school), because she needed to buy corn." When she was 9 years old, Carmelita's family was forced to flee for Honduras. But although Carmelita attended school in Mesa Grande, she says that she "could not learn there." "I believe," Carmelita explained, "that the problem is that I cannot grasp the sounds of the letters. I went to school for almost 7 years, and I couldn't ever really learn." Carmelita also added that the conditions in Mesa Grande made it very hard to study, naming such factors as very few food resources and the constant threat of military invasion.

Since attending the class in Papaturro, however, Carmelita had begun to show some progress towards attainment of literacy skills, although she continued to struggle to grasp basic phonetic and sight word skills in ways that most of the other students had. When aided, however, and asked to read slowly, or to slowly write out her thoughts, Carmelita was able to read or write several sentences.

Consistent with her shy behavior, Carmelita rarely participated in class discussion unless invited, and even when invited, would look down and hide behind a very large smile, ultimately saying that she had "nothing to say." When encouraged, however, Carmelita was always able to contribute to the dialogue in some way. In a similar manner, Carmelita had more trouble than most determining what to write when asked to "write out your own thoughts" on the generative theme of the day. When encouraged and aided, however, Carmelita was always able to produce either a phrase or a sentence that would relate to the class summary sentence.

Esperanza

Esperanza Leino was another quiet and shy member of the literacy class. She, like Carmelita, did not speak out in the class very often, or in any other community gathering. When invited and encouraged, though, Esperanza shared thoughts and feelings reflective of her experience of the war, a very formative time in her life that continued to impact her physical health and her view of the world around her. But Esperanza had another side to her. In unexpected moments, she would surprise the class with a funny comment or a joke. The women eventually knew to look to Esperanza when they wanted to laugh, knowing just what to say to spark this aspect of her.

Esperanza was 37 years old, one of the younger members of the class. She was married to Lolo, and they had seven children, one of them a war orphan they "adopted."[8] Lolo's position with the *directiva*, heading the education and recreation programs, impacted Esperanza in several ways. She was exposed to many aspects of the community's education programs and was required to attend to visitors to the community who were affiliated with those programs. Esperanza, a thoughtful and generous woman, was eager to share what little food she may have with visitors. For this reason, her class attendance was intermittent. Esperanza also often missed class because she needed to attend to the illness of a child, or because she must attend to her responsibilities as manager of one of the community's *tiendas*[9], small supply stores stocking things like batteries, eggs, sweet bread, and tortilla chips.

Like Carmelita, Esperanza was always nursing an infant. At the start of the class, she was nursing Myra, and a year later, newborn Beatriz. There were usually several other of her younger children who hovered near the open-air classroom, curiously observing Esperanza as she studied, and occasionally interrupting her to inform her of a visitor or a vendor who had come to sell her a product for the *tienda*. Whether nursing or paying momentary attention to her other children, however, Esperanza did not appear to be distracted from her attention to reading and writing. Nursing infants and attending to children seemed to be a natural reflex for Esperanza, and when she was able to attend class, she seemed intent on concentrating on the task at hand.

Esperanza, unlike most of the other students, attended school as a young girl. She explained that the school was far away from where she lived, and there were several streams to cross that were high and wide during the rainy season. But Esperanza had several other siblings, and this freed her from needing to stay at home to help her mother with the daily survival tasks. "My family was very poor," Esperanza added, "so we didn't have notebooks like we use today. But my family bought packing paper, and from this, we made our notebooks."

Esperanza attended school for 3 years, but she says that she never learned to read and write. She blamed herself, saying that "I never really paid close attention. I cared more about playing."

Esperanza did not attend school again until she was in the refugee camp in Mesa Grande. There she "studied the vowels," and learned to write her name and a few other words. Although these classes were "very nice," Esperanza felt that she did not learn very much at that time. Again, she blamed herself. "The teachers were very nice," Esperanza explained, "but I am not a good student, not very able to learn." There were also many distractions, she added. In addition to the distractions of the military presence and the need to work for basic survival, the several small children she had to attend to "never let me really concentrate and study."

These eight women formed the regular core of the literacy class in Papaturro over the course of the study. Although others began the class, they did not make ongoing commitment to it for a variety of reasons, including domestic and field duties and personal or family illnesses requiring their attendance, often in another community, which left them no time for daily attendance at the 2-hour class.

Robin believed, however, that the critical underlying explanation for their failure to continue was a firm belief in their inability to learn. This came, according to Robin's understanding, from previous brief, but significant, experiences with pedagogy that failed them. Although a few of the women who tried and then quit returned to try again when a new basic literacy class was begun a year later, none of them persisted in that class either. It was an ongoing problem in Papaturro and other communities.

IMPLICATIONS FOR ADULT EDUCATION

Several issues are raised in this chapter that reflect key quandaries facing adult education efforts world-wide, including the United States. The first of these is the difficulty in recruiting adult literacy students to programs. Wagner (1992) pointed out estimates that only 1 in 10 Americans in need of basic skills training was receiving or had received such training as of 1990.

Recruitment

Comments made to Robin by her potential students reflect some of the factors behind the difficulty of recruitment, even when such programs are available (as may not be the case in developing countries and certain areas of developed countries). Unlike children who are learning to read and write, adults who need to further their literacy abilities are stigmatized by societies like the United States where universal education is available for all children (Wagner, 1992). Or, as was the case for the women of Papaturro, they had previously attempted to learn and had failed to progress. These low-literate adults feel like failures and are, understandably, loathe to put themselves in situations again where they will fail and reinforce their feelings of unworthiness. When asked, many of these adults make it clear that they do not believe that they can learn to read and, perceiving no reward for the sacrifices to their time and their pride (by declaring to a teacher or a group of other adults that they cannot read), they see no point in even making the attempt. Many adult educators are familiar with the experience of announcing the advent of adult literacy help in the form of a new class or tutoring program to the community and then sitting back in dismay as no one, or only a few, shows up.

Several possible solutions to this are suggested by the experience in Papaturro. One element that seemed to stand out in the data was the degree to which the literacy classes and their potential students were supported by the community. Although Robin was an outsider, the advent of the classes was clearly a community effort, and it was presented as such to the entire community. Further, attendance at the classes was framed by the leaders of the community as an opportunity to help the community and its people in their drive for social justice and economic and personal well-being.

This "initiation from within" a community avoids many of the problems that come from attempting to impose a solution on people from without: feelings of patronization that feed existing feelings of failure and inferiority, resistance of minority to majority cultures and their solutions (Ogbu, 1974), and misapprehension on the part of the outsiders as to the nature of problems and possibilities for solutions.

With the support and encouragement of their communities, adult learners can feel empowered, accepted, and understood as the real people they are with their full potentials. It is one thing to be asked to leave your community and approach a teacher who represents the culture that previously failed you and ask for another chance and quite a different thing to step forward within your community, as a member of your own group, and assume the responsibility of working on your literacy skills so that the community as a whole will benefit.

There do exist similarly framed participatory, community-based, adult literacy programs in countries around the world, including the United States (Auerbach, 1996; Flecha, 1997; Heaney, 1989; Heller, 1997). We suggest that, as contradictory as it may seem, international and national organizations working for the advancement of adult literacy seek to find ways to frame programs so that the impetus and the rationale for each is based in the individual communities from which the potential students come.

In addition, many adult educators will recognize the value inherent in the face-to-face visits that Robin, Sylvia, and Lita made to their potential students. By visiting with each woman and urging her to attend the class, they began to establish the trust and relationship that was so needed to help these women overcome their feelings of unworthiness and fear to the extent that they would appear at the first class. Whether it's a visit (or visits) by the teacher or personal recruitment from a friend, this type of personal contact that says "I care" and "I believe that you can do it" possibly is responsible for the majority of cases within which adult learners make the initial commitment to an adult literacy class. Initial teacher–student visits have a strong impact toward making the teacher more a part of the community and less an outsider who is accessible only within the four walls of the class. As we as a field begin to talk about professional standards and training for adult teachers, we believe that this aspect of the teacher–student relationship must be taken seriously and that providers be given the skills to develop these types of relationships and the wherewithal to apply these skills in their recruitment of students.

Teacher as Community Member

The value served by Robin's decision to live within the community cannot be overstated. As upcoming chapters show, this allowed her to learn about her students and their culture, language, and ways of being to a much greater depth than if she only appeared from the outside just before class and left the community when the class ended each day. The relationship and trust she established proved to be a critical element of the program.

To what degree is this possible for other programs and other teachers? Probably not very. But we feel that the power in having teachers become members of their students' communities needs to be acknowledged.

Archer and Costello (1990), in describing and analyzing the successes and failures of literacy campaigns throughout Latin America, concluded that a key factor in the failure of some popular literacy campaigns was the distance (both physical and psychological–cultural) between teachers, recruited to teach in outlying rural areas, and their students. Transportation difficulties, lack of commitment that grew over time to people far away, and general unfamiliarity with the daily challenges faced by their students resulted in many instances where teachers would miss classes at increasing rates and eventually stop appearing altogether (by which time most of the students had given up).

Clearly, it is highly unlikely that we will ever return to the days when teachers lived in the communities they served. However, if we analyze why such arrangements carry such positive rewards and then work to establish ways to achieve these same rewards in other ways (or at least get as close as we can to the same effect), we believe that the efficacy of adult literacy programs will be greatly increased. We address this issue again in chapter 7.

Problems and Challenges

Another whole set of issues raised in this chapter serve to remind us of the many difficulties shared by adult literacy programs in both highly developed countries like the United States and developing ones like El Salvador, although on different scales: lack of materials, scarcity of adequate classroom space, the supreme obstacles to attendance created by the demanding life responsibilities that adults face, and the effects that life's stresses, particularly those associated with oppressed and marginalized people, have on the adult student's ability to learn when in class.

As discussed in chapter 1, the national and international organizations concerned with raising world literacy levels in developed and developing countries are being challenged to address these issues through major structural and economic changes (Draft Summit Document, 1997). Until real change is achieved, however, we as adult educators need to become increasingly aware of the impact that factors such as these have on our programs and work to find ways to achieve our goals within them.

ENDNOTES

1. An *asamblea* is a community-wide meeting, generally called by the community president. It is the forum for discussing all social and political issues, local, regional, and/or national. It is also the forum for discussing various aspects of the community's collective work, and for assigning responsibilities.
2. This term refers to that which is "of the people," that which comes from the people, their local culture. It is often characterized by such things as the incorporation of local leadership, and/or local songs, art work, or dance.
3. At this time, most of the men who signed up for education classes in Papaturro signed up for either the sixth- or ninth-grade classes that were being offered simultaneously. Most of these students were youths, ages 15 to 20. Other men, generally those over the age of 30, eventually participated in a third–fourth-grade class that the literacy program *Fundación-16* (F-16) initiated approximately 1 year after the start of the basic literacy class. This reflects the fact that more males were able to attend school when in the refugee camps.
4. The following year, F-16 offered a literacy class in the evening. Each of the male students who dropped out of the first class began to participate in that class.
5. This kind of attitude is a common Salvadoran cultural trait, particularly among the *campesina* women. It is more reflective of a value of humility, however, than of a sincere lack of belief in one's skills or value.
6. While the Salvadorans suffered from the cold in Mesa Grande, they also suffered from the heat in their first refugee camp, located in La Virtud. The operative factor is that the extreme poverty that characterized the conditions in all of the refugee camps resulted in tremendous physical suffering.
7. A significant proportion of the postwar Salvadoran economy is comprised of money sent to relatives by Salvadorans residing and working in the United States.
8. In keeping with the culture/values of the community and the generosity among the Salvadoran *campesinos*, it was common for families to "adopt" children who because of the war were without parents.
9. In Papaturro, there are currently five *tiendas* (stores). Most often, these are small mud shacks or simply a designated part of someone's home. From these tiendas, one can buy such items as corn chips, cans of juice, dried milk, eggs, and batteries. Those who manage these stores often travel long distances to supply them, carrying everything on their heads as they make their way on foot down the long road to Papaturro.

PART II
THE LITERACY
CLASS

4

The Literacy Class: Engaging With Social Reality and Print to Effect Change

The new literacy programs must be largely based on the notion of emancipatory literacy, in which literacy is viewed "as one of the major vehicles by which 'oppressed' people are able to participate in the sociohistorical transformation of their society." In this view, literacy programs should be tied not only to mechanical learning of reading skill but, additionally, to a critical understanding of the overall goals for national reconstruction.
—Freire and Macedo (1987, p. 157)

A Day in the Class

It is just before 2:00 p.m. as Deonicia quietly makes her way down the path, clutching a plastic bag filled with her literacy notebook, math book, and loose papers, ready to sit under the branches of the *pepeto* tree and wait for the other students to arrive. Despite her age and frailty, she offers to help Robin and Sylvia carry the blackboard out from the school building. They carefully place it against the largest tree, talking over the day's events as they wait for the rest of the students to arrive. Deonicia soon begins work on some simple math problems Robin assigns her, knowing that they will need to wait at least 15 minutes for the others to arrive in order to begin class. Sylvia takes this opportunity to explain to Robin what they had done in class the day before while Robin had been away, observing a literacy class in a different community.

As Tomasa, Francisca, Celia, Margarita, and Esperanza straggle in over the next 15 min, Robin greets each one with a kiss and the customary *buenas tardes*. Tomasa brings word that Carmelita has "asked permission" to miss class today, needing to stay home and attend to a sick child. At this point, everyone but Chunga has arrived. Everyone knows that Chunga will arrive late, so Robin begins the class, starting as Sylvia and she always do, writing the date on the top of the board. Quietly, with concentration and the comfort of familiarity, all of the students engage in copying the date into their notebooks. Robin had learned early on that this activity was one that grounded the students; it was a simple gesture that oriented them, allowing them to feel that they were "in school" and ready to begin to study.

Robin begins today by explaining to the students the function of dialogue in a literacy class. She is responding to recent comments that some students felt that there was "too much talking in class" and not enough of the activities like syllable instruction, dictation of spelling words, and the copying of words and phrases from the board.

"I know that some of you feel that maybe there is too much 'talking' in the class," Robin begins, "so I want to try and explain to you why I am teaching the class the way that I am. I know that it is very different than what you are used to." Many students nod their heads in agreement. "One thing is that I believe that many of you have important opinions and insights about your lives, the past, and the present. I think it is very valuable that we make these part of what we are learning in the class."

"I also believe," Robin continues, "that it is really important that the class be very engaging, very interesting—that there be a spark, that there be energy. In this way, you all will have a greater desire to read and write about what we are studying. And, as I have said before, I believe that you will learn to read and write *most effectively* if you spend a lot of time reading and writing. And in this way," Robin adds, " we will also be able to develop our skills at speaking out in groups, skills at better being able to express ourselves, and not be so shy to say what we are thinking." Seeing that many students were again nodding their heads in agreement, Robin determines that she can now begin the class, starting with a dialogue of a new generative theme

Beginning With the Generative Theme

Yesterday, Sylvia had just completed all of the activities surrounding the generative word *comunidad* (community). So today, Robin begins class with the next generative word in the F-16 Facilitator's manual, *tierra* (land). Putting up a poster-size photo of a *campesino* doing agricultural work on a piece of land, with the word *tierra* printed in bold underneath, Robin initiates the discussion by reading a short paragraph written in the teacher's manual.

> The history of the ownership of land in our country has passed through a series of changes; changes that have favored a privileged minority, who struggle, to this day, to maintain their domination. In the times of the Conquista and colonization, many people were stripped of their land and their possessions, and reduced to slavery.
>
> In the past century, the ancient forms of collective land ownership have disappeared, such as communally owned land and the *ejidos*. The *campesino* people have been marginalized, and they have been denied the possibility of access to the land. This is the point that, over the large view of history, has been the cause of diverse uprisings, starting with Anastasio Aquino and the rebellion of 1932, up to the conflict that has recently ended. Regardless, in spite of this, the dispute continues between those that produce from the land and love the land as they love their life, and those who use the land in order to increase their wealth. We, as Christians, think that in order to avoid future conflict, it is necessary to have a just distribution of the land that carries with it the fertilization of the efforts towards peace and democracy that we long for (based on Isaiah 42, v 5). (From *Manual Facilitador,* p. 74; written by the NGO *Alfalit* and distributed by the NGO *Fundación-16*).

Oral Discussion and Dialogue

Robin begins the discussion. "What does this make us think about?" she asks. "Is this true, what it says here about the way that land has been owned and the conflicts that occurred as a result?" Several students begin to speak, quickly and with enthusiasm. Tomasa and Celia confirm the historical reality of the "14 families" that owned most of El Salvador's land and resources, stating flatly that it was the poor *campesinos* who worked on the land but did not receive a fair wage for their work. Celia agrees, adding that God created the world and all that it contains, creating it for all people to enjoy. "It is not right," she argues, "for some people to be owners of so much of God's earth and for others to suffer from a lack of resources."

Robin asks people to respond to what Celia and Tomasa are saying. Chunga, who has arrived by now, contributes that the war began as a result of the fact that the poor eventually began to protest this unjust distribution of the land. Margarita joins in, pointing out that the war started because of the way that the Salvadoran Army massacred all of the *campesino* people who tried to protest this injustice. Murmurs of agreement sweep through the class.

Directing the conversation toward their own community, Robin asks, "What does this say to us about what we can do, here in our own community, to bring about more justice? What can we do to help create a society that is more of what we want, what we believe in?" Tomasa speaks about the fact that they work in a cooperative manner in Papaturro, explaining that people do not own the land individually, but that the land is owned in common by all members of the community. "The land here is owned cooperatively," Tomasa said. "The government wants to parcel it out individually, but not all of the land is good. Some of it would not produce crops, and so it is better that we own it cooperatively so that no one person has the bad land. For this reason, the land is owned communally, and we work as a united community, so that there is more equality."

Celia adds, "If we owned it individually, we would not be able to afford to pay for it either. We can only afford it because we work together."

Robin solicits other opinions about this. Deonicia says that she thinks this is very good. "It is important that there is equality."

This allows more unity, more fairness, and, in the end, they can all accomplish more because they have worked together, Celia says. "Because of this, we make sure that no one goes without, no one suffers from hunger. There are some people who cannot do the work, the widows, the *ancianos* (elderly), and because we divide the land fairly and work it collectively, we can share with those who cannot work or who do not have a good piece of land."

Chunga adds, "In Mesa Grande, we lived this way. It is there that we started. We learned that this is how we can survive, how we can care for one another."

Writing and Reading the Group Sentence

As the discussion draws to a close, Robin asks, "Who can give me a sentence that summarizes what we have been talking about?" Celia offers, "*La tierra colectiva es necessaria porque todos trabajamos igual y todos recibimos igual*" (The collectively owned and worked land is necessary because all work equally and all receive equally). Robin writes it on the board.

Pointing to each word, Robin leads the women in three choral readings of the sentence, the third time independently. "Very good!" Robin responds, affirming the students' ability to read independently, specifically pointing out to them that they are reading.

Individual Composition

"*Bueno*," Robin continues, "now I would like you to copy this sentence into your notebooks. After you are done, I would like you to continue to write out more of your own thoughts on the theme of our dialogue. And remember," Robin emphasizes, knowing what the women are thinking as she is saying this, "I do not care about your spelling or your penmanship. The most important thing is that you try and write words that express more of what you think. Write the words whatever way you can," Robin adds, reinforcing the concept of "invented spelling" that she encourages in every writing activity. "Really, it does not matter to me if you spell words correctly."

After 5 min, Robin begins to circulate, sitting down next to each student, asking her to read aloud what she has copied. Several students stumble on the word *igual*, but most are able to read the sentence. Margarita, though, needs more help. Robin, instantiating a form of "echo reading," reads with her. When it is Deonicia's turn, she is able to read the entire sentence, stumbling only on the two instances of *igual*. Robin celebrates by announcing her success to the entire class!

The students continue for another 20 min with their independent writing. At times, Robin, in response to different requests for help, adds words to the large sheet of paper she has constructed and hangs on a tree, *el diccionario*. She also refers students to this collection to help them correct incorrectly spelled words.

For the first time, Margarita and Deonicia join the class in completing at least one other sentence. Margarita insists that she "can't" do it, but Robin asks that she try. When Robin sees Maragarita glancing up at her nervously while asking Tomasa for help, she reassures her that it is okay to ask others for help. In the end, Margarita writes, "Working united is better."

Deonicia does not leave any spaces between the words in her sentence, and she relies heavily on inventive spellings. But she is able to read the sentence back to Robin, and it reflects content relevant to the generative theme of the day: "The land helps us to live."

Tomasa appends the copied class sentence with, "But if we work in collective, we don't lose work, and others don't go without." Francisca adds the sentence, "The land, we need it very much." Celia writes, "We the women, we work from 5 in the morning and they say we don't do anything." And Chunga writes, "The land is very important because with the land we have life because it gives us many fruits (products) so that many classes of things can be maintained."

Reading One's Own Words

Each student reads her writing to Robin, one-to-one, and to the entire class as a whole at the end of this segment of the class, laughing nervously and protesting their inability to read. Each, though, responds to Robin's encouragement, with the exception of Margarita who begs not to have to read her writing aloud. Deonicia too balks at this, saying that she cannot "remember" what she has written. But Robin tells her that she doesn't need to remember, she needs to read her words and that she (Robin) will help her. She reads her sentence with only two instances of help. Each writer's efforts are enthusiastically applauded by the group.

Learning the Graphophonic Code

Robin now turns to a list of syllables that they have studied. These include the syllable families for the letters n, l, m, b, s, r, rr, and m (e.g. na- ne- ni- no- nu). Led by Robin, the students read through the syllables together, and then independently, as a group, and individually. Robin then asks the students to give her words that contain these syllables. As the students dictate the words, Robin writes them on the board. Robin then guides the women as they read these words, again as a group and then individually. Robin reinforces the concept that "the words we speak and write are made up of syllables, combined together."

As each student is called, she goes to the board and writes a word that contains one of the syllables. They are all successful, pointing to each syllable and saying the word aloud. Then as a group, they read all of the words on the board, concluding with each woman reading the words on her own.

In response to Margarita's "I can't" after she has read the words successfully, Robin explains that "One way that we learn to read is by learning the sounds of the letters, breaking words down into their parts, and sounding these parts out in order to finally read the whole word. In the beginning, some will only be able to read the words that contain the syllables that we have studied. But little by little, we will be able to read more."

Feelings of Progress and Hope

The students copy the words on the board into their notebooks, and then it is time to go. As several students gather their materials, they comment excitedly that they feel they are learning. "We're learning to read and write, aren't we?" Robin tells them how proud she is of them and reminds them that she is learning a great deal as well, repeating the Freirean philosophy, "No one knows everything and no one knows nothing."

The student all leave their open-air classroom under the branches of the *pepeto* tree and make their way home to make the evening's tortillas and feed their families.

WHOLE-PART-WHOLE SHAPE OF INSTRUCTION

The overall, guiding structure of the literacy class reflects what is called in some U.S. curriculum studies, "Whole-Part-Whole" (McIntyre, 1996;

Purcell-Gates, 1996b). In the U.S. context, the "whole" refers to holistic literacy events, usually for authentic purposes, such as reading a story for enjoyment or an article for information. The "part" refers to a focus on skills teaching and learning, with the skills being taught in the context of the preceding whole. The final "whole" in the whole–part–whole approach refers to the application of these skills back into whole texts for reading and writing. The key element here is the idea that skills teaching should be in the context of actual reading–writing events—emanating from and being applied to these events so that they are never viewed by the learner as separate and decontextualized. The instantiation of this in the Salvadoran context involved all of this, as well as a Freirean lens for the whole.

ENGAGING IN CRITICAL DIALOGUE

As can be seen in the portrait presented above, Robin began each class with a dialogue focused around the generative theme for the day, usually suggested by materials she had obtained from *Fundación 16 de Enero*, who used materials produced by another NGO, *Alfalit*. Robin came to firmly believe that all learning in the class was inspired and guided by these dialogues.

Engaging at the Emotional and Analytical Levels

Effective dialogues, according to Robin, engaged the women on an emotional and analytical level. They focused on topics that were central to the lives of the women and about which the women knew a great deal and cared deeply. The dialogues emanated from the points that created a "spark" in the women, those issues that particularly engaged the women in thought, feeling, and critical reflection. Robin, as facilitator, would look for this kind of engagement and consciously move the discussion in that direction. Within this, Robin facilitated the dialogues in such a way that encouraged an analysis of their past as well as their present-day lives, their lived realities. And, reflecting Freire's essential connection of reflection to practice and action, Robin made sure that she always helped the women connect their thoughts to personal action, to a thinking through as to what they could personally do to shape their futures and the future of their people.

In the first months of the class, when the students were at the level of basic literacy, many of the dialogues began with a generative word, such as *tierra* (land) or *derechos* (rights). As the students developed some basic reading skills, however, and, as Robin came to know her students better, she would sometimes use short excerpts from different texts to spark discussion. In keeping with Freirean thought, these texts were always considered to be generative texts, functioning in the same way a generative word or theme would.

Two categories of text were particularly effective in connecting with the lives of the women and in facilitating analyses of their sociopolitical realities with plans for future action. These were texts that dealt with the experiences of the *campesinos* during the war and texts that were religious in nature.[1] Robin often tried to provide copies of these texts for each student, printed in large print for students with poor vision. If this was not possible, she provided enough copies so that the women could read together in pairs. She always began by reading the text aloud, asking the women to follow along. She then instructed the entire class to read aloud, in a choral fashion. She then asked the women to read silently, in preparation for the dialogue that would follow. Given the various literacy levels of the students, Robin often paired particular students, asking Margarita or Deonicia to read with someone like Tomasa or Chunga. The remaining students read independently.

When Robin ascertained that the women had, through the dialogue, become highly engaged with the topic and had been able to develop a degree of critical reflection, she would ask them to suggest a summary sentence for her to write on the board. This sentence was to capture the essence of the discussion, that is, what the women felt had been a central theme of the dialogue, what they believed and had been reflecting on and expressing in their talk. Sometimes the students generated this sentence collaboratively, and sometimes one student would provide it for group approval. Once it was determined, Robin would write the sentence on the whiteboard. As she wrote, she spoke the words aloud while the women followed the unfolding text with their eyes and either silently or orally spoke the words along with Robin.

With the sentence written on the board, Robin would then lead the class in an oral reading of it, pointing to each word as they read. Three times over they would read their words, written and visible to them. Robin would then ask each woman individually to read the sentence aloud. When they hesitated out of fear or shyness, she found ways to support and encourage them. These ways often included both establishing physical closeness and support while verbally expressing a belief in their ultimate ability to read and write. The following report from Robin to Vicki illustrates one such event early on in the study:

> Then I asked Deonicia to read the sentence. She insisted that she could not read, several times. I believed that she could read this sentence, so I told her that she could, and drew close to her. Together we read it, and then I had her read it alone a second time. She was cautious and timid the first time and read with a significant degree of success the second time.

WRITING AS A CONTINUATION OF DIALOGUE

Following the reading of the summary sentence, Robin instructed the women to first copy the sentence into their notebooks and then continue to write out their thoughts, working on their own. While the women wrote, Robin and Sylvia went around, observing, answering questions, and encouraging the students as they struggled to encode their thoughts and words. It was at this point in the class that the women engaged with print in ways that allowed them to see its true relationship—in a semiotic[2] sense—to them—to their thoughts, their beliefs, their actions, and their words.

A Key to Development

In many ways, Robin saw this activity of writing as one of the most important and powerful components of the class, as it allowed the students to further discover and develop their voice, their dreams for the future, and their belief in their own power to help create that future. In one of her field notes to Vicki, Robin referenced Freire (1985):

> During a discussion of a problematic situation—like a codification—educators should ask peasants to write down their reactions—a simple phrase or whatever—first on the blackboard, and then, on a sheet of paper. While participating with the educator in "decodifying" a codification (generative word, photo, and/or their own writing), peasants analyze their reality and in their discourse they express levels of seeing themselves relative to an objective situation. They reveal the audiological conditioning to which they were subjected in the "culture of silence." From whatever angle we address it—be it form or content—this significance and richness involve a linguistic analysis that in turn includes ideology and politics. (pp. 24–25)

Robin then went on to explain the relevance this particular point had to her work. At this time she wrote:

> There is tremendous amount of data that I have collected that illustrates this point. Over and over, the literacy students in Papaturro wrote out statements that were rich with social and political meaning. These statements often reflected a great capacity to analyze their social and political reality. Many times, there were also many writing samples that specifically address the issue of how the women had been silenced by their culture, either for reasons of sexism, or because of the behaviors and policies of a repressive government. The dialogue seemed to help them discover this experience, and their writing seemed to allow them to name it and further analyze it, as well as look to the various ways that they have been working (and can continue to do so) to break out of the silence and develop their voice.

At a later time, Robin again wrote to Vicki some of her insights on this particular point:

> I am increasingly convinced that having the students write out their thoughts on the generative theme is absolutely essential. It is vital that there is dialogue, but always in combination with reading and writing activities. I contend that dialogue in isolation is not of essential value, and, clearly, that the instruction of reading and writing in isolation of dialogue and engaged, critical thought is also not effective education. Education is at its most potent, most effective, when there is dialogue in combination with writing (and reading) activities.

Individual Help

At this point in the class, while the students were engaged in their writing, Robin and Sylvia began working with each woman on an individual basis, helping them grasp and use essential principles of encoding language, always aware of where each woman was in her development as a reader–writer. While Deonicia was struggling with the concept of word boundaries, often needing to be reminded to put spaces between her words, Celia needed help in spelling *heroes*, and Margarita needed to be reminded of how to write the letter *s*. Robin and Sylvia answered each woman's questions and tried to extend each woman's understanding and ability. In Vygotskyan terms, they were able, during this individual writing time, to work with each woman within her zone of proximal development.

As the women finished their writing, Robin asked that they read what they had written for the class. Again, she always supported their efforts and refused to accept their stated beliefs that they "could not" read or write. Over time, we documented the growth of each woman in the class, particularly through the writing they did in their personal notebooks.

PART IN CONTEXT OF WHOLE

While the instruction up to this point had followed a whole–to–part–to–whole progression, with the summary sentence being pulled from the whole of the dialogue and then leading in to the whole of each woman's personal written text, Robin and Sylvia further broke down the whole into the basic phonemic and word levels in each lesson. This instruction usually followed the individual writing portion of the class.

Syllable Instruction

For syllable instruction, Robin wrote the target syllable family on the board. These syllables always came from the generative word for the day or played a central role in whatever text they had used for their dialogue. For example, the syllable family, *rra, rre, rri, rro, rru*, accompanied the generative word *tierra* (land); the syllable family *na, ne, ni, no, nu* accompanied the generative word *comunidad* (community); and the syllable family *ba, be, bi, bo, bu* accompanied the generative word *basura* (trash). Robin always wrote the generative word first and then the syllable family underneath it, pronouncing each and explaining the part–whole relationship between the syllables and the word.

Connecting to Own Words

Following this, Robin asked the students to tell her words that they knew incorporating the syllables on the board. As each student contributed words, she wrote them under the appropriate syllable. Again, she took pains to pronounce each word and discuss the relationship of the syllable to the word. Robin then had each student go up to the board and write words that she (the student) knew that utilized any of the five new syllables. The class read each word, with Robin's guidance, after it was written. Robin encouraged applause for the writer each time. Whenever a student struggled, Robin encouraged her to isolate and hear the syllables in the word she wanted to write. Robin was always intentional about trying not to set a student up for failure, always seeking a balance between encouraging the students to overcome their shyness and low esteem as learners and responding to genuine need for help. Each woman then copied the generative word into her notebook, accompanied by the five syllables, and all of the words that had been written on the board.

PREVIOUS FAILURE TO UNDERSTAND PARTS IN RELATION TO WHOLE

Robin believed that a central weakness to the Freirean-influenced adult education pedagogy prevalent in the country was a failure to grasp the essential link between a dialogue of a theme (one loaded with political/personal/social meaning for the students) and the instruction of reading and writing skills. Writing to Vicki late in the study, Robin reflected:

> I have acted out of the belief that the most vital kind of education is one where the educator generates a dialogue based on a generative theme, and from there guides the students in reading and writing acquisition activities, be that syllable instruction or actual writing of sentences. Most important, perhaps, is that I have found this to be essential to what has made the class in Papaturro most "effective." Conversely, the greatest weakness that I have observed in other classes (taught by teachers recruited and trained by Robin) is the *alfabetizadora*'s failure to understand this principle and to ultimately apply it. The idea of learning

parts within the whole, that is, learning to read and write by actually engaging in the process in a meaningful manner, and from there extracting a few relevant "direct teaching" lessons of some "parts," is completely foreign to the traditional education process here in El Salvador. The basic principles of "popular education" (which are fairly widely accepted) encompass the idea of incorporating a theme of social–political importance to the past and future of the students. This is truly the strength of the materials and knowledge that exists here and surpasses that which we have in the United States. Simultaneously, while traditional education in El Salvador also seems to embrace the idea of studying syllables, grammar, etc, this aspect of educational practice is most often weak and limited. Ultimately, it seems that the greatest weakness in the educational practice here is a lack of understanding of how these two pedagogical components can work together.

Education and Teacher Training an Absent Privilege

Robin attributed her understanding of the relationship between the two educational components (whole–theme and part–decoding or encoding) to the education she had previously received in the United States in the field of literacy development and instruction. She understood her educational experience to be a reflection of her privileged status, in that she had access to formal schooling and advanced teacher training. Conversely, she recognized that these types of educational opportunities are something that many people throughout the world do not have access to.

In El Salvador, there are no formal education courses in adult education, so even those in top positions in the field lack this exposure. Compounding this is the fact that in the field, the majority of those who are *alfabetizadoras* do not have more than a third- or fourth-grade education, nor do they have the opportunity or resources to obtain further education, despite the strong desire that many have. Their poverty, the lack of schools, the lack of good roads or transportation systems, and the lack of time to dedicate to anything other than basic survival are all significant obstacles.

Moreover, there is little, if any, government funding toward adult education. Consequently, these *alfabetizadoras* receive a stipend, not a salary, and work with extremely limited materials and resources.

PROCESS TEACHING AND AUTHENTIC LITERACY EVENTS

Robin brought to her work in El Salvador a thorough understanding of, and deep belief in, the efficacy of teaching reading and writing from a process perspective (Goodman, Smith, Merideth, & Goodman, 1987). She had learned through her graduate studies that "you learn to read by reading and to write by writing."

Further, she had been taught that learners should not simply be involved in isolated reading and writing activities. Rather, they should engage in authentic literacy events from the beginning, with *authentic* defined as those print activities that are engaged in by literate people to accomplish social and personal communicative goals, over and above learning to read and write, such as communicating over time and space, gaining or transmitting information, participating in group activities, exploring other worlds through literature, and so on.

Process and Authenticity Unfamiliar Concepts

The notion that one must engage in the process being learned in order to learn it was totally unfamiliar within the context that Robin found herself. Her fellow adult educators did not understand it, the *alfabetizadoras* whom she was training did not understand it, nor did her students (who based their conceptions of what learning "in school" was all about on their limited and scattered experiences with schooling in their youth, in the refugee camp, or both) understand it. One serious result of this unfamiliarity with process learning was the total lack of materials for the women to read and the almost total failure of the available materials to incorporate actual reading and writing in the learning activities. Nonetheless, Robin was determined to incorporate what to her was basic, good methodology for learning to read and write: authentic literacy events that allowed for as much reading and writing as possible.

Ascertaining "Authentic"

Robin approached this issue from several angles. One of the first things she did was to survey class members as to their motivations for learning to read and write. As a result of this survey, she began to ascertain what would constitute authentic literacy events for the women. She learned that one of the most important desires held by almost every student was to be able to read the Bible. They wanted to be able to read it on their own, in their own homes, as a way to further understand their faith. They also wanted to be able to read and study the Bible as a way to better prepare themselves to participate in the community's religious services, the Celebrations of the Word. The students also expressed a desire to be able to read the songbooks that are used in these religious services.

Robin also learned that many women had relatives and close friends in other communities and the United States. They wished to be able to read the personal letters they received from these people and to write to them in return.

She also learned that many women felt as if they were "blind," easily deceived by others because of their illiteracy. They were therefore determined to develop the necessary skills to read such things as basic governmental forms, health care information, road signs, and informational flyers.

Further, several students expressed the desire to learn to read books. They explained that they believed that this would be a pleasurable experience, giving them the opportunity to forget about some of the hardships of their lives.

Within this search for authentic literacy events in the lives of her students, Robin also decided that, given the need to read and write as often as possible, she would incorporate their repeated readings of all of their personal writing as well as repeated reading of the words containing the new syllables being taught. In other words, her students would read and reread everything in print in the classroom that they and Robin could provide.

Religious Text as Authentic

Early in the study, during the second month of literacy classes when none of her students were fluent in any sense of the word, Robin incorporated a religious text with Biblical passages into the class lesson, reading it to them in response to their beginning reading status. In this illustration, both the use of authentic, relevant literacy events and practice at reading and writing can be seen as they were instantiated in their full interaction. Robin wrote:

> I wanted to give a short exam to see what the students have learned and what we need to review. I decided to do this at the end of class, so I tried to create an activity at the beginning which would reflect their interest and continue to provide opportunities to read and write, and think critically about their present social–political world and their future. I chose an excerpt of one of the stories from the *"Tiempo de Recordar y Tiempo de Contar"* book (a compilation of short, oral testimonies of Salvadoran people's experiences during the war). I chose one that incorporated and referenced a Biblical reading. I had Lita read it aloud, slowly and clearly. I then facilitated a discussion of their reactions, focusing on how they identified with it, what their opinions were of a question posed within it (i.e., "What is God's plan for us, *campesinos*?"), and how they could make that happen here in our community. The discussion was lively. Everyone participated, with me soliciting their thoughts only in the first 3 or 4 min. Even after I tried to end the discussion and ask for a sentence, they continued to respond to the central points of the discussion. In the end, Deonicia gave the following sentence:
>
> > *Dios que quiere es que miremos con cariño a todos, pero más a los necesitados* (What God wants is that we look upon all others with warmth and kindness, but most especially on those who are the most needy).

At this point, I had us read it together twice and asked that they read it alone once. I then asked that they copy it in their notebooks, and afterwards, that they continue writing more of their own thoughts.

Celia had arrived late, not hearing the reading, so I offered that she could either write more of her thoughts or read the reading. She chose to read. She read the entire text (sweating because of her effort, but completely absorbed with no desire to stop). I gave her only occasional help in sounding out some words such as *valor, tienen, básicos, raices.*

Sylvia and I went around asking that everyone read their copied sentence, and later that they read their own sentences. We did this for over an hour. I again wrote some of the words they were unable to spell, but were using, on the newsprint paper on which I had written *el diccionario* (our "word wall") and had been writing words over the past several classes. I indicated to several individuals that I was doing this so they could try and self-correct.

Eventually, I directed everyone's attention to the dictionary, and we read all the words, me reading first, then the students. I asked particular individuals to read certain words alone, specifically asking people to read words that they had used in their own writing. Some were able to read these independently, but the majority needed a little prompting and aid from me.

At this point, most of the students copied the words into their notebooks. Sylvia then came into the classroom, and I took this opportunity for another reading activity. I had each one stand up and read what she had written. Again, many said, "I can't," but smiled and laughed nervously. I assessed that they were nervous, but excited and proud. They read independently, with only Deonicia and Carmelita needing a little help. We applauded each effort and all of the students had large and bright smiles on their faces!

Text Becomes More Complex

Three months later, with most of the students having achieved a solid, if rudimentary, ability to read, Robin's incorporation of Biblical text to generate dialogue reflected decreased reading support as well as text that was more complex. Robin maintained the dual instructional principles of relevant, authentic literacy events and practice with reading and writing:

> We are now in the Catholic liturgical season of Lent, and in El Salvador this means many things. In general, it is said by many that the poor of El Salvador identify in a very strong way with the passion and crucifixion of Jesus (which is the focus during the time of Lent). The Salvadoran people both have very strong Christian roots in general, and they have suffered in a way that they see as very parallel to the suffering that Jesus endured. Therefore, many people here say that the celebration of Lent is central to the life and faith of the Salvadoran people.

Along with that, here in the Suchitoto area (which includes the 60 repopulation communities), they are reviving the Base Christian Communities (BCCs) that were once very active in the late 1960s and 1970s. Most all of the leaders and participants were brutally killed during the time of the war, and for this reason the BCCs dissolved and people have been fearful about starting them up again. The movement to start up, however, is now very strong. Consequently, in Papaturro we have both weekly BCC meetings and we have a re-enactment of the Stations of the Cross every Friday. (The latter is a re-enactment of the passion and crucifixion of Jesus, done in 14 steps. In most cultures it is only re-enacted on Good Friday, but in this cultural context it has always been a tradition to re-enact the Stations of the Cross every Friday.)

For these reasons, combined with the fact that (a) the women in the class have always said that they long to be able to read the Bible, (b) that they are most interested in reading the "Three Stories of Jesus" book (a small pamphlet, which I requested that a friend send because there was almost no other source of actual reading materials), and (c) that a few of the women in the class volunteered to help coordinate one of the three BCCs that we have in Papaturro, I have decided to incorporate the Lenten Biblical readings into our class. I have taken each of the readings that will be studied in the BCCs as well as the Biblical readings that correspond with each of the 14 stations of the cross, and I have typed them up on the computer and printed them in very large letter size. (Many of the women in the class have poor vision, never having had an eye exam or the opportunity to obtain corrective lenses.) I have made enough copies so that most every student has her own, with a few exceptions where I have asked people to share.

Today we studied the first "Station of the Cross." I had Sylvia read it aloud to the students, who were able to follow along with their own copy. I went around and made sure that they were able to follow along. After she read, I asked that they each read it on their own, or pairs (assigned by me).... I then wrote words on the board that I had noticed the students having difficulty with, either being able to read them, understand them, or both. I facilitated a discussion of the meaning of these words. I then had the students decode the words and study their syllable combinations. I tried to invite the participation of everyone, and although in the end I achieved this, Celia was most able to participate when it came to explaining the significance of the various words. She was able to give both a definition of the word and an explanation of the concept that it referred to in relation to both the social, historical, and cultural context of the reading as well as that of the Salvadoran people. I had each student underline the word that we were studying, on their copy of the text, wanting them to be sure to understand that this activity was a part of their developing the necessary skills to be able to adequately read and comprehend the text we were reading.

I then asked that the students again read the text to themselves as they had before (i.e., alone or in their pairs). They did this and were all engaged in the activity. After 10 minutes of reading, however, I had to interrupt them and ask them to stop so that we could discuss the text and then write about it.

We had a very full discussion, involving the input–participation of all of the students. In my facilitation of the dialogue, I focused on the theme of their understanding of the actual text and then their understanding of how this resonated with their own past or present. Although people had a great deal to say about the text (Jesus being condemned to death by Pilate for being an agitator and teaching particular religious doctrines), the student participation became most lively when I fed the students off of each others' comments about their personal experience of the war, and that of people they knew, specifically reflecting on the accusations that they were *subversivos* (agitators) and the many ways that they suffered because of this, some unto death.

At this point, I asked for a sentence that could sum up some of their thoughts. I invited several to give it to me, but when they didn't, Celia said:

> *Tenemos el ejemplo de Monseñor Romero y otra gente Salvadoreña* ... When I asked that another student complete that sentence, Francisca added *que también sufrimos lo mismo.* (We have the example of Monseñor Romero and the Salvadoran people who also suffered the same [as Jesus]).

At this point, we did the same as we most often do: They copied the sentence; Sylvia and I went around and asked that they read it to us, and the students then continued to write out more of their individual thoughts related to the theme. (Field note March 16, 1995)

Personal Letters as Authentic Text

Eventually, late in January, Robin assessed that the students were ready to learn another authentic literacy skill that many students had expressed as a goal. At this point, Robin began to teach the students how to write a personal letter, something that none of the students had ever before learned to do. Robin announced this activity several days prior to the class. Not a single student missed class on the designated day, each of them arriving particularly energetic and excited. Their talk was characterized by typical expressions of self-doubt. "I cannot do this!" "I will never be able to write a letter!" Yet, it was clear to Robin that these statements did not accurately reflect their desires and their hopes.

Robin began the class by reminding the students that they had all said that they wanted to learn to write letters to their friends or children. She then asked who had never written a letter before, and every student raised her hand.

After assuring the women that she would help them with their spelling as they were writing, she showed them the lined writing paper she had brought to class and explained that they would write their letters in draft form in the notebooks first and then, after they had worked on it, would copy it onto the writing paper. She also informed them that she would take the letters in their envelopes[3] to the capital the next day and mail them from the post office.

This lesson proved quite successful, with all of the women feeling rewarded and excited about actually writing to a friend or relative on their own. All of them were familiar with the functions of personal letters as they had received letters themselves that family members had read aloud to them. Many had even sent letters by dictating them to family members who could write. Now, they were learning to write them themselves. Robin reported that from that point on, many of the class members began to incorporate this literate activity into their lives, writing letters to family members and friends who live far away. Reflecting on this class, Robin wrote:

> In my assessment, this was a great class, for all of us. In part, I attribute this to the fact that we worked on an activity that has obvious, recognizable and practical significance in the lives of the students. Also, it is an activity that came from the students' own expressed goals–interests as determined in a verbal assessment I facilitated when we first began the class. It also struck me that this activity was a particularly significant and powerful one because of its emotional value: the students were writing letters to people who they care deeply about—their children, their dear friends. This was the first time ever in their lives to be able to do this, and in this, they were discovering a new world of communication and connection with people who are very important to them. This activity also seemed very powerful simply because it was the first time ever that the students were able to write a letter, and their ability to successfully do this was clear not only to me, but to each one of them as well.

Ultimately, Robin found that this activity increased the students' motivation toward the class in general, in that it was a source of tremendous self-esteem for the students, as well as an experience of the tangible results of their efforts to become literate. In a culture where women tend to have appropriated a poor self-image and where the benefits of literacy skills are not obvious, this kind of activity and the results it produced proved to be particularly powerful. Within this, Robin noted, it was also particularly effective because the culture in Papaturro is very family and community oriented, with these relationships being a central and compelling force in people's lives.

WOMEN'S POSITIVE RESPONSE

The women truly responded to this type of instruction, described earlier. As they began to experience their success with reading and writing, they would literally tremble with emotion. Never before had they "got it," i.e., seen the nature of the relationship between their spoken words and print. Slowly over the course of the 2 years, comments and stories about previous experiences with trying to learn to read and write came out for Robin to record. Her reflections on these indicated a belief on her part that they were beginning to recognize that their success and/or failure was not attributable to themselves (as unfit learners), but rather the way in which they were being taught.

Deonicia and Celia both shared with Robin some of the experiences with a literacy class that had been previously held in the community.[4] Both of them had attended this class and neither had learned a thing, they reported. They both stopped going after a few classes. But now, they said, they are learning, and Robin agreed, noting in a field note that their "I can'ts" in class when asked to read and/or write were decreasing. The women attributed this to "dynamic and animated" conversations and discussions that were held in the class and to their teacher's general enthusiasm and energy.

Providing more details of the previous program, which all agreed was similar in content and form to the classes they attended in the refugee camp, Celia said that the teacher would "just write all of the words and syllables on the board, and then have us copy them. She didn't even explain what the letters sound like, and she never asked us to write any of our own thoughts or words." Deonicia went on, describing the classes in the refugee camps. "It was the same way in the refugee camps. The teachers would just write everything on the board and ask us to copy it. They didn't explain anything—the sounds, what they said, *nada* (nothing)! And we never did any other kind of writing. That's why most of us didn't learn anything there either. Except how to copy, or to practice writing letters," she concluded with a smile and a laugh.

We discuss the nature of the progress the women in the literacy class made—and its relationship to the instruction—in greater detail in chapter 8. It is worth noting here, however, that this instantiation of Freirean pedagogy, with its blend of dynamic dialogue situated within the people's sociopolitical reality, whole–part–whole approach to skills learning, and inclusion of much process reading and writing, was received by the class (after some hesitation) with enthusiasm and delight at having finally begun to learn to read and write.

INSIGHTS FOR ADULT EDUCATION

Forms of Adult Literacy Instruction

This chapter described the basic form taken by the literacy class established by Robin and the women. Clearly, the class incorporated both process-based teaching and learning and critical engagement with significant issues related to the sociopolitical underpinnings of the marginalization and impoverishment of the students. Critical pedagogues around the world repeatedly make this point: A focus on instructional methods, alone, without the inclusion of critical engagement with issues of class, race, and gender results in an empty instructional shell, a technology of instruction rather than the heart and soul of true education. This is an issue which, although having been raised by critical theorists, has yet to be adequately dealt with, or even truly understood, by the majority of educators involved in adult education with the very best motives of improving the lives of their students. We address this issue in greater depth in chapter 5.

For now, it is most instructive to look at what we actually know about the forms of adult instruction being actualized in the United States and around the world. Unfortunately, with the exception described below, virtually no systematic research has been done on this topic. The general belief is that the form of instruction utilized by literacy programs in the United States varies widely, being at this time under no centralized oversight or direction. In many ways, the loose network of programs in El Salvador, which are predominantly staffed by low-paid or volunteer workers, is similar to adult literacy efforts in the United States and other countries around the world (NCAL, 1995). Responding to calls to begin to sort out and describe these different approaches to adult literacy instruction (National Center on Adult Literacy, 1995), Purcell-Gates, Degener, and Jacobson (1998) conducted a survey of adult literacy programs across the United States and created a typology of programs along two instructional dimensions that were directly related to the type of instruction instantiated by Robin in the Papaturro class: (a) life-contextualized/decontextualized and (b) dialogic/monologic. Life- contextualized/decontextualized reflected the degree to which the programs reflected real-life, authentic reading/ writing activities and materials in their instruction. Dialogic/monologic reflected the degree to which the power relationship between the teacher/program administrators and the students was one of mutuality (dialogic). Programs judged to more dialogic were those that incorporated the input of the students in issues of course content, assessment, procedures, and so on. The researchers used a short questionnaire with questions designed to elicit information regarding these dimensions in a triangulated manner.

Given the increased calls for programs that reflect and incorporate the lives, languages, and authentic literacy needs of adult students, the results of this study were surprising (see Endnotes for chapter 8 for a description of how coding for the categories was done). Out of 271 responding adult literacy programs, distributed across the United States,

73% of them were judged to reflect the life-decontextual/monologic quadrant of the two-dimensional grid. These were programs that were self-described as more teacher-directed and using materials and activities, such as skill sheets and workbooks, that did not reflect real-life purposes for reading and writing. Only 8% of the responding programs were judged to be life-contextual/dialogic, dimensions that describe Robin's Papaturro class.

The concept of life-contextual can be more complex and more difficult to understand than may appear to be the case at first glance. The incorporation of activities and materials that reflect real-life literacy purposes is supported by research on the powerful role of context in learning and in retention of learned skills (Brizius & Foster, 1987; Sticht, 1988) The authors of the typology define this construct as "literacy work grounded in the life of the student outside of the classroom" (Purcell-Gates, et al., 1998, p. 2). They make the point that what may appear to be authentic literacy activities may, in fact, be rendered inauthentic in adult literacy instruction. This would be the case if activities and materials that are mass produced and mass prescribed are actually distanced or nonexistent from the individual students' lives:

> Given the diversity of life situations among adult learners, this could easily happen in the adult literacy classroom. For example, a thematic unit centered around the use of checkbooks—considered a "real life" activity mediated by print by most middle-class people—would not be contextually relevant for students who do not have checking accounts, have never had checking accounts, and have no realistic plans for opening checking accounts in the near future. (p. 3)

One strategy, obvious and perhaps necessary, to avoid this type of scenario is to survey the students as to the purposes for which they want and need to improve their literacy, as Robin surveyed her students. The adult literacy teacher who is in touch with the literacy needs and goals of her students will be more likely to provide instruction that is immediately relevant and, thus, compelling. Another aspect of this familiarity with the literacy needs of students is knowledge of the types of literacies that mediate their social and work lives. This means coming to know and understand the communities and lives of the students. We discuss this further in chapter 8.

Balanced Literacy Instruction

The whole–part–whole aspect of the Papaturro class is reflective of the increased movement toward what many are calling *balanced literacy instruction*, that is, instruction that blends both holistic, process-driven activities and instructional stances with focused skill instruction.

While many view this movement as the result of dissatisfaction with totally holistic methods, in fact many teachers and theorists who recommended holistic approaches to literacy learning had always included skill work in the context of process driven reading and writing. It was with this latter, whole–part–whole framework that Robin began her work in Papaturro. Even though the professional focus on balanced literacy instruction has been, for the most part, centered in the K–12 field, the theories and rationale for such a blend apply equally to adult education; the inherent issues are beginning to be addressed by adult education researchers and practitioners.

The rationale behind balanced literacy instruction is that people learn language (and thus reading and writing) best by using it to get things done, things that language does. Reading and writing, as language activities, are learned most effectively by using print to accomplish communicative ends that are best served by print, for example, conveying information to an absent audience, reflecting on one's thoughts, expressing personal feelings to friends and loved ones who are not present, learning regulations, experiencing another's reflections and thoughts, and so on. While reading and writing are best learned in process, that is, by actually reading and writing, they differ from the learning of oral language in that one needs to be shown how to read and write. One must be instructed in the ways to understand and use the relationships between print and speech. Clearly, both of these elements—process-based reading–writing and explicit skill instruction—need to be present in effective literacy instruction (McIntyre & Pressley, 1996).

As the Purcell-Gates, et al., typology revealed and as ongoing research into adult literacy instruction is confirming (Purcell-Gates, 1996), much of adult literacy instruction tends toward the skills-based-only instruction, with, we believe, resultant problems with transfer, retention, and actual literacy growth—long-standing problems associated with the adult literacy field (NCSALL, 1996). As we will discuss in greater depth in chapter 7, the Freirean-based instruction instantiated by Robin in Papaturro provides a dynamic example of how skill instruction can be an inherent piece—necessary but not sufficient—of process-based literacy instruction.

The synergistic blending of both process-based and focused skill instruction can be viewed as particularly critical to *adult* literacy instruction. People who have previously received literacy instruction yet still cannot use print to accomplish their goals have often missed learning crucial aspects of the process, either because of poor or inadequate instruction or because of individual difficulties with one or more of the strategies needed to successfully develop as a reader and writer.

Jenkins (1995), in a report of her work with a woman named Anna, described one such case. Anna bloomed under Jenkins' tutelage, which included many opportunities to connect reading and writing with her own life through such activities as recipe writing and journal writing. These activities, according to Jenkins, began to convince Anna that she was capable of learning and that her life held important experiences on which she could draw as she read and wrote. However, her spelling and decoding abilities were very weak, and she was often frustrated in her attempts to write out her thoughts. She requested more skill instruction and Jenkins responded with lessons on phonograms (particularly those regularly encountered in the books she was reading) and dictation activities with linguistically regular sentences. Jenkins reported, "Anna loved having control over print and she beamed with pride over her dictations. The integration of this skills-based instruction into the holistic learning framework seemed to meet Anna's need." (p. 69)

It seems to us that the key to the successful integration of process reading and writing and focused, explicit skill instruction is the delicate balance the instructor maintains between the two elements. Our report and analysis of Robin's instruction provides one successful example of this integrated approach. However, we firmly believe that the balance between process and skill work, between invention and convention, must be individually accomplished by individual teachers scaffolding and responding to individual students within specific conditions and contexts. Therefore, we cannot recommend a method of balance, nor can we script teacher and student roles. Rather, we put forth the power and efficacy of a synergistic integration of process-based reading and writing instruction with focused, explicit skill instruction as needed to accomplish and develop literacy ability.

ENDNOTES

1. Careful analysis of the data leads us to reject the possibility that the choice of religious texts was primarily due to Robin's interest and academic background with religion and Liberation Theology. As we discuss later, Robin took careful inventory of the personal motivations and interests held by her students in wanting to learn to read and write. The overwhelming first choice of literacy functions for these women, and others who did not continue with the class, was to be able to read the Bible on their own. This reflected the deeply religious, yet politically aware, nature of this population (see chapter 2). It was in response to this desire that Robin provided Biblical texts for the literacy instruction. The fact that her background made it relatively easy for Robin to critically read religious texts reflects the co-constructive nature of a Freirean-based literacy class.

2. Semiotics, in its most general sense, is the study of sign systems. Our use of the term here follows from the work of Peirce (1998), who wrote:

> There are three kinds of signs. Firstly, there are *likenesses*, or icons, which serve to convey ideas of the things they represent simply by imitating them. Secondly, there are *indications*, or indices, which show something about things, on account of their being physically connected to them. Such is a guidepost, which points down the road to be taken ... Thirdly, there are *symbols*, or general signs, which have become associated with their meanings by usage. Such are most words, and phrases, and speeches, and books, and libraries. (p. 5)

It is the third type of signs that concern us here. It is by engaging with key words, with symbols, that these women took an active role in a print-mediated relationship (of self and social world). Peirce noted that "The symbol is connected with its object by virtue of the idea of the symbol-using mind, without which no such connection would exist" (p. 9). Thus, the written word, as a symbol, points both to an object and to a symbol-using mind. It is the existence of this symbol-using mind that is often denied.

3. Traditionally, letters and notes sent within the country take the form of folded notes, sent by way of any person going to the destination community.

4. Two years previous to when Sylvia and Robin initiated the class in Papaturro, the *Movimiento de Mujeres* had initiated an adult literacy class in Papaturro. At this point, the program was coordinated by a person who had many responsibilities throughout the zone, which limited her ability to devote much time to the program. Also, her background was with elementary education and not with adult education. At first the class was taught by a 14-year-old girl, who was ultimately asked to step aside because she did not teach the class on a consistent basis. At that point, a young man from the community began to teach the class, but he was also asked to leave the position for similar reasons. These *alfabetizadores* had very little training. Students recounted that their instruction involved a great deal of watching the *alfabetizador* write letters and words on the board, and then being asked to copy these words into their notebooks. Each of these classes lasted less than 6 months and very few students attended.

5

Learning Through Dialogue: Reading and Writing the World

Reading the world always precedes reading the word, and reading the word implies continually reading the world.... this movement from the word to the world is always present; even the spoken word flows from our reading of the world. In a way, however, we can go further and say that reading the word is not preceded merely by reading the world, but by a certain form of writing it or rewriting it, (that is, of transforming it by means of conscious, practical work. For me, this dynamic movement is central to the literacy process).
—Freire and Macedo (1987, p. 35)

The very essence of the success of the literacy class in Papaturro lay in the dynamic interplay between the critically engaging group dialogues and the reading and writing that fed, extended, and reflected the meanings and the reality of the world of the participants. It was this complex synergism between the vital engagement of the learners (impelled by the decoding and rereading of their world, their experiences, and their poverty and marginality) and the cognitive benefits afforded by the activities of writing and reading their writing that we believe best explains how the Papaturro women became fully literate within the context of the Freirean-inspired literacy class.

Oral dialogue, in and of itself, in isolation, is not of essential value in learning to read and write, Robin concluded. Nor is instruction in reading and writing in isolation of dialogue and engaged critical thought effective. In a written memo to Vicki late in the analysis stage of the study, Robin stated, "A prime insight and conclusion that I have come to is that education is at its most potent, its most powerful, and its most effective when it is a combination of dialogue and the reading and writing activities that spring forth from this."

To illustrate how this dynamic worked, we present in this chapter selected dialogues, oral and written. We use the term *dialogue* in the Bakhtinian (Todorov, 1984) sense, viewing dialogue as exchanges of utterances within given social milieus, utterances shaped by social contexts and presupposing listeners or readers as social linguistic partners. Thus, we consider both the oral exchanges and the written expressions to be dialogic and examples of dialogue.

The oral dialogues brought to consciousness and focused the women's thinking on specific aspects of their realities. In dialogue with Robin and with each other, they engaged with critical analyses of the topics before them. They also became engaged readers and writers (Baker, Afflerbach, & Reinking, 1996; Wigfield & Guthrie, 1995). These oral dialogues, along with their activated meanings and affective engagement, moved into written forms as each woman turned to writing to continue her reflections and analyses.

Freire (1985) emphasized the importance of participants using, through and with language, analysis of their reality. "From whatever angle we address it—be it form or content—this significance and richness involve a linguistic analysis that in turn includes ideology and politics" (p. 25). We can see this process at work repeatedly in the writings of the Papaturro women. Over time, their notebooks filled with written expressions that were rich with social and political meaning. The women of the Papaturro literacy class thus reflected their capacity to analyze their sociopolitical reality across several dimensions: poverty, oppression, sexism, and voice. As this all came together, each woman moved increasingly toward full literacy.

SAMPLE DIALOGUES

December 9, 1994. Topic: God's will for the campesinos and for society

Robin (reading from text): "What is God's plan for us, *campesinos*?" Carmelita?

Carmelita: To unite ourselves like brothers and sisters. To work together, bettering ourselves.

(Silence from the others.)

Robin: Why do you think this is important?

Celia: If we weren't united, then it would continue to be as it is now, with some who are rich and others who are poor. God does not want it this way.

Tomasa: God says that we are all equal, and it should not be that the poor are beneath while the rich are above.

Celia: Yes! God does not want that there are poor and rich! God wants that there is equality, that the rich move toward the middle and so do the poor, so that we can all live in an equal way.

Tomasa: Yes! Like how some cannot read because we have not had the same opportunities to study, to go to school. *This* is not what God wants! *This* is not how God wants it to be.

Robin: What is it that you can do, as a community, to make things be as God wants, as you want? Francisca?

Francisca: We must pray; we must do penance. And we need to struggle, to work together, reaching out our hands to those who are the most needy, those that suffer the most.

Deonicia: We must struggle; we must work hard!

Carmelita: Yes. Because the poor are those that think more about God, who pay more attention to God.

Tomasa: We need to come together. We need to value one another and not fail to appreciate one another.

Celia: We need to unite; we need to all come together as a community. And we must not carry around hatred, nor should we leave anyone behind, leaving anyone with less that the rest.

The oral dialogue ended with the following summary sentence written on the board:

Dios que quiere es que miremos con cariño a todos, pero más a los necesitados.
(What God wants is that we look at all with kindness and warmth, most especially with those who are needy.)

The written dialogues then commenced, with each woman spending the next 20 to 30 min copying the class sentence and continuing to write out more of their own thoughts in their notebooks. Note that the entries are presented in the following order: (a) student's spelling, (b) conventional spelling, and (c) English translation:

Celia:
Es de los porres
Es de los pobres. (He is of the poor.)

Deonicia:
tenemoalFeneDioslavaa.
Tenemos la fe en Dios. Él va a
(We have faith in God. He is going)
ayadar
ayudar
(to help)

Francisca:
nodeciandomal al Projimo
No deseando mál al projimo.
(Don't desire bad for the neighbor.)

Tomasa:
Dios ilavirjenmaria lamadre
Dios y la virgin María, la madre
(God and the Virgin Mary, the mother)
de nuestroceñor Jesuscristo
de nuestro Señor Jesús Cristo.
(of our Lord Jesus Christ.)
nostro Ceñor senpre loama
nuestro Señor siempre lo ama
(Our Lord always loves,)
y el notienerecor es usera ñor
y Él no tiene rencor. Es nuestro Señor.
(and He does not have rancor. He is our Lord.)

Carmelita:
yo le Pido a Dios que medememoyia*
Yo le pido a Dios que me dé memoria
(What I ask of God is that He gives me memory)
para poder leer.
[Dictated to Robin who then wrote the words]
(So that I can read)

*Carmelita also received help from Sylvia as she was writing.

February 24, 1995. Topic: organización (organization)[1]

Robin (directing the students' attention to the word *organización* that she had written on the board): What would life be like if all the students had was their national government?"

Chunga: If all we had was our government, and not our *directiva* or any *asambleas*, we would be dying of hunger and sickness and we would all remain illiterate.

Celia: We would be oppressed.

Tomasa: Yes, if this were true, we would all be very unhappy. The government does not care about us. The government is on the side of the rich, not on the side of the poor. The poor, they are putting forth their work, they are not waiting for the government. They are organizing their work in order to move forward with their lives. Also, we, the poor, we are receiving the help of international organizations as well.

Francisca: Yes, if all we had was the government, if all we did was wait for them, our life would be terrible. We would have nothing.

Deonicia: We have our *asambleas*, and there we evaluate the good and the bad of the community. There we organize the collective work, and there we make decisions.

Margarita: In the *asambleas* we evaluate the good and the bad of the community, we organize the work that we need to do as a community, and we make decisions about important issues.

Robin: Do you all feel that what you say and want matters to the *directiva*? Also at the *asambleas*, do you feel that you can speak out, that you can talk about what matters to you? Or do you think that there are only some people who can talk at these meetings, that there are only some people whose opinions really matter?

Margarita: Well some of us are very shy and self-conscious, and so we don't say anything. But yes, we all have the right to speak, and we are all welcomed and invited to speak and to participate.

The summary sentence was solicited and written on the board:
"La organización y las asembleas de la comunidad nos ayuda a organizarnos y hacer el trabajo colectivo." (Organization and the *asambleas* of the community help us to organize ourselves and the collective work).

For 20 to 25 min of individual writing time, the students wrote the following sentences:

Chunga:
El govierno queire ganar
El gobierno quiere ganar
(The government wants to win)
el puesto nesesito todo
el puesto. Necesita todo
(the place [the favor]. It needs all)
los pobres entonces
los pobres, entonces
(the poor, therefore)
les ofresia muchas cosas
les ofrecía muchas cosas
(they offered many things.)
Cuando ce sentio con todo
Cuando se sentió con todo
(When they felt with all)
el poder entonses trataba
el poder entonces trataba
(the power, they tried)
de enganar y el que no
de engañar y él que no
(to deceive and he that did not)
avia botado por elo en-
habia votado por él en-
(vote for [the government])
tonses lo multaba
tonces lo multaba
(therefore they fined him)
para espremir le el
para exprimirle el
(so that they could squeeze out)
poquito de sudor
poquito de sudor
(a little sweat.)

Deonicia:
asisetravagavine
Asi se trabaja bien.
(This works well.)

Tomasa:
no sotros los Savadorenos de
Nosotros, los Salvadoreños de
(We, the Salvadorans of)
Las comunidades que los organisamos
las comunidades que nos organizemos
(the communities, we should organize ourselves.)
el govierno no los ayuda en nada.
El gobierno no los ayuda en nada.
(The government does not help us with anything.)
Calderon es con los ricos no
Calderon (Sol, the country's president) is with the rich not
es con los pobres poreso no lo
es con los pobres. Por eso no lo
(with the poor. Therefore he does not)

Celia:
la organizaciañ
La organización
(Organization)
esInportente
es importante
(is important)
par salier de la Ioram sia
para salir de la ignorancia
(in order to become free of ignorance)
y node Jarlos enganar
y no dejarlos engañar
(and not be left deceived)
del govierno nidepolicticas
del gobierno ni de politicas.
(by the government or politics.)
tenemos que ser listas.
Tenemos que ser listas.
(We have to be prepared, intellectually.)

February 26, 1997. Topic: A continuation of the generative theme
<u>*organización*</u>

Robin began by reading a short narrative text which appeared in the students' workbooks:

> *Muchas veces no podemos solucionar los problemas de la comunidad, por estar aislados unos de otros.*

> *Unamos nuestras ideas y organicemonos para mejorar poco a poco.*

> *Si estamos organicamente unidos, estaremos preparados para crecer juntos espiritual y materialmente.*

> *Decidamos las tareas en forma democrática. A todos nos gusta participar cuando se nos toma en cuenta.*

> *De entre nosotros mismos pueden salir los lideres para que orienten el trabajo. Así podemos obtener ganancias de beneficio colectivo.*

Many times we cannot resolve the problems of the community, because we are isolated, one from another.

We unite our ideas and organize ourselves in order to improve, little by little.

If we are organically united, we will be prepared to grow spiritually and materially.

We decide the tasks in a democratic form. We all like to participate when we are taken into consideration.

From within ourselves (our own communities), can come our own leaders who can guide the work. In this way, we can obtain earnings for collective benefits (earnings which will benefit all).

Robin (Rereading the first sentence): *Muchas veces no podemos solucionar los problemas de las comunidades, por estar aislados unos de otros.* (Many times we cannot solve the problems of the community because we are isolated one from another.) What does this mean to you? How do you understand the word *aislado*?

Deonicia: This is when people do not have communication with another ... when they live in a way that is apart from one another.

Robin: Yes, very good! What else does this word, in this context, mean to us?

Tomasa: *Aislado* is when people do not work together ... when they live and work in a way that is separate from the others in the community.

Robin: Anything else?

Celia: If we lived this way, we would be just like before (the war). We would be poor just like before. Before, all we did was work individually. We did not have collective work. We have to be united; we have to work together. We have to communicate with one another.

Robin: What does this mean for our community?

Celia: Organization is a right of everyone! The collective community work comes out of the *asambleas*. It is here that we decide what the work will be and who will do it. This is organization.

Tomasa: And in this way, we work in a united way.

Celia: Yes, the *asambleas* are where we talk about and decide about the collective work.

Chunga: And this is for the benefit of the whole community. *This* is community.

Celia: It is very good and important that it is not just words, that the collective work is something that is actually done, and done as a service to the community.

Robin: How do you feel about the way that the *asambleas* and the community leadership functions in Papaturro?

Celia: Well, everything doesn't function *completely* well …

Margarita: But yes, it functions very well. Really, the majority of it all functions very well!

(Nods of agreement from all of the students in the class.)

Margarita: Yes, we coordinate all of the work, and it functions very well.

Celia: The *viejos*[2] work more than the others. The youth have other commitments, other things that they do. Before (the war), the men that worked individually, they sacrificed a lot, their work was very hard, they suffered very much. The youth do not know this, they have never had to live and work this way. (This other way), it required more, it took a lot more out of people. Yes, the adults, they are the ones who know about this. And that is why they work harder (than the youth) now.

Robin: As we have talked about before, let's think about what we can do to make the changes we want in our lives. How can we be the protagonists of our own lives, deciding what change we want to see and then being the ones to make them happen?

Celia: The *viejos* think a great deal of the future of their children. We think about the illiteracy that exists. We think about the education of our children. We are concerned that they are not trapped in ignorance, that no one can deceive them (as we have been). And we think about organizing ourselves, about creating the collective work.

Tomasa: Yes! As parents, we give support to our children so that they can take advantage of the opportunities that exist ... the things that we never had. As parents, we can make sure that they go to school, that they study.

Robin: All of you, as parents, are working hard to create a new future for your families, for your community, for society. You make sure that your children go to school, you support the *maestras populares*, and you are studying yourselves, developing your understanding of your social and political reality. You are trying to teach your children about all that has happened and all that you have learned in your lives, everything you know. Ok, so we have talked a lot about this theme. Who can give me a sentence to summarize what we have said?

Celia: *Nosotros como madres, les contamos a nuestras hijos como era la vida de antes.* (We, as mothers, we tell our children what life was like before.)

For 20 to 25 minutes of time for individual writing, the students wrote the following, in addition to the class sentence:

Chunga:
Nosotros el tienpo pasado
Nosotros el tiempo pasado
(We in the past)
no podiamos denunsiar nada
no podíamos denunciar nada
(we couldn't denounce anything)
porque no teníamos vos
porque no teníamos voz.
(because we did not have a voice.)
todo era cayado
Todo era callado.
(Everything was kept quiet.)
en el tiempo de hoy es me-
En el tiempo de hoy, es me-
(In the time of today, it is)
jor porque todo lo que nolos
jor porque todo lo que no los
(better because everything that we do not)
gusta es denunciada para
gusta es denunciada para
(like is denounced so that)

solusionar los problemas.
solucionar los problemas
(we can solve the problems.)

Celia:

los hiJos sealmira
Los hijos, se admiran
(The children, they admire us,)
de nosotros lo padres
de nosotros los padres.
(their parents.)
pensamos en el Futuro
Pensamos en el futuro
(We think of the future)
de los hijos
de los hijos.
(of the children.)
que tiene queorganizarse
Que tiene que organizarse.
(They (we) have to be organized.)

Deonicia:

La vida de nosotros, la vida era pobre. *
(Our life, life was poor.)

August 4, 1995. Topic: Text from Matthew 14, verses 13–21

Throughout the Suchitoto region, there had been a resurgence of BCCs. The regional church had begun to train local community members to facilitate reflective discussion of Biblical text, within the context of Celebrations of the Word religious services. As a result, the students in Papaturro's literacy class had begun to ask Robin to use Biblical text as part of their literacy instruction. Coming to see that class dialogue was fostering their abilities to analyze written text and verbally express their opinions in a public setting, the students told Robin that it would be very helpful for them to discuss in class the Biblical reading that was to be used in the weekend's BCC. Consequently, Robin began to use the week's Biblical text as the generative text on a weekly basis. It was clear that this fu-

---

*Deonicia dictated all of these words to Sylvia, who then wrote them in Deonicia's notebook. Previous to this class, Deonicia had been writing independently after the class discussions. Unfortunately, Sylvia did not fully understand the importance of having the students write independently, and Robin was not able to intervene and re-explain this point to her, as Robin was unaware that Sylvia was writing for Deonicia.

eled student engagement and motivation, as the students were increasingly aware of the impact that their participation in class was having on their experience of daily life, outside of the class.

On August 4, 1995, the class discussion revolved around the text from Matthew 14, verses 13–21. This particular text presents the scene where Jesus chooses to draw away from a multitude of people so that he can pray in quiet. In response to the persistent requests of the people who have gathered, however, Jesus chooses to return and be with the crowd. Jesus takes time to heal the sick who have gathered. He eventually preaches to the crowd. Evening nears, and Jesus indicates that people should not worry about going home for food; he will create enough food to feed the multitude using five pieces of bread and five fish. According to the text, Jesus offers a prayer to God in heaven and produces enough food to feed everyone who has gathered. It is also written that there was a significant amount of bread and fish that was left over, even after all had eaten their fill.

Robin had produced copies of the text for each student, printed out in large letters so that the women with poor eyesight could read it. She initially read the text aloud, asking all students to follow along. Given that the students' literacy levels had increased, Robin then had the class read the text aloud, chorally, along with her. Finally, she paired stronger with weaker readers and asked that the students read the text one more time.

At that point, Robin began the discussion. Using the questions that were to be used in the BCC meeting, she began with simple questions, soliciting a retelling of the details of the narrative.

Robin: Francisca, why do you think there were so many people who gathered when Jesus arrived?

Francisca: Because they became happy and went to listen to what Jesus had to say.

Robin: And Tomasa, it says that Jesus drew away, going to an area that was less populated, in order that he could be alone. But the people followed him, coming from all over. How can we understand this, that Jesus drew away to be alone, but in the end, chose to return to the group, heal the sick and speak to the crowd?

Tomasa: He wanted to pray, alone, but the people followed him because the people always followed him wherever he went.

Robin: Thanks. Very good. The reading also says that "Jesus had compassion and healed the sick." Celia, could you tell us what you think, how you understand this part of the reading?

Celia: Yes, what I think is that Jesus had compassion for the people, because he pulled away at first, wanting to be alone, but he came
back to them when he saw that they needed him and wanted
to be with him. I believe that the people followed him, because
they loved him and had faith that he was a mediator for the
poor, for the people. And because the people always loved him,
had a great deal of faith in him, he always loved the people,
healed the sick, offered consolation.

Margarita: As for me, what I understand of compassion is that we should
have compassion, one for another. If we look upon another
who is needy of us, we have to give them a hand, have compassion for that person. If we have something to share, we should
share it, with those people who need it.

Robin: I'm going to read to you a commentary on this text from *La Biblia
LatinoAmericana* (the Bible used in the community). I ask that
you listen to this and speak about your understanding of it.

> From God comes bread. God has put on earth all that humanity needs for nour-
> ishment and development, but if we do not know how to listen to the Word of
> God, we will not find solutions to the most urgent problems of the world, such
> as a good distribution of the riches, such that everyone has enough. And to have
> faith in the promises of God, so that we can overcome privileges, selfishness,
> and obtain for all bread, peace and freedom. This is to say that selfishness and
> privileges are the obstacles that do not permit us to distribute and share bread as
> God wants. (pp. 68–69)

Margarita: The rich do not want to share what they have, as the more the
rich have, the more they want, and the more they exploit the
poor in order to make themselves more rich. Yes, all of this
makes us think very much. To me, it makes me think of when
we went about during the war, fleeing, far from our own
homes. We had nothing, *nadita*! So people went about looking
for food, asking for food from other families who were also
very poor, and for this great multitude of people, there was
enough food from the little that we collected. It was a little,
but we felt full. *Imagínese*, this makes me think a lot, because
this reading is just like the life that we lived, these (Biblical)
readings that we read are just like our lives, exactly!

Celia: Amongst the poor, we have always shared, one with another. But
the rich, they do not want to share their riches. What
Margarita says is the reality. In the time of the war, when we
were fleeing the military, when we had nothing to eat, the
leaders of our communities would leave us, hidden, while they

went into other (rural) villages to look for food for us to eat. They would bring back oranges, small pieces of sugar cane, whatever people had to give them. And they would share whatever they had with all of us who were waiting.

Tomasa: In this way, we were living out the Word of God. Some people have done this and continue to do this. It would not have much meaning to leave things (of this world) as they are. No, we have to continue to follow the Word of God, until we arrive at the goals that Jesus set for us, for all of his children, for the poor. This is what we have looked for, what we continue to look for.

Robin: No one is saying that they want that wealthy people suffer, but the reading is very clear. There is enough for everyone, if one can overcome selfishness and the advantages of privilege, and be more willing to share. And so, it seems that if we are listening well, analyzing what we read, we should act a little differently, right? What do you think of this, Chunga?

Chunga: The wealthy have privileges, and we, the needy, we have had to be without opportunities to study. But God has helped us, sending us some teachers so that they can teach us. Because of the rich, we have had no schools, because our parents never even had what would have been most necessary and basic to be able to send us to school. We do not have resentment for the rich. We do not wish suffering for them, but we do wish that they had more compassion so that there was more equality, and less suffering for the poor. Our parents, they had to work for a very basic, minimal salary, and because they had to pay a census for the use of the cornfield, what they harvested was a very small amount, just enough to barely get by. If we sold *una arroba* [3] of corn or beans, what we earned was to buy a small little bit of food for everyone to share, and then we were left without any money to even buy clothing. The money was never enough. And still, we had to go work in other places, one week here, another there, just so that we would not die from hunger.

Robin: Do you think that God wants that some people have opportunities to study, and that others stay behind, without opportunity to study?

Francisca: God sees everyone equally. God does not see one person as more than another. No, God sees everyone equally.

Robin: And to have faith in God, so that we can overcome selfishness, privileges? What does it mean, saying that these are obstacles in the path of obtaining, for everyone, bread, peace and freedom?

Celia: *Bueno*, when we were young girls, we didn't have the opportunity to study. In the first place, we were poor, and our parents did not have what was necessary to buy us pencils and notebooks. God does not want this, that we the poor remained illiterate. No! What God wanted was that all the earth's riches were shared equally, for the benefit of all. In the Old Testament, it says that God made the world in 6 days. And He didn't make the world for just a few, but God made the world for all of humanity, everyone who lives in this world. Because it says that "God had compassion on the poor," but the government, the government of the Republic does not have compassion for the poor. They only treat us in the manner of seeing us as less. And the more they view us as less, the more they oppress us. Because let us say that this president, Calderon Sol, we can see that he has it so we are very badly off. Because he has opened up the (economic) market, to other Republics, so that they can bring their crops and fill the market here in El Salvador. And still, the poor (Salvadorans) have so many loans out with the banks, and yet now we cannot sell our crops. Therefore, there is this situation that the poor are there with their work, but cannot sell their crops, because their crops no longer are worth very much. And this is not what God wants. Because this is an injustice, what the wealthy are doing in relation to the poor. Because the wealthy, they have everything they need, but the poor, without being able to sell their crops, we don't eat. So, this thing of not being able to sell our crops, this has us very badly off. This is a form of repression, *bien grande*, that the government is imposing. And the other thing, ever since the government raised the sales tax again, everything is very expensive. Because what used to be worth 5 *colones*, today is worth 15 *colones*. And this makes it so the poor, we can barely buy anything. This is what this reading makes me think of. *Gracias.*

Robin: Let's focus on our future. We never want to end (a class discussion) just thinking of the difficulty and problems of our lives. Therefore, reflecting on this Biblical reading, what can we see that we can do in order to bring about this "multiplication of bread" in our community? Let's look at our own community, what is it that we are doing here? What more can we do?

Tomasa: Yes, as we said in the beginning, we can help one another. If someone is sick, we can give them a hand. For we the poor, this is what we must do, help one another. Because to say that we can bring something to eat, or money and other things, well, since we have very little food, and we have no money, we cannot give in this way. What we have is no more than love and warmth and caring, and we can help one another, giving a hand. We can offer to help with the daily tasks. Because one who is poor, whatever we have, we will share. Share with one another, and help in whatever way we can.

Deonicia: And if anyone is sad, give them *ánimo*, a little energy, so that they can go forward and not remain sad.

Robin: Thanks very much, Deonicia. And Carmelita, what do you think? Maybe you could comment a little about how it is that we can help inspire each other, how we can work together in the community in order to be able to move forward. For example, maybe you could talk a little about the work of the *maestras populares*, the teachers of the children.

Carmelita: They are teaching the little that they know to the children and to us, too.

Francisca: Yes, what I see is that Sylvia, she has love for the children and for the elderly because she is young, but still she is sharing with all of us what she knows.

Robin: Sylvia, what do you think about your work as a *maestra popular*, and the work of the other teachers who work with the children? How does it all relate to what we are talking about today?

Sylvia: Well, I see it as I am working and the other teachers are working because we have love for the children and for all of us, the poor, in our community. We are not earning a salary; what we earn is not very much. What I mean is that everything that we do, we do because of love and because one has a consciousness of the needs of the children, the needs of the community. Whatever we know, be it a little or a lot, we try and pass that on to the children, and there is where one is sharing that which she has. There were five pieces of bread, and, from these five pieces, a lot of people ate. This can be us too, that we are teaching the children from the little that we know, and everyone is learning. Too, in this class here, I see that it is the same because from the little that I know, I am teaching, and we all are sharing and learning. I feel that we are all equals; we all have capacities and abilities, but we share from what we know, and we all learn together.

Celia: Yes. What Sylvia says makes me think a lot. Yes, the work of the *maestras populares* is very valuable in El Salvador. Like Sylvia says, everything that they have learned, they are sharing with the poor—the poor sharing among the poor. They are teachers, and we call them *maestras populares* because they do not have the ambition of trying to earn a big salary. No, they do their work because of their love, because what they earn, a stipend, is very simple, very little,[4] but what the work they are doing is large, it is incredible. I have noticed, too, that they almost never miss a day of teaching. Five days a week, they are working. And I have been able to observe that the certified teachers,[5] that are earning more than c 2,000, how many times they miss teaching their classes! But, in comparison, the *maestras populares* are faithful to their classes. And we, too, we commit to help with this work. *Fíjase*, for example, I have committed to watching Lita's[6] children every day while she teaches. And when she goes to teacher training, too. We all try and support the work of the teachers in ways that we can because we believe our support is important, and we believe in the work that they are doing. We believe that this work is for the good of the whole community.

Robin: *Bueno*. Thanks so much, everyone. Let's think of a sentence now so that we can continue to write out our thoughts on this valuable theme.

Tomasa: *En las comunidades, lo poco que tienen los pobres, comparten con los de más pobres.* (In the communities [villages], the little that the poor have, they share with others who are poor.)

Each student then became absorbed in copying over this sentence, and either adding to it or creating other sentences, as a way to continue to develop their thoughts. As always, Robin had each student read their writing to her when they finished. Following is a transcription of this reading for this particular dialogue (the written samples were unavailable):

Tomasa: "In the communities, the little that the poor have, they share with others who are poor. This is an example, with the popular teachers, that they are sharing the little that they have learned."

Celia: "In the communities, the little that the poor have, they share with others. God has love for all of His children. He wants that we are all equal."

Francisca: "In the communities, the little that the poor have, they share with others who are poor, like the poor of El Salvador."

Chunga: "In the communities, the little that the poor have, they share with others who are poor. We, when we could share what I had, I have always done that. But when people looks for something they need, it is much better to offer. When someone looks (for something), and it is there, you cannot deny them."

Deonicia: "In the communities, the little that the poor have, they share with others who are poor. We, the poor, we have faith that God helps us, that we will overcome the war."

Carmelita: "In the communities, the little that the poor have, they share with others who are poor. Wash (the clothes) of some people in the community who need help."

CRITICAL LITERACY: ENGAGEMENT AND PROCESS

Over time, the women in the literacy class learned to engage critically with the issues of their lives, first in oral dialogue with each other and Robin, and then, with increasing skill, in written dialogue. Their ability to think critically about their reality, and their familiarity with critical textual analysis, had its genesis in the critical gestalt of the prewar years, particularly as instantiated in the BCCs. However, they had never before synthesized this with their expectations, gained through experience, of the classroom. Thus, as the early dialogues revealed, they were nonplussed by Robin's inclusion of so much "talking" in the class and by her insistence that they express their own ideas in writing. As we have seen, though, they accepted Robin's pedagogical rationale, drew from their experience with critical analysis in the BCCs, and engaged with their lives through oral and written texts, learning to read and write in the process.

Critique, engagement, process: These three factors made literacy possible for the Papaturro women. They learned to read and write by reading and writing about that which deeply engaged them, that which energized them, that which truly mattered. The engagement came first, the *energy*, as Robin termed it, the power and strength that came from the critical dialogues through which they came to see themselves as agents of their own lives, as subjects rather than objects, as actors rather than the acted upon. This engagement, this energy, enabled them to overcome the years of educational deprivation, the negative beliefs they possessed regarding their own abilities to learn. This engagement impelled them past the difficulties inherent in learning a new symbol system, with its new semiotic conventions and rules. They learned to spell and read words and sentences because they *cared* about what those words and sentences meant to them, to their lives, to their realities.

As the women wrote out their own thoughts, following the oral dialogue, they *created* their critique, their written language, and their visions for their own futures. This creative act was accomplished with the help of their teachers who were there to facilitate each woman's individual creation. This process of creation is at the heart of Freirean pedagogy, crucial to the assumption of Subject status by those who had previously lived as Objects. Freire (Freire & Macedo, 1987) wrote:

> (As a teacher of adults) I would find it impossible to be engaged in a work of mechanically memorizing vowel sounds, as in the exercise "ba-be-bi-bo-bu, la-le-li-lo-lu." Nor could I reduce learning to read and write merely to learning words, syllables, or letters, a process of teaching in which the teacher *fills* the supposedly *empty* heads of learners with his or her words. On the contrary, the student is the subject of the process of learning to read and write as an act of knowing and of creating. The fact that he or she needs the teacher's help, as in any pedagogical situation, does not mean that the teacher's help nullifies the student's creativity and responsibility for constructing his or her own written language and for reading this language (p. 35).

INSIGHTS FOR ADULT EDUCATION

Engagement and Motivation

The recent work done by the federally financed National Reading Research Center (NRRC) on motivation and engagement provides an excellent literacy development frame for our conclusion that the essence of the success of the Papaturro literacy class lay in the interplay between the engagement of the oral and written dialogues and the process reading and writing in which the women participated. Although the NRRC focused exclusively on the K–12 population, we find their insights and theoretical frames to be equally applicable to the adult population when considering explanations for literacy development.

NRRC researchers Guthrie and Wigfield (1997) stated that the traditional view of reading development focused almost exclusively on cognitive and linguistic factors, with little attention to the role of motivation in literacy acquisition or on the interactions, or interplays, among motivation, cognition, and language in this process. They pointed out that findings from different lines of inquiry suggest a central role is played by motivation and engagement in literacy acquisition. The first of these are studies that conclude that cognitive strategies for reading are deliberate, conscious, and effortful (Pintrich & Schrauben, 1992). Because such cognitive activities demand effort, persistence, and desire, posited Guthrie and Wigfield, they are dependent on motivation.

Secondly, other research highlights the significant relationship between reading frequency and increased reading achievement (Guthrie et al., 1995; Stanovich & Cunningham, 1991). Guthrie and Wigfield claimed that asking what accounts for amount of reading is essentially a question of motivation.

A third line of inquiry is that which links motivation to academic achievement. This research is framed by expectancy-value theory (Wigfield & Eccles, 1992), self-determination models (Deci, 1992), goal-oriented research (Dweck & Leggett, 1988), and studies of interest in text (Shraw, Bruning, & Svoboda, 1995).

The engagement perspective, as constructed by the NRRC researchers, involves a view of readers as motivated, strategic, knowledgeable, and socially interactive (Baker et al., 1996). They link engagement–motivation to reading and writing that is personally meaningful. Thus, personally meaningful reading and writing facilitates and makes possible the cognitive and language development needed for the acquisition of literacy.

The studies done by the NRRC highlight the need for literacy practitioners to understand the critical linkage between engagement and literacy development. Further, they stress, and we agree, that teachers, once they understand these relationships, need to explore ways to make engagement and motivation central to their instruction. They need to find out what motivates their students to learn to read and write. They must learn ways to engage their students in these topics or content in such a manner that the motivation is intrinsic and drives the reading and writing. Robin's "energy" must be created in different classrooms with different students and teachers. This undoubtedly implies that the processes of creating, or facilitating, such energy will vary with the contexts. But the central need for such energy, such engagement seems absolutely clear.

Critical Engagement

The question that arises is, of course, engagement with what? As briefly discussed in chapter 5, adult educators who espouse a critical pedagogy stress the need to keep the critical engagement and reading of one's own life and condition central to the educative process. "Education is not reducible to a mechanical method of instruction," proclaimed Shor (1993) in an essay on Freire's intent regarding critical education (p. 25).

Much of the pedagogy prevalent in the United States and several other developed countries at least partially reflects this belief, albeit without the focus on social justice that Shor shares with other critical educators. "Learner-centered" instruction has enjoyed a long and popular tenure in these countries. Progressive educators have believed for quite some time that education that centers around the topics of interest to their students and those with which their students have some knowledge and experience are best for promoting the learning of skills and strategies. This has, for the most part, been translated into teaching routines that involve the teacher in introducing a topic, or theme, leading a discussion, and then either making assignments or facilitating the choice of activities that relate to the theme and involve the learners in reading, writing, calculation, research, and so on.

"Theme-based" teaching, according to critics from the critical literacy field, has been too often concerned with the routine, or technology, of learner-centered education with little or no consideration to the importance that should be assigned to the theme under consideration. When engaged with literacy education with marginalized or oppressed people, practitioners need to focus their themes on issues central to their students' oppression and marginalization. To do less is to continue to marginalize the students by wasting their time with superficial topics which, by their noncritical natures, affirm the status quo and trivialize the educative process.

In a critique of adult education, Briton (1996) quoted Darkenwal and Merriam regarding the misdirection of many adult education programs:

> Many adult education practitioners engaged in the daily tasks of program planning, administration, or teaching have little time to reflect upon the meaning and direction of their activity. The educator is generally more concerned with skills than with principles, with means than with ends, with details than with the whole picture. Yet all practitioners make decisions and act in ways that presuppose certain values and beliefs. Whether or not it is articulated, a philosophical orientation underlies most individual and institutional practices in adult education (Darkenwal & Merriam, 1982, p. 37).

The implication of such critiques of progressive methodology is that the very nature of the engagement experienced by the students is watered down, weaker, or (perhaps) nonexistent when content is used that does not critically examine the social and political contexts of the students and the contexts' consequences for their lives. Organizing reading and writing experiences around topics such as "favorite foods" or "exotic animals," thus, would not engender the type of energy described by

Robin, the type of energy needed to carry the students past the difficult aspects of acquiring the skills and strategies needed for literate activity.

Even adult educators who may consider themselves "Freirean," according to Macedo (Freire & Macedo, 1995), may reduce Freire's notion of dialogue to a mechanistic methodology, reducing "the epistemological relationship of dialogue to a vacuous, feel-good comfort zone" (p. 202). Macedo pointed out that simply involving students in discussions of their own personal life experiences, without connecting such discussions to conversations of culture, power, and ideology, results in a form of group therapy that fails to proceed beyond the psychology of the individual. According to Macedo, this is a reductionist view of Freirean theory, "leading Henry Giroux to point out that such pedagogy leaves identity and experience removed from the problematics of power, agency, and history" (p. 204).

These are actually two separable issues, interrelated but not identical. One is a question of degree and type of engagement needed to promote literacy development. The other concerns the very nature of critical pedagogy and literacy development within that frame. We can see them as two issues within this discussion because we are highlighting literacy development as a process within a Freirean-based project, rather than focusing on the critical theory and social and political aspects of such a project. The degree to which these two issues—(a) engagement and (b) the presence of social and political foci within critical pedagogy—implicate each other is a question that is, or should be, paramount within the field of adult education today, and is one which we present as worthy of greater consideration, discussion, and research.

One argument heard from informed and concerned adult educators relevant to this discussion concerns the nature of the relationship between teacher and student. To what degree does the teacher direct the choice of topic, activities, procedures, assessment, and so on? It is generally agreed that a truly dialogical relationship between teacher and student involves a mutuality of power, a sharing between equals in the shaping of the educational experience. As experienced and instantiated by different Freirean-based practitioners, this sharing of power entails student input—on an equal level of influence as program directors and teachers—regarding all aspects of the program, including meeting times, topics, assessments, materials, teacher-student roles, and so on (Auerbach, 1996; Kirkwood & Kirkwood, 1989; Purcell-Gates et al., 1998).

Within this, committed adult teachers have reported their struggles with their responses to expressed student interests that do not appear, at least from the teachers' perspectives, to involve or deal with issues related to the students' social and political realities in ways that could result in greater empowerment. When students reject such topics for ones like "ice cream flavors" (E. Jacobson, personal conversation, September 1997), it feels more appropriate, given concerns related to student agency and self-direction, to follow that lead rather than impose one's own beliefs of appropriate topics, topics which are explicitly rejected by a class of adult learners. This, according to some adult educators, results in a more truly participatory educational process. To impose explicitly rejected topics is not empowering and does not lead to greater student agency, a goal of Freirean pedagogy (Ellsworth, 1989).

Freire (1993) may respond to this by pointing out the reality of the participation of the oppressed in their own oppression:

> ... at a certain point in their existential experience the oppressed feel an irresistible attraction towards the oppressors and their way of life. Sharing this way of life becomes an overpowering aspiration. In their alienation, the oppressed want at any cost to resemble the oppressors, to imitate them, to follow them (p. 44).

Certainly, leading critical theorists such as Macedo, Giroux and others view this teacher dilemma within the larger issue of teacher abdication of responsibility (Freire & Macedo, 1995). Again, these are significant questions in the field of adult education worthy of greater inquiry and dialogue.

ENDNOTES

1. In the Salvadoran context, the term *organization* has a very specific meaning. It is extremely central and vital to the grassroots movements among the poor. Organization implies that the poor will develop leadership and broad participation from among themselves; it implies that they be united and strong; it demands that the poor continually cultivate a vision of an improved future for themselves with specific goals and plans of action as to how to achieve their vision.
2. The literal translation is "the old people," but in this context, as in many uses of the word, she is referring to anyone who is older than a *joven* (a young person between the ages of 15 and 25, approximately).
3. This is an antiquated form of measurement, equaling approximately 100 kilos.
4. The *maestras populares* earn a monthly stipend equivalent to $37, combined with an additional $27 meant to cover travel and food expenses related to their mandatory, monthly teacher trainings.
5. Certified teachers are those who have earned a teaching license through studies at a university. They earn a monthly salary equivalent to $250. The predominant experience among the rural villages is that these teachers frequently show up late for their classes, or, more often, do not show up at all. The situation has improved over the past 50 years, but it remains a serious problem.
6. Lita is Celia's daughter who works as a *maestra popular* in Papaturro.

Literacy class students (L to R): Deonicia, Celia, Margarita, Tomasa, Robin, Francisca, and Chunga holding the first letter they've ever written. (Photo courtesy of Molly L. Graver)

Robin listening to Celia read her writing in class. (Photo courtesy of Victoria Purcell-Gates)

Margarita, Chunga, and Robin during the writing portion of the class. (Photo courtesy of Victoria Purcell-Gates)

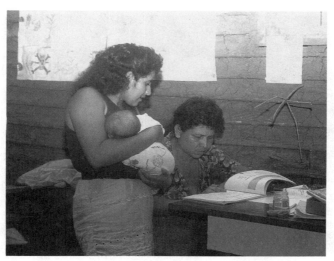

Sylvia (standing) and Esperanza in class. Sylvia was the
teacher in Papaturro who Robin trained and who taught the
class several days a week while Robin worked in other parts
of the region.

Celia often pulled apart from the class to write
out her thoughts on the generative theme.

Celia washing clothes in the stream.

Tomasa and Carmen carrying firewood for cooking.

Celia preparing the ground corn
to make tortillas.

A group of Papaturro's children dressed up for school.

Lolo (Esperanza's husband), a member of the *directiva*, working on the preparations for a new school in Papaturro.

Blanca, an *alfabetizadora* (literacy teacher) in another community. The sign reads: "For a more just and humane society. Neither men without land nor land without men."

Lino, former *alfabetizador* (literacy teacher) in the refugee camps and current member of Papaturro's *directiva*.

The entire literacy class (minus Esperanza and Margarita). From L to R: Deonicia, Carmela (childcare worker), Chunga (and grandson), Carmelita, Francisca, Robin, Tomasa, Celia, and Sylvia (*alfabetizadora*). (Photo courtesy of Patricia Lawless.)

6

The Language
of the People: Issues
# of Language and Power

I learned to read and write on the ground of the backyard of my house, in the shade of the mango trees, with words from my world rather than from the wider world of my parents. The earth was my blackboard, the sticks my chalk.
— Freire and Macedo (1987, p. 32)

I have always insisted that the words used in organizing a literacy program come from what I call the "word universe" of people who are learning, expressing their actual language, their anxieties, fears, demands, and dreams.
— Freire and Macedo (1987, p. 35)

Words From Our Hearts

The shaft of late afternoon sunlight streamed softly through the small window opening of the house where the new basic literacy class was gathered. Robin had taken over the lesson from the new *alfabetizadora* in order to model the teaching strategies she wanted her to employ. The three women, Simona, Marta, and Elsa, gazed bemusedly at the chalkboard on which Robin had written the syllable family, *sa, se, si, so, su*, taken from the word *casa*. They had tentatively repeated the syllables orally with Robin, who had then asked them to think of words they knew which had those sounds in them. Repeatedly, Robin stressed that the written syllables they were learning came from *their* words: the "words in our hearts; the words from our mouths."

Simona could not think of any words with one of the syllables to contribute. Robin pressed her. "Simona, I know that you know a word. I am sure that you know a word. There is one word with the 's' sound that you know very well." Suddenly Simona's eyes lit with wonder and her face creased with joy! "*Mi nombre! Sí ... mi nombre! Simona,*" she murmured shyly. "*Simona.*"

The connection between the printed words and the women's own(ed) words was central to Robin's instantiation of the Freirean–based pedagogy. It was one of the areas where Robin's U.S.–acquired training and Freirean theory met and reinforced each other. That the women must learn to read and write their own words first was critical, Robin concluded, not only to their understandings of the links between language and print, but also to their engagement in learning to read and write and to their abilities to think critically about the many issues they dealt with in their lives. Specified by Freire, it was also a practice that was not understood by other area teachers and educators to the degree that Robin understood it.

Despite the fact that virtually all of the adult literacy materials made available to Robin, and on which she consulted over the 2 years, included the Freirean generative word, there was little else in the prescribed pedagogy to involve the learners' language. Robin was intentional about using the women's own words at all levels of her instruction, from the syllable instruction to poems and narrative texts written in the "popular" format.

For the syllable instruction, Robin insisted on soliciting words from the women to use as examples (as she did with Simona, above). This was not as easy as it may sound to the U.S. reader. Whatever experience the individual women had had with schooling, it had never included this type of involvement or participation. When Robin first asked them to think of words they knew with the relevant syllables, they were totally bemused and silent. A great deal of support and encouragement on Robin's part was required before they would venture forth. Her description of this during one of the earlier classes is telling:

> I told the students that I was going to call them up to the board to write a word that has one of these five syllables. I called the most advanced student first. She was very nervous and initially unwilling, saying that she could not do it. I put my arm around her shoulder and faced the class, and said, "Chunga, we are here to work together, not to judge. We will work together with *amistad*, warmth and friendship." Then I asked the class if they were in agreement. They responded with enthusiasm and large smiles. So, Chunga went to the board and wrote a word. I asked the class to read it, and then we all applauded Chunga. Four others came up, with the final woman being Deonicia, one who can barely

write more than her name. She volunteered herself, coming up with a sense of conviction. I aided her by simply helping her recognize the sound of the letters she wanted. She wrote the word *misa* (mass, as in a Catholic religious service). We applauded her as we had the others.

Copying Other People's Words More Familiar

Robin noted that she had never seen a student workbook or teacher manual in El Salvador that suggested this type of student contribution to syllable learning. Instead, she observed, the teacher manuals offered lists of words that the *alfabetizadoras* were to write on the board and then read with the students. Afterward, they were to instruct the students to copy the words from the lists into their notebooks. "It was clear to me," Robin wrote, "that when the *alfabetizadora* did this, the students once again did not engage intellectually or emotionally, politically or psychologically."

The gap between the schooling experience of Salvadorans and the practice advocated by Freire and Robin also made itself apparent in the difficulty felt by the *alfabetizadoras* in carrying out Robin's training in this regard. During each monthly training Robin repeated her injunction to solicit words for the syllable instruction *from the women learners*, demonstrating and staging model lessons. Yet, when observing the actual classes in the communities, she discovered that many of the women had not fully understood these educational practices so as to be able to appropriate them. It was more than a year before Robin did not observe, in virtually every literacy class in her district, the *alfabetizadoras* listing words on the board for the students and instructing them to copy them in their notebooks.

The Power of the Personal Sentence

The power inherent in using the language of the students for beginning reading and writing instruction is perhaps more visible when the students are involved in reading and writing at the level of the sentence and beyond. Robin's practice of soliciting a dialogue-summary sentence from the students to write on the board, as well as providing space for them to write out their own thoughts on the generative theme following the oral dialogue, demonstrated this power. Repeatedly, as the class struggled to construct a summary sentence, the often scattered remarks and commentary of the oral dialogue would coalesce and sharpen to capture in a more incisive way the *conscientización* that emerged during the dialogue:

El gobierno estaba de acuerdo con los ricos, pero con los pobres, no.
(The government was in agreement with the rich, but with the poor, no.)

Cuando no hay otro trabajo, podemos trabajar con artesanía.
(When there isn't other work, we can work with arts and crafts.)

El derecho de nosotras las mujeres es que organicemos.
(The right of we the women is that we organize ourselves.)

Exigir que haya otro projecto de construir casas dignas.
(Demand/ask that there be another project to build dignified houses.)

Jesús fue pobre, igual que nosotros.
(Jesus was poor, the same as we.)

Ayudar los niños que se vayan a la escuela. Ayudar uno al otro.
(Help the children so that they go to school. Help one another.)

Como nos teníamos amor, no había preferencia.
(As we had love, there were no preferences.)

La organización y las asembleas de la comunidad nos ayuda a organizarnos y hacer el trabajo colectivo.
The organization and the *asambleas* (community-wide meetings) of the community help us to organize ourselves and to work collectively.

Nosotras como madres les contamos a nuestras hijos como era la vida antes.
(We, as mothers, tell our children what life was like before.)

Tenemos el ejemplo de Monseñor Romero y otra gente Salvadoreña que también sufrieron lo mismo.
(We have the example of Monsignor Romero and other Salvadoran people who also suffered the same [as Jesus].)

Cargamos la cruz como Jesús, pero encontramos esperanza en Dios y los internacionales y nosotros mismos.
(We carried the cross like Jesus, but we found hope in God, the international volunteers, and in each other.)

Quedaron algunas personas del proceso revolucionario que todavía están trabajando para que se cumplan los acuerdos de paz.
(Some people have remained from the revolutionary process who are still working so that (the government) fulfills the Peace Accords.)

The linguistic and cognitive effort needed to synthesize their thoughts and discussion into a sentence to be written and read reinforced for the women the powerful bridge between their lives, their language, and print. Print was no longer out of their reach, mysterious and powerful in its ability to deceive, control, and exclude. Rather, it now belonged to them; it became their tool, their reflection, their expression of beliefs, of concerns, of lives lived. It slowly became extensions of themselves and their world. Rather than being the epiphany this description may make it seem, however, it was the slow result of great effort and will.

Effort Required to Counteract Past Experiences

This bridge building between the lives and language of the women and print resulted from a powerful synergism among Robin's beliefs, efforts, and emotional support and the women's acceptance of this and their subsequent willingness to trust and take unprecedented risks. Robin spent months cajoling, encouraging, insisting, applauding, and praising as she sought to elicit the women's thoughts and words and translate them into texts for them to read and from which to learn about print. Responding to their warmth and relational natures, she would hold them close while she read their written words with them, kiss them on their cheeks after their efforts to decode their written words, and lead the class in smiling applause after each woman read in a trembling and shy voice.

The women of the literacy class similarly struggled with Robin's imperative to "write out your own thoughts" during the written dialogue portion of the class. Initially, of course, they were constrained by their limited knowledge of spellings and written conventions. Several of the women were unable to begin at all because they were unable to adequately use a pencil or they were still unfamiliar with the basic syllable families. In these cases, Robin asked them to dictate their words to her or to Sylvia who would scribe for them. The other women slowly progressed from limiting their writing to those words and phrases they could encode, approximating spellings as best they could. Over time, though, their writing increasingly expressed their continuing thoughts on the topic being discussed, deepening their thinking and crystallizing their beliefs. At the same time, they were consolidating their writing and spelling abilities as they pondered what to write and how to encode their words.

SPELLING AND DIALECT

Distance Between Written System and Oral

Because the women were writing out their own words, their spellings often reflected dialect variations present in their speech. *Campo* (rural) dialect was a regional dialect and thus displayed phonetic, syntactic, and lexical variations specific to its users and different from the standard Spanish reflected in most written texts and in the phonetically regular spelling system.

Learning to spell by applying just-learned graphophonic principles to one's own words is made more complex by the fact that no spelling system completely captures the variations in people's dialects. This is especially true, and especially crucial, for sociolinguistic groups who exist outside of the power structure and whose language is thus considered "substandard" as well as "nonstandard." With the virtual absence of language and spellings reflecting one's dialect in printed materials, and with the inconsistencies between taught spelling patterns and one's own speech, learners from speech communities outside of the margins of power easily conclude that their language provides no help in the decoding and encoding of the language of print. Their ultimate success, then, resides to a great degree in the knowledge, ability, and sensitivity of a teacher who will help the learner see the ways in which their language can help them in the acquisition of literacy and the ways in which print language differs from their own oral language, this latter requiring special attention.[1]

Teaching to Bridge the Gap

Robin's documentation of her teaching and of her student's progress reveal this type of teaching in process. Within a few months of instruction, the women in Papaturro were attempting to spell words they wished to use in their written reflections by applying the syllabic instruction they had been receiving. As they read their writing to her, Robin recognized the spelling errors they were making as evidence of both their learning from the syllable instruction and areas in need of special attention and a different type of instruction.

Discounting the spelling difficulties presented by syllables not yet taught and ambiguous consonant or vowel pronunciations specific to oral Spanish[2], almost all of the spelling errors noted in the women's writing reflected dialect variations. For example, in the *campo*, people greet each other with the phrase *bueno dia* instead of the standard *buenos dias*, reflecting a tendency by *campesinos* to drop the final /s/ from words. This tendency appeared in their writing with such spellings as *los rio* for *los rios* (the rivers) and *nos vemo* for *nos vemos* (see you later). In other cases, the *campesino* tendency to drop the medial /r/ from words would affect the spelling of phrases like *para que* (for what? or in order that), which was written by Esperanza as *pa que*, a spelling which more closely captured the local pronunciation. Similarly, the *campesino* pronunciation of /ll/ as close to /g/ was reflected in Francisca's spelling of *gina* (Salvadoran slang word for flip-flop sandals) as *llina*.

Robin's reactions to these types of spelling behaviors revealed her grasp of the need for teachers to appreciate the language knowledge possessed by learners and provide direct instruction on those written language units that do not correspond with the students' implicit language knowledge. She would always agree with the student that their dialect-related misspellings "made sense," given their pronunciation, and then would provide the "correct" written version for the student to learn by sight. She made sure that Sylvia, as the teacher in training in Papaturro, understood that there were logical, linguistic-based reasons for these types of errors, best dealt with directly through acknowledgment and explanation rather than simple correction.

Exemplifying this stance, this description begins with Carmelita having difficulty reading to Robin what she has written, partially due to many spelling problems:

> When I got to Carmelita, she had trouble reading the sentence that she'd written. I sat with her, and we tried to figure it out. Soon enough we did, and she read it to me. At that point, I wrote out for her the sentence that she had wanted to write, writing it below the other. I carefully pointed out to her the missing letters and tried to help her to learn these sounds or recognize why it was that she had left them out or written a different letter. Some of her mistakes were: "esdo" for *estoy*, "pedo" for *puedo*, "co Te ta" for *contenta*, "cha" for *Ya*.

> I called Sylvia over and we went through this together, the three of us. I explained (to Sylvia) that it was best to simply write out the words with correct (i.e., conventional) spelling, and try and determine why the mistakes were made. I told her it was best not to erase what the student had written. In this case, I explained that two of these mistakes were probably made because some people's pronunciation (i.e., out in the *campo* where we live) is such that the sound of /d/ would be similar to /st/, and /ch/ to the /y/ in *Ya*. I pointed out that it's words like these that we need to study separately and try and help the students to memorize (i.e., sight words).

READING AND DIALECT

Reading Other People's Words

Dialect issues also presented themselves in the reading of texts written by others. Because the Freirean-based instruction began with the words and thoughts of the students—a support which was extended by Robin's inclusion of text for reading that was either dictated or written by the students—this stumbling block did not present itself until other texts were introduced into the class. These latter texts included the Biblical text so beloved by the students and the texts provided in the instructional materials.

Teaching to Bridge From the Known to the New

As with the writing and spelling issues, Robin's responses to dialect-related difficulties with decoding, comprehension, or both were key to the continued progress of the women. With an appreciation of the legitimacy of the local dialect as well as of the profound effect of implicit language knowledge on the processing and comprehension of print, Robin could accurately assess the meanings of different students' difficulties with reading specific texts. She could decide whether a decoding–reading problem was related to a lack of knowledge of a particular letter–sound pattern or to an unfamiliarity with a particular word or phrase not used in the *campo*. As such, she could more accurately judge a specific student's progress, or lack thereof, and make informed instructional decisions for the future. This assessment procedure is illustrated in a field note in which Celia's success at reading a letter from Patty (sent through Robin), written from the United States, is described.

> Celia came to my home this evening, and I had a letter for her, written by our friend, Patty, which Patty had sent to me. (There's no post office in Papaturro, and it's easier to send it through me.)
>
> Celia and I sat down, and she read it out loud, by candlelight. Patty had written it on the computer, and had printed it in "extra large" letter/font. There were only two instances where Patty had handwritten some words, i.e., *"Para Celia, con cariño, Patty"*, thus signing off. Even though Patty used large print here, Celia could not read it.
>
> The rest of the letter, which was three pages long, Celia was able to read with very little help. I had to "give" her only three words, as she became frustrated with sounding them out and asked me to tell her what it said. One of these words, *apropriada*, is a word not used in the *campo*, and Celia did not recognize it even after I said it.
>
> She read with incredible concentration, barely looking up and barely commenting. She worked hard to sound out almost every single word, and even when I offered that she finish it the next day, she practically ignored me as she continued to read. She paid particular attention to the use of the letter *h*, commenting to me that she was noticing that it is silent. There was only one word (out of the entire letter) that she did not try and sound out: When she came to the word *cerveza*, she read it without hesitation or an attempt to sound it out.

Her greatest difficulties were with confusing *y* when it is a word (it means "and") and when it is in a word (it sounds different) and "I"; confusing the two small words *el/le* and *se/es*; and a few double consonants and double vowels.

Patty is someone who learned Spanish "in the streets," and therefore does not always use correct spelling and grammar. For example, she often misspells subjunctive verbs. When Celia came across words that Patty had misspelled, she would balk, with a doubting, confused look on her face, pronouncing the correct letter but reading the one that Patty had written. I always quickly interjected that Patty had made a mistake. In some instances, Celia also simply "read"/said the word as it should be, ignoring that Patty had misspelled it.

I praised Celia's first moment of ever reading a letter and sincerely told her that I was overjoyed and amazed at how well she could read. She beamed and laughed and gave me a very long and strong embrace.

Observations/Insights:

Truly, I think it is a sign of incredible progress that Celia could read a letter of such great length, that appeared to include a vocabulary that Patty would normally use with her friends in San Salvador.

It was very clear that it made a significant difference that the letter was written in computer print with a large font. It is safe to presume that Celia would not have been able to read it if it had been handwritten in Patty's usual writing (as shown by her inability to read P.'s few words of affection and goodbye at the end). Celia has glasses that she needs in order to read, but these are simply used glasses that someone donated, she tried on, and now uses. I would guess that her main obstacle is that her prescription is not sufficient. To some degree, it is also probably a factor that as a new learner she simply has some problem reading peoples' handwritten (as opposed to typed) messages.

I am convinced that Celia recognized *cerveza* as a sight word, and that all of the other words she managed to read by decoding. She works at a small store in the community and there she sells *cerveza* (beer). I believe that Celia recognized this word because she has seen it on the bottles as well as on the side of the trucks that contain the beer that deliver and sell beer to the owners of these small stores.

Within this I feel confirmed in my recent assessment that the students of the class rely very heavily on decoding and very little on sight words. I explained my thoughts on this in my class notes of Feb. 15, but they essentially relate to a lack of materials as well as an absolutely complete absence or even an acknowledgment of the need for sight word development in the materials that we have. I need to think more about this and give more thought to how to better incorporate this into the class, but also try and determine what is the actual importance of learning sight words in the work of (Spanish) literacy.

I think it is very interesting how Celia dealt with Patty's mistakes with the use and spelling of subjunctive verbs. She employs her decoding skills to such a pervasive degree, that she ended reading the printed letter *a* as she was reading the word *encuentra* for example, yet she balked because she knew that it should be *e*. (She knows, from her orally learned understanding of sentence grammar, i.e., that *encontrar* (to find, meet), as it comes after the word *espero* (I hope), should be conjugated as *encuentre* (and not *encuentra* as P. wrote). Essentially, I attribute her balking and confusion to the way that one's orally learned understanding of sentence grammar functions in our efforts to learn to read: It functions as an aid, predisposing us to know many things about print. And I attribute those moments where she "misread" Patty's incorrect spelling to some of the same logic and to the fact that she did not feel a need to finish decoding the word with absolute care and concentration all of the way up to the last letter.

I had taught the letter *h* that day in class because I had been observing that many students have been having trouble with it, quite consistently. (It is silent.) Celia's noticing of the presence and functioning of this letter is a direct reflection to me of how well she pays attention in class, which is at least in part a reflection of her great interest in learning and in the class. It also is a sign of her intelligence as reflected in her ability to assimilate and apply what she is being taught.

The Word Wall

Robin dealt with the issue of sight words by instituting a practice recommended by P. Cunningham (1991) and used at the Harvard Literacy Lab when Robin had done her clinical training. Obtaining some large-sized butcher paper from the Ministry of Education, she began writing words on it—words which the students tried to use in their writing but which gave them problems for any or all of the reasons just cited: letter patterns as yet untaught, ambiguous letter–sound correspondences, silent letters, letters with alternate sounds, and dialect-related pronunciation differences. As candidate words came up in the students' writings, Robin would add them to the growing list on the word wall. Referring to this list as *nuestro diccionario* (our dictionary), Robin would encourage the women to consult it as they wrote and to memorize the spellings.

Robin used the word wall for reading purposes as well as for writing. At the end of each class, she would engage the women in choral reading of the words on the list. She would then ask them to try and read some of the words, orally, on their own. Review of these words continued until the women knew them as sight words.

Keeping with the Freirean intent to bring the women's awareness of their conditions to consciousness and to make the proper attribution of their literacy underdevelopment, Robin tied her work with the word wall to explicit discussions of why such work was needed. She described this in a written reflection on the issue of materials:

I specifically point out to the students what I am doing and why, explaining that there are some words which are difficult to spell–write and that we simply need to memorize them. I explain that because they have had very little exposure to printed text in their lives (because in the *campo* there are very few books, sign posts, newspapers, and other such things as phone books, a post office, etc.), that it is especially hard for them to be able to know how to correctly spell words that contain difficult letters such as b/v, c/s, y/ll, z/s. Therefore, I need to help them by writing these words on our word wall (which I actually label *el diccionario*) in order to expose them and help them learn and memorize the correct spelling. I explain this primarily to help the women understand that their inability to spell many words is not because of any lack of intelligence, but, once again, because of a lack of the same opportunities that many other people have had. I also explain that our work in the class is a large step toward giving them the opportunity to tap into the potential and intelligence that they have, so that they can learn to read and write.

Over time, however, the word wall fell into disuse. This was due primarily to the lack of permanent classroom space, which made the transportation of the wall from class to class difficult, particularly during the times that the class met outdoors under the *pepeto* tree. Finally, the wall became lost, rolled up and tucked away into some forgotten crevice. In its place, the women had begun keeping separate lists of "problem" words in their writing notebooks.

FROM ONE'S OWN WORDS TO THOSE OF OTHERS—CRITICALLY

The power of beginning with the very own words of adult students, whether dictated or written inventively, is apparent; the need to move beyond their words, however, to the words of other writers is crucial to literacy development. Freire (Freire & Macedo, 1987) declared that this does not mean literacy development requires the use of text embodying the intentions, meanings, and agendas of others. Not only are these types of texts less engaging to readers, but they also perpetuate the marginalization and disempowerment of those students who do not exist within the dominant culture. A Freirean-based curriculum, thus, would incorporate text that is of the subculture of the students until the students can read both technically and critically well enough to handle texts that embody the language and culture of those in power. In this way, the students are able to increase their literacy skills at the same time they're being equipped to critically analyze text such that it will no longer have power over them.

Increasing the Distance

During the 2 years of this study, thus, the women of Papaturro began their move away from themselves as their own readers and writers to increasingly more distant communicative partners.[3] At the same time that Robin began to incorporate a greater variety of texts, written by a wider array of authors, the new texts continued to emanate from and address the concerns and realities that were central to the lives of the students.

During the early stages of the literacy class, Robin and Sylvia always used generative words reflecting the realities of the women to begin the discussions that would spark writing and the reading of that writing. Soon, this was accompanied by short narrative texts, read by Robin, which also served to generate critical thought and reflection. Robin, noting the women's high interest in Biblical text and reflection, interspersed these materials with Biblical texts that she modified for use in the class.

Even with the women's familiarity and experiences with the contents of these two types of text, the students sometimes encountered unfamiliar words whose meaning required definition and linkage to what the women already knew. This was the beginning of their move from their own texts to those of others.

Lack of Materials to Read

It was at this juncture that the severe shortage of materials became so critical. As their ability to decode print grew, the women were soon ready to read texts other than their own. Recognizing this, and believing strongly in the value of actual reading to advance reading ability, Robin cast about desperately for materials for the women to read.

Following one abortive attempt at providing the few children's books available in the community (the women were unable to read them), Robin discovered a book containing writings by survivors of the war. This collection, titled *Tiempo para Recordar y Tiempo para Contar* (Time to Remember and Time to Tell) had been compiled by a Jesuit-sponsored NGO called *Servicio Jesuita para el Desarrollo Pedro Arupe*. Because the stories had been written by *campesinos* and were about experiences with which many of the women in the class could identify, Robin judged that these stories were more readable than the children's books. Robin made photocopies of the stories that she believed the women could most relate to and began to use them in class. Three months into the class, some of the women (Celia, Tomasa, Chunga and Esperanza) could read these stories independently; the others needed to follow along as either a fellow student or one of the teachers read them aloud.

During this time period, Robin searched in vain for materials for adults who were just beginning to read. There were none available in the country, and, despite pleas to supporters in the United States, very few were ever located. Robin continued to rely heavily on the women's own writings for their reading material.

New Texts; Familiar Stories

Robin did, however, locate and create several other types of texts during the first year of the study, supplementing the writings of the women. One of these was a small booklet containing three simply written stories about Jesus, *Tres Historias de Jesuscristo*. The stories were familiar to the women, and reading them provided excellent opportunities to apply their newly learned decoding skills.

When Robin first received this booklet, during the fourth month of the class, she paired the two less advanced readers each with a more adept reader: Margarita with Tomasa and Deonicia with herself. For these pairs, Robin orchestrated an echo-reading-type format[4], with encouragements that the students stop and discuss their thoughts about the text as they wished. The other students read independently, and, as Robin describes it, they all benefitted from this opportunity to read published text:

> I also had Deonicia and I stop and discuss what we were reading. Her comprehension was excellent. She understood all that we read, giving substantial reflection–comments about how this related to her own life. She also gave general comments on the subject, and related these to the larger social–political realities of the Latin American poor. Margarita and Tomasa seemed to really enjoy reading together. Tomasa seemed to include Margarita and help her to feel that they were reading together. All of the students stayed on past 4:00 p.m., as they were very engaged in their reading. When someone told them that it was almost 4:15, however, they started to get up and leave, knowing that they needed to begin the work of preparing the evening tortillas.

Reaching the Other Side of the Gap

By the end of the first year of the class, all of the women, except Margarita and Carmelita, were reading the following texts on their own, with only minor scaffolding from Robin: Biblical text, prepared by Robin on the computer in large font; short poems, of *popular* themes; letters from various correspondents, including Patty and a group of nuns from Mexico; children's books; a Stations of the Cross booklet; and journal entries written by Robin and Sylvia in the students' dialogue journals.

The students' move from their own words to those of others was well underway. They had developed a firm foundation for a genuine understanding of the linkages between language, thought, intention, and print.

INSIGHTS FOR ADULT EDUCATION

Emotional Power of Language

Robin's tenacious belief that the literacy instruction must be rooted in the language of her students, and the ways in which she instantiated this belief, carry several implications for adult education in other settings. To begin with, the analysis just presented illustrates, we believe, the crucial synergism between motivation–engagement (the affective domain) and cognition and language development (the cognitive domain) discussed at the end of chapter 5. Many of the adults in literacy programs have experienced years of failure at learning to read and write in formal educational settings.

These same adults, for the most part, also have as their first language either a dialect or a language that is considered nonstandard or substandard. It seldom "matches" the academic form of language used in schools or in written texts. It is fairly common for these students to feel that their own language is wrong and, in some way, responsible for their failure to learn when they were in school. Jenny, the urban Appalachian mother in *Other People's Words* (Purcell-Gates, 1995), taking her cue from ill-informed teachers, phrased it thusly: "That's why it was a little hard for me startin' to like … sound my words out … 'cause I talk different … 'cause I'm you know … countrified. And my words don't come out the way they're supposed to" (p. 100). Believing that her speech was wrong, Jenny had never understood that she could write it or read it. Thus, she was denied the very foundation block every potential literacy learner needs: her implicit knowledge of language.

Freire and Macedo (1987) focused on this and stressed the need for adult educators to respect and build on their students' language, to respect and legitimate the students' discourses, their own linguistic codes, "which are different but never inferior" (p. 127). First, and foremost, these adult students who have come to believe that their own language is inferior and harmful to their literacy development must be confronted directly by a teacher who explains to them the powerful role their own language must play, and can play, in their learning to read and write. To accept this is to accept and begin to believe in themselves as language learners and to begin to trust their own readings of their realities.

To deny students access to their own discourse is to deny their meanings of their realities as constructed through that discourse, according to Freire and Macedo (1987). "… it is through multiple discourses that students generate meaning of their everyday social contexts. Without understanding the meaning of their immediate social reality, it is most difficult to comprehend their relations to the wider society" (p. 154).

This deep connection between self and language is needed when learners attempt to acquire another language, or discourse, such as that of print and written language. Simona's emotional recognition of the sounds encoded by the unfamiliar print as the same as those in her name provided a powerful moment of learning and acquisition and a basis on which she could develop as a reader and a writer. If print is always perceived as encoding "other people's words," this affective engagement is lost and, thus, the entire learning process is seriously, if not fatally, weakened.

Scaffolding the Distance Between Print and Oral Language

Those who worry that speakers of nonstandard dialects will not be able to sound out the words as they read or write fail to understand the relationships between oral and written language and the differences[5]. Print, and the conventional phonics rules for going from print to sound, fails to match anyone's spoken language perfectly. Even within standard dialects, sound variations are the most prevalent markers of regional differences.

We believe that the effective teacher helps his or her students understand that phonic relationships between letters and sounds are imperfect and that, in order to decode, the reader needs to rely on phonic regularities and approximate whenever possible. When writing, it helps to remember that even phonetically regular languages like Spanish have ambiguous sound–symbol relationships and the developing speller needs to learn those problematic words by sight. In graphophonetically more complex languages like English, spellers have a more difficult job and must learn to spell words by employing a range of strategies, including sounding out, learning by sight, learning morphological derivations, and so on.

The distance between learners' oral language and that encoded in print will vary by dialect. Teachers must help learners bridge this distance. In order to do this, teachers need to know the language of their students. They need to know, and respect as legitimate, the syntactic system of that dialect, the lexical and semantic system, and the sound system. Before teachers can help learners bridge the distance between the language they speak and that encoded in print, they must know what that distance is and what aspects of the learners' language it involves.

Teachers cannot do this if they adopt an elitist stance toward the language of their students, refusing to acknowledge it as "language" and insisting on the exclusive use of the "different" print language with no explanation of which cognitive and linguistic strategies are needed for the learners to move between their own language and language knowledge and that of print language.

Materials

Also raised as an issue in this chapter is that of materials. The availability of materials for low-literate adults to read has always been problematic; this is a particularly severe problem for adult educators working with learners whose language is different from that of typical printed material. In many instances, low-literate adults speak different languages than that of the official print world. For example, in several Central and South American countries, marginalized populations speak various native Indian languages rather than Spanish, the language of colonialization and domination. In the United States, groups of immigrants from Haiti or Cape Verde speak Creoles for which there are no, or few, printed equivalents[6]. The challenge facing adult educators is to develop such materials so that they can be used by their students to acquire basic understandings of, and strategies for, reading and writing.

Learners who speak the language represented in print also suffer from the scarcity of materials written at levels at which they can read. Particularly in developing countries, but also in developed ones, few resources are targeted for adult literacy materials beyond the ubiquitous workbooks and worksheets.

Although Robin would have had an easier time finding appropriate texts for her students in the United States, it still would have presented a challenge. Her solution (using the writing generated by her students either on their own or through language experience[7] activities) is growing in popularity among adult educators after years of use with younger learners. Adults bring with them many years of experience and knowledge building that can be elicited and used to introduce them to the strategies needed to read and write print. Further, by using the language of the adult learners, teachers are assured that the distance between the learners' language and that encoded in print is as narrow as it can possibly be, thus ensuring early success and positive feedback for adult learners.

The Move to Other Discourses

A greater concern, and bigger issue, for most adult educators is that of moving their students to proficiency in discourses other than their own. While the value of starting with the students' own language is acknowledged, the real challenge, and goal, of most adult basic education is to increase the students' ability to read, write, and, in some instances, speak in standard and academic discourse. This move from the student's own language to that of those with more formal education is the subject of debate, concern, and considerable angst among teachers of students from marginalized groups.[8]

This angst comes from the recognition that the acquisition of a discourse different from one's own involves more than just learning new linguistic rules. It includes issues of self-esteem, group identity, power, and political positioning. From her vantage point as an influential Black educator in the United States, Delpit (1990) discussed this move in the following way:

> A nonstandard language variety is a stubborn thing. Teachers seeking to help students acquire standard English as a second dialect sometimes think that all they are asking of their students is some technical linguistic achievement. They forget that students' community speech patterns are loaded with emotional investment for those students. They forget, also, that speech style is not just composed of discrete linguistic elements, but is also composed of broader styles of interaction and expression. Finally, teachers sometimes forget that speech which may deviate from some standard does not necessarily reflect thought patterns that deviate from any logic. Ability to learn is not hindered by the boundaries between language varieties. (p. 247)

Freire (Freire & Macedo, 1987) also underlined the complexity and ramifications of shifting discourses. Along with urging continued and basic respect for students' own discourses, he concluded (as this applies to Black Americans) that "The legitimation of black English as an educational tool does not, however, preclude the need to acquire proficiency in the linguistic code of the dominant group" (p. 127). Oppressed groups, according to Freire and Macedo, need to learn the discourse of the dominant group in order to both truly understand their own domination and to effectively fight it.

Delpit (1990) fully agreed with this position and suggested a stance much like one of "translation" for teachers who face the need to help students acquire other discourses. She suggested explicitly telling the students that there is more than one way to talk or write about things: the first, the way one talks at home, and then, second, the way of the mainstream. Whereas neither is better than the other, the home way of speaking is more comfortable and useful in certain situations. The more academic way is better in other situations, however, situations that may lead to increased agency and power for the students. She provided the following example of a teacher of Athabascan Indian students in Alaska:

> Martha Demientief ... finds that her students, who live in a small isolated village, are not fully aware that there are different codes of English. She analyzes their writing for features of the dialect that have been referred to by Alaskan linguists as "Village English." Half of a bulletin board is then covered with words and phases from students' writing, which she labels "Our Heritage Language" (e.g., "We go store."). On the other half of the bulletin board she puts the equiva-

lent statements in standard English, which she labels "Formal English," and sometimes refers to as "political English." ("We went to the store.")

She and the students savor the phrases and discuss the nuances of their "Heritage English," as she says to them "That's the way we say things. Doesn't it feel good? Isn't it the absolute best way of getting that idea across?" The class then turns its attention to the other side of the board. Martha tells the students that there are people, not like those in their village, who judge others by the way they talk or write:

> We listen to the way people talk, not to judge them, but to tell what part of the river they come from. These other people are not like that. They think everybody needs to talk like them. Unlike us, they have a hard time hearing what people say if they don't talk exactly like them. Their way of talking and writing is called "Formal English." We have to feel a little sorry for them because they have only one way to talk. We're going to learn two ways to say things. Isn't that better? One way will be our Heritage way. The other will be Formal English. Then, when we go to get jobs, we'll be able to talk like those people who only know and can only really listen to one way. Maybe after we get the jobs we can help them to learn how it feels to have another language, like ours, that feels so good. We'll talk like them when we have to, but we'll always know our way is best. (pp. 157–158)

According to Delpit, stances such as this one support and legitimate students' own language or dialect while at the same time provide them with an additional one. This type of approach also makes it explicit to the students where and how they can shift between discourses. It gives them the detail of knowledge needed to successfully acquire and use the second discourse. Explicit explanations such as these are much more powerful and effective than expecting students to acquire new discourses and effectively shift cultures through limited exposure to academic discourse. Adult students are aware and intentional about why they are seeking further education and are likely to benefit from such explicit instruction.

ENDNOTES

1. See Purcell-Gates (1995) for an in-depth case study analysis and discussion centered on this issue.
2. In Spanish, students most commonly have difficulty distinguishing between the letters *b* and *v*, as these letters sound almost identical; the letter *h* also causes great difficulties, as it is silent; confusing the *c* and *s* is also common, as these letters sound the same in some words.
3. Early in 1996, the NGO *Fundación-16* established a second literacy class in Papaturro, aimed at grade levels 3 through 5. Lino, a Papaturro resident who had taught literacy in the refugee camps, taught the class. Several women from the original literacy class (taught by Sylvia and Robin) moved into this class. In the

new class, Lino used *Fundación-16* materials (which Robin helped write) that contained readings such as excerpts from the Salvadoran political documents, national health promotion materials, text outlining various aspects of Salvadoran history, and excerpts from expository text discussing the themes of education, democracy, and human rights.

4. This technique is also sometimes called the Neurological Impress Method (Heckelman, 1966, 1969). It involves the teacher or a partner reading the text aloud with the student who reads a beat or two behind. Lipson and Wixson (1991) recommended specific guidelines:

   1. The teacher should maintain a reasonable, fluent pace of reading. The point is for the student to match the fluency of the teacher not vice versa.
   2. The teacher runs a finger smoothly along the print as it is being read.
   3. The teacher does not launch a discussion of comprehension and does not use this experience to teach word recognition or word analysis strategies. (p. 528)

5. See R. Horowitz and S. J. Samuels (1986) for a compendium of articles dealing with different aspects of the similarities and differences between oral and written discourse and the implications of these for learning to read and write.

6. Increasingly, community activists for such groups are attempting to create printed texts in these languages. However, they are few and far between and do not provide enough practice (due to scarcity) or functionality for adult teachers to be able to rely on them as texts from which to teach reading and writing.

7. Language Experience is a technique, useful for beginning readers and writers of all ages, wherein the student is asked to "say" or dictate a text for the teacher or aide to record in writing. This text is then used for reading and for literacy instruction by the student. Strengths of this technique include (a) content that is developmentally appropriate, familiar, and of interest to the student; and (b) language that is familiar to the students as it is their own.

8. J. P. Gee (1989) theorized about such moves. He framed his work within a theory of discourse that views one's first language as one basic Discourse. According to Gee, Discourse involves not only language, but also one's way of being, acting, dressing, speaking, reacting, thinking, and so on. It is a sociocultural identity kit. Gee does not believe that Discourses can be learned through overt instruction that deals with the superficial aspects of grammar, style, and mechanics. Rather, they must be learned through enculturation in social practices through scaffolding and social interaction with people who have already mastered a Discourse.

7

Dialogic Practice: The Teacher as Student and the Student as Teacher

One cannot expect positive results from an educational program which fails to respect the particular view of the world held by the people. Such a program constitutes cultural invasion, good intentions notwithstanding

—Freire (1993, p. 76)

Freirean theory calls clearly for a stance of inquiry on the part of the teacher, inquiry driven by the need to understand the world from the learners' perspective. And this need to "get inside the learners' heads and hearts" is itself driven by the imperative for mutual respect and dialogue between the students and the teacher, the dialectical opposite of a banking approach to teaching–learning. Dialogue, according to Freire, is not a mere tactic to involve students. Rather, it is an epistemological necessity; it is a way of knowing, a way that acknowledges the social character of knowledge building (Freire & Macedo, 1995).

In *Pedagogy of the Oppressed*, Freire (1993) described the many ways that "investigators" need to go about learning about a particular community of learners before they begin the process of designing an educational program in collaboration with the students:

> ... the investigators set their critical "aim" on the area under study, as if it were for them an enormous, unique living "code" to be deciphered. They regard the area as a totality and visit upon visit attempt to "split" it by analyzing the partial dimensions which impress them. Through this process they expand their understanding of how the various parts interact, which will later help them penetrate the totality itself.... It is essential that the investigators observe the area under varying circumstances: labor in the fields, meetings of a local association (noting the behavior of the participants, the language used, and the relations between the officers and the members), the role played by women and by young people, leisure hours, games and sports, conversations with people in their homes. ... (pp. 92–93)

To establish and maintain an on-going, dynamic, dialogical relationship, Freirean-based teachers must be learners, or students, as well as teachers. This concomitantly means that the students in a Freirean-based class must also be teachers, as well as learners. As Robin was consistent in pointing out to the women in the literacy class, "No one knows everything, and no one knows nothing."

LIVING AND LEARNING IN THE COMMUNITY

Robin, as noted in her statement of location (Appendix A), had always felt strongly that as a teacher she needed to live with her students in their world, and she had done this for several previous teaching assignments. When she took on the responsibility of directing *El Moviemiento de Las Mujeres de Cuscatlán*, she very naturally sought out and found a place to live in one of the *comunidades* in the *campo*. This, bolstered by her research commitment, resulted in her following Freire's prescriptions for learning about a community almost to the letter.

Robin's growing, deep knowledge of the world of the Papaturro women was reflected in virtually all of her educational decisions: choosing generative themes, locating compelling texts, planning for functional literacy instruction, selecting pedagogical activities for her students. To acquire this knowledge, she actively assumed a learner stance of observing, recording, questioning, acknowledging, synthesizing.

GENERATIVE THEMES

A key need impelling cultural learning with a Freirean-based literacy program is the choice of generative themes. The generative theme must emerge from, and connect with, the learners' reality: their history, their culture, their social and political lives. These themes serve as the focus for dialogue and subsequent learning. They engage the learners and impel reading and writing. A theme that does not emerge from, and connect with, the learners' reality is not generative, but merely a theme in a technical sense, disconnected from the learners and used by the teacher to manipulate and stage discussion and writing–reading events. It has no power to transform.

Time and again, Robin documented the insight gained through her learning about the culture and lives of her students as it impacted on her choice of generative themes. Within the context of Robin's assignment, there were adult literacy materials available for her use, all of which were already formed and sequenced with the attendant generative themes, words, and codes. But this did not mean that she simply proceeded through them, page after page in a simplistic, blind sort of way. Rather, Robin actively exercised control over whatever materials were provided by making on-line decisions to abandon certain themes and substitute others, or to create her own entirely. This decision-making emanated from her growing knowledge of her students and their lived realities.

Teaching-Moment Decisions

Changing Texts in Response to Students' Knowledge and Interest.   An on-the-spot decision made during classtime in early February of the first year illustrates both the way in which knowledge of the culture and sensitivity to the students can play out in a dialogical relationship. While waiting for others to arrive to class, Robin and Sylvia were conferring about what to do with the class that day. The women who had arrived early had chosen to read their book, *The Three Stories of Jesus*, while they were waiting.

When the rest of the students arrived, however, Robin chose to assign a different narrative text. She passed out some small pamphlets containing Biblical stories that were rewritten using "popular language" (i.e., simpler discourse, "of the people") and printed in particularly large letters. Each story contained several illustrations. Robin suggested, and Sylvia agreed, that each student would first read one of the stories silently (the one that Robin had enough copies of so that each woman could have her own copy), and then take turns reading aloud. They would then discuss the text and write out more of their thoughts on the central theme that surfaced.

> The books I had the most copies of were based on a reading from Daniel. Sylvia and I looked it over and … neither of us found it very interesting, or compelling;

the theme had to do with foods, which were acceptable to eat, etc. It certainly did not contain anything that we could easily discern as that which would provoke a lively dialogue and social–political analysis. Meanwhile, some of the students started asking us who Daniel was, saying that they were not familiar with that part of the Bible. Between these two occurrences, I indicated that the women were not obligated–assigned to necessarily read the book on Daniel. Several decided to read their "Jesus" book. Given that each have a copy of that, I asked that everyone put away the Daniel book and take out their "Jesus" book. Most of them explicitly expressed that they were very happy about this decision. They said, "I love this book!"

The lesson proceeded with this text. Robin later reflected on this event:

I think the students' reaction to my choice to use the popular education book on a Biblical reading from Daniel was very revealing. I believe that the books are valuable to the extent that they are in a popular education format,[1] but were clearly not valuable for our class because they did not have a theme–topic that had social–political significance, nor one that touched their life experience or that which is familiar to them. I'd actually speculate that these books ultimately would fail to accomplish the goals of any popular educational activity–class because of this fact. (I.e., I can't imagine that their content would be of political–social significance to any poor community.)

Ultimately I learned an important lesson: I allowed myself to be misled by the fact that the books were, to a degree, created in the popular education format, and that they were based on a Biblical reading. I now know that I should never give my students something to read before I have read it and reviewed it, making sure that it is of a theme that will provoke thought, reflection, discussion, and ultimately, of course, personal and social transformation.

Changing Generative Themes to Reflect Student's Knowledge and Interest. The *chilate* incident, recorded in Appendix B, similarly illustrates this playing out of the dialogical relationship between Robin and her students.

Midstream during a lesson from the materials she had been given to use, she abandoned the theme of traditions with *chilate* as the code and shifted it to the students' experience of traditions during the *guinda*, the period of time during which they lived in the mountains, constantly fleeing the Salvadoran army. Her knowledge of the culture so far, and the responses of the women to her questions, told her that *chilate* was not a common term, or drink, in the community. Her observations of the responses of the women to their experiences of this generative word also told her that they were not as compelled and engaged with it as they were with other manifestations of themes from their lives. So she diverged from the suggested discussion questions (as presented in the teacher's manual) and began to facilitate a discussion about how they felt when there were on a *guinda*, "... refugees on the run and had to live without them (their traditional foods, drinks, etc.)."

LITERACY GENRES

Purposes and Functions of Print in the World of the Students

What to teach literacy for, that is, which functions and forms of print were authentic and relevant for the women, was another decision(s) aided by Robin's active stance as a student of the culture. Almost immediately, Robin ascertained through direct questions of the class and of individual women what purposes they had for learning to read and to write. As they related their feelings of "blindness" without literacy and their experiences of vulnerability to oppression and deception, Robin built her knowledge of her students' motivations and socio–political histories. As she noted what things they wanted to be able to read and write (street signs, prescription bottle instructions, personal letters, the Bible, etc.), she began to plan for lessons.

Robin was also observing and learning about the community-wide functions for print. As such, she noted that participation in the governance of the community required literacy skill with particular forms.

Print for Community Governance.   Literacy was required for members of the *Directiva* because most of the business attended to by the elected members was mediated by print. Letters were received and read from outside of the community and responses were written as a result of action taken. Agendas were written by many and brought to the meetings. Also, someone always took notes.

At the *asambleas*, written materials were also often referred to as part of the business and proceedings. As with the *Directiva*, someone took notes at the *asambleas*, recording the topics and the decisions arrived at by the assembled members of the community. Outside of meetings, community members presented *Directiva* members with written notations of concerns and issues they wished raised at community meetings.

Print for Personal Communication Within and Between Communities.
Although the community was without a postal service, a local system of written communication existed. This system employed the use of notes and human couriers.

It worked in this way: a person who wished to get a message to someone living in another community, or less often within the same community, would write the message on a piece of paper, fold it over several times to make a tight package (not unlike the folded and tucked-in notes often passed in school among students in the United States), and give it to someone who was traveling outside of the community in the near future. If the person was going to the destination community, he or she would personally deliver the note. If not, a succession of passings may take place, with, for example, someone boarding a regional bus and asking of all passengers if anyone is going to the destination community or knows of anyone going to the community. Robin found this system to be quite efficient and used it herself on many occasions.

Creating Curriculum From Community Knowledge

Robin worked many of these functions and genres of print into the lessons for the literacy class. She taught a lesson on letter writing, and each of the women wrote her own letter to a friend or relative which Robin mailed for them when she went into Suchitoto. She helped the women create a list of health concerns that had emerged from a class dialogue about health problems in the community. A written letter, listing the concerns that the women wanted raised at the next *Directiva* meeting, was produced in class and later presented to the President of the *Directiva*. Building on her new understanding of the note-passing procedure among communities, she created a lesson for inclusion in a literacy text that she was helping to create on *El Recado*, a small written note communicating information like "I can't come to the meeting today."

Robin also incorporated Biblical text and discussion into the class, and as the women began to assume leadership roles in the BCC meetings and Celebration of the Word services, she used the class as a way to study the reading and writing that they needed for these roles. Connecting with the yearly celebration honoring the life of Monsignor Oscar Romero, Robin incorporated into the literacy class the text of a poem written for the occasion by a member of the community.

CULTURAL WAYS OF SAYING–WRITING

A Moment of Teacher Learning From Students

A striking instance of cross cultural learning by Robin occurred in the midst of the lesson on personal letter writing. Within this episode was also a dramatic example of the culturally based genre knowledge that community members can have of a written genre, knowledge that precedes their ability to employ it by writing themselves.

Robin had ascertained that no one in the class except Chunga had ever written a letter. They all had, however, received letters or knew people who had received them. The students had always heard these letters read aloud, as it is a common custom for the literate members of a community to read and write letters for those who cannot do it themselves. After explaining that each woman would be writing a letter to a friend or family member with Sylvia's or her help, and displaying the nice stationary on which they would each write their final draft, Robin began to directly instruct the women on form. She first put the day's date on the board, explained its function, and how it is written.

I then wrote out *"Querido___* ("Dear___), after checking with Sylvia if that is, in fact, the customary way to start a personal letter, and explained that this is the customary way to address the person to whom the letter is being written.

I then began to give a general explanation of the body of the letter (thinking of the letters that I myself write), and Sylvia, as well as some of the students, asked me about the part for the *saludo*, the greeting. I quickly realized that it is a custom for Salvadorans to include some sort of opening sentence, as several students proceeded to say out loud almost the same exact sentence (*Te mando un salud cariñoso, y espero que te encuentres bien, a lado de tus hijos y tus amigos.* "I send you a very warm greeting, and I hope that you are well, at the side of your children and friends.")

At this point, I simply wrote out on the board the sentence they were giving me, word for word. I then had us read it out loud together, and then had them read it alone.

Before having them continue to write, I began to ask for ideas of the kind of things that one would include in the general body of a letter. There was no quick response, and shortly after, Esperanza said, "We don't really know because we've never written a letter before." So I began to directly teach them some of the things that one could include in a letter, trying to draw from things I knew about their lives. At this point, I asked each of them to give me suggestions of what they would like to write about, and after doing this in a random way, I went around and had each one say what she herself was actually thinking about writing (trying to help them prepare their thoughts in this way).

At this point, I asked that they copy what I had written on the board, as a way to start their letter. I also asked that after they finished copying this sentence, that they continue to write several sentences about the kind of general things we had mentioned. I then noticed that none of the students had done what I had instructed. Instead, on her own, each student attempted to write a sentence saying, "After this short greeting, I will go on to the rest" as a segue sentence after the initial greeting, before the body of the letter. Meanwhile Sylvia had begun to write this sentence on the board, at Francisca's request. Initially I did not recognize that Francisca had requested this help because she knew this sentence to be an essential part of a personal letter (in the Salvadoran culture). I told the students, therefore, that while a transitional sentence had value, it was not necessary. Sylvia, responding to my role as a teacher who is training her, immediately proceeded to erase this sentence from the board. But as I later read each student's writing, I noticed that all of the students had written in this transitional sentence, using the same exact words.

Teacher Reflection on What Has Been Learned

As Robin reflected on the events of the lesson, she noted:

> I found it quite interesting to note that here in this culture there are some commonly used ways to frame a personal letter. My lack of awareness of this, and the way I discovered it, reinforces the fact that (1) I am always learning and need to be ever-conscious of that fact, and (2) I always need to be especially aware of how Sylvia, because she is from the culture of the students, can provide me with some very valuable information concerning the best way to conduct the class. Within this, for example, I was obviously wrong to say that the transitional sentence didn't matter—and Sylvia was correct in her choice to put it up on the board (thereby recognizing its value and importance for the students).

CULTURAL WAYS OF LEARNING

Robin's respect for the culture of her students and the ways in which she, as one participant in a dialogical relationship, must learn from it and incorporate it into the class resulted in a modification of her approach to literacy learning, brought with her from her own culture in the United States.

Opposing Pedagogical Paradigms

As described in Appendix A, Robin had learned about teaching and learning within a theoretical paradigm that assumes that learners actively construct their own knowledge through activity and social interaction. Within this, she had been taught, and firmly believed, that one learns to read mainly by reading and to write by writing. This process approach, dominant within the North American context, ran counter to the pedagogy played out in many Central and South American schools where copying and writing to dictation predominate much of the literacy learning in classrooms.

The constructivist, process approach to learning to read and write incorporates such student-generated activities as invented spelling, which involves the students in encoding their thoughts as they work to figure out the graphophonic relationships of the words they wish to use. Accuracy is not the first and final goal within this paradigm. Rather, miscues and approximations are celebrated and used by the teacher as indicators of development and growth toward conventionality.

The very opposite assumptions about learning underlie the practice of copying and writing to dictation. By copying from preexisting text, students are expected to learn how to read and write words accurately. Beginning readers and writers are not assumed to be able to read and write. Thus, they must copy other people's writing. Repetitive copying and writing to dictation are assumed to result in learning to read and write through practice and mastery.

Initial Resistance.   Robin initially strongly disagreed with and avoided these practices, called *planas* (repetitive copying exercises) and *dictados* (dictations). They did not fit at all with her beliefs about literacy learning, and she believed that they were in fact partially responsible for the failure of so many adults to attain literacy.

Robin also felt strongly that they were not reflective of Freirean philosophies, even though many of the materials that were developed with Freirean-inspired generative themes and codes and presented in the popular education format instructed teachers to use dictation and *planas* in each lesson. Her primary concern here was that the strong cultural proclivity toward copying would result in teachers choosing to overemphasize the dictation and copying components of the lesson, and underemphasize the component of dialogue and subsequent reading and writing. In her observations of the literacy teachers that she was training, Robin's concerns proved valid: She consistently saw that the *alfabetizadoras* gravitated toward the dictation sections in the teacher manuals, supplementing these activities with several *planas*, that is, copying over single words multiple times. In doing this, their instruction showed limited emphasis on, or understanding of, the discussion of the generative theme and any subsequent reading and writing activities.

The lack of understanding of the relationship between Freirean thought and the use of copying also revealed itself in the literacy materials that existed in El Salvador. When Robin first began to work in El Salvador, she discovered that there were no literacy texts that included any component of student writing: The dictation component was what was considered writing. As a result, Robin made a concerted and persistent effort to talk with educators in the field regarding this aspect of literacy development. She worked as part of several teams of educators in the creation of new literacy materials.[2]

Pedagogical Response to Different Paradigm

Eventual Response.   The power that these familiar activities had for the women could not be denied. Even after they became convinced that the dialogues and subsequent writing of their thoughts were resulting in impressive literacy gains, the students continued to seek opportunities to engage in *planas*. By her third month of teaching, Robin recognized the significance of this need for the familiar and began to respond to it. A direct request from Tomasa sparked her first incorporation of this practice.

> Tomasa asked that I send her home with *un plan* which is a typical kind of exercise where one writes out a syllable or a word and has the student copy it over for the entire page. I do not see this as very valuable—the students do not need penmanship practice. So, I sent her home the homework of doing a half page of this *plan* and then assigned that she write out at least three words that contain each of these new syllables and I gave her examples.

In her reflection on the events, Robin explained:

> I assigned that Tomasa do some bit of a *plan* so that I would allow her some of what she is used to. Being here in this foreign environment has allowed me a sensitivity to the need to have some aspect of that which is familiar. And in general, I recognize that it would not be good educational theory to take away all that the students are used to.

Working in Students' Ways of Learning for Own Purposes   As time went on, Robin used *planas* (copying exercises) more and more to reinforce phonics lessons and for sight word practice. Having recognized the power that these activities held for Salvadoran literacy students, she began to assign her students *planas* as homework. She would ask that they copy over, multiple times, the syllables that they had been studying. She would also assign students, on an individual basis, the homework of copying over sight words that they had difficulty with in the writing that they had done on the day's generative theme. With each of these assignments, Robin added to the conventional procedure, however, by also asking that the students practice sounding out or reading all that they were copying. She believed that this would allow her to draw from the power of the familiar as well as draw from a valuable aspect of literacy acquisition, studying and memorizing particular syllables and sight words. She observed that the women enjoyed this kind of homework, and as a result, were committed to completing it. This experience reinforced for Robin the recognition that one of the most valuable aspects of literacy development is not necessarily the educator's belief in the value of a particular methodology or activity, but the degree to which students are engaged by it and will, therefore, spend "time on task."

Robin also began to recognize the value that dictation exercises could have within literacy development in El Salvador. She began to use dictated lists of words, both sight words generated by the students' writing and words containing new syllables that she was teaching, as a part of her class instruction. These dictated word lists, therefore, became a valuable assessment tool. Robin would dictate particular words at the end of a class and then evaluate the results as a way to see which words and syllables she needed to continue to teach, and which words and syllables the students had already mastered. It was immediately clear to her that this form of on-going evaluation was an essential component of her literacy instruction. None of the literacy materials available in El Salvador guided the *alfabetizadoras* to conduct such on-going assessment, and as a result, teachers often moved students through the books, chapter after chapter, without any cognizance of whether the students had actually learned the new syllables and could apply them in their attempts to read or write. In fact, none of the materials, nor any of the training for literacy teachers, addressed the need to incorporate on-going evaluation into instruction. Robin was particularly pleased, therefore, to discover a way to incorporate dictations, which the students enjoyed and frequently asked for, in a way which proved to be so vital.

Robin also discovered the value of using dictated word lists as part of the formal exams that she created for her class, as well as for all of the literacy classes involved in the program *El Movimiento de Mujeres de Cuscatlán*. Traditionally, the Ministry of Education created formal exams meant to measure if students had passed particular educational levels, such as First Level Literacy, Second Level Literacy, and so on.[3] Passing these exams, and receiving the corresponding certificate, was very important to the students. Working toward the goal of passing these exams, therefore, contributed toward motivating student attendance. The exams, however, often did not reflect the content of the classes in Papaturro or the others in the *El Movimiento de Mujeres de Cuscatlán*. This was largely due to the fact that these classes were based on the Freirean belief in using generative themes reflective of the students' realities, and they were not, therefore, based on the more generic curriculum created in isolation by the Ministry. Fortunately, Robin was able to convince the Ministry to allow her to create her own formal exams for the students of Papaturro and those of *El Movimiento de Mujeres*. In doing this, Robin wrote exams designed to measure all aspects of literacy skills. One of these components was a dictated list of words that reflected the particular syllables and sight words that students had been studying.

As these examples show, Robin learned from her students. She came to realize the value of using what they know, their cultural ways of knowing and learning, to forward their literacy development. At the same time, she maintained control over when, where, and for what purposes these culturally based practices were best incorporated.

TEACHER AND STUDENTS LEARNING FROM EACH OTHER: CO-CONSTRUCTION OF CURRICULUM

Freire and Macedo (1995) made the point that a dialogic relationship between teacher and student requires that both partners maintain their *subject* status in the relationship. Thus, the teacher is as active and directive as is the student, and each respects and learns from the other. A dialogic relationship does not lead to laissez-faire pedagogy. The teacher must teach with all that she knows and believes about learning and development. Freire explained:

> ... way to proceed is to assume the authority as a teacher whose direction of education includes helping learners get involved in planning education, helping them create the critical capacity to consider and participate in the direction and dreams of education, rather than merely following blindly. The role of an educator who is pedagogically and critically radical is to avoid being indifferent, a characteristic of the facilitator who promotes a laissez-faire education. The radical educator has to be an active presence in educational practice. But, educators should never allow their active and curious presence to transform the learners' presence into a shadow of the educator's presence. Nor can educators be a shadow of their learners. The educator who dares to teach has to stimulate learners to live critically conscious presence in the pedagogical and historical process. (p. 379)

Robin's assumption of the teacher's responsibility to decide how to use the *planas* and *dictados* illustrates the playing out of this delicately balanced relationship, with the responsibilities and roles of each—teacher and student. From the stance of an equal, Robin learned from her students about cultural ways of being and incorporated those into her instruction. But she did not do this blindly or without knowledge of how these modifications would transact within the totality of the literacy instruction. Rather, as an active teacher–subject she controlled the direction of her instruction, made judicious decisions at critical moments, and constantly reflected on the theory and praxis connections relevant to these decisions.

None of this would have been possible without the input from the people of Papaturro, in general, and the literacy students, in particular. If they had failed to assume their subject status in the dialogical, teacher-student relationship, if they had, instead, assumed a passive, object role as empty vessels waiting to be filled by the all-powerful teacher, then an entirely different experience would have resulted. Robin could not have learned from them the crucial cultural information that ultimately informed the instruction and gave life and possibility to the class. Thus, they could not have been active agents in their own transformations. And Freire's vision of a dialogical relationship would instead have been another instance of a banking concept of education.

But the women did assume their subject status, and Robin assumed hers, and they both engaged in dialogue such that they became teacher-students and student-teachers (Freire, 1993). As Robin always reminded the women, "No one knows nothing, and no one knows everything."

INSIGHTS FOR ADULT EDUCATION

Dialogue and dialogical relations between teachers and their students are at the heart of Freire's vision of empowering and liberating education. This chapter dealt with the ways in which Robin and her students worked toward this. It focused particularly on Robin as a teacher from outside of the culture who worked in very specific ways to learn about her students in the deep, sociocultural way advocated by Freire. We believe several issues raised in this chapter are relevant to adult education in other contexts.

Scarcity of True Dialogue in Programs

As the results of the typology report revealed (Purcell-Gates et al., 1998), very few adult education programs in the United States reflect the mutuality between teacher and student that Freire had in mind with this concept and for this epistemological practice (see chapter 4 for a description of the procedures and overall findings of this typology). Of the total responding programs ($N = 273$), only 3 (1%) were judged to be "highly dialogic" and only 26 (10%) were judged to be "somewhat dialogic."[4] The remaining 89% of adult literacy programs were judged to be more reflective of what Freire refers to as the "banking concept of education," dominated to varying degrees by the teacher as authority who makes the critical decisions about what the student need to know and how they need to learn it. While we have no data on this dimension for programs outside of the United States, we strongly suspect that the situation is highly similar. This scarcity of dialogical practice exists despite widespread recognition of the need for meaningful action to realize this goal.[5]

Teachers Becoming Learners

Unless an adult education program emerges from within the community of learners who desire and maintain control over it, it is the responsibility of the teacher, or program director, to create a dialogical space within which teacher and student can learn together. As part of this process, the teacher needs to become absolutely familiar with her students, their lives, their histories, their languages, and their present sociocultural contexts. This is very rarely done, at least to the degree dictated by Freire (1993). Almost all programs that described themselves in ways that Purcell-Gates et al. (1998) judged to be dialogic learned of their students' interests and goals through in-class discussions and surveys. None involved the type of anthropological study described by Freire and played out by Robin.

Recently, in response to the charge to make U.S. ABE programs more student-centered, and as part of NIFL's Equipped for the Future (EFF) initiative, NIFL conducted a survey of more than 1,500 ABE students of their goals and needs.

> Their goals fell into four basic categories: to have access to information and orient oneself in the world; to give voice to one's ideas and opinions and to have the confidence that one's voice will be heard and taken into account; to solve problems and make decisions on one's own, acting independently as a parent, citizen, and worker, for the good of one's family, community, and nation; to be able to keep on learning in order to keep up with a rapidly changing world (Draft Summit Document, December 1997, p. 11).

Plans and procedures are now being strategized to meet these goals, and teachers, researchers, and students are involved in designing curricula and assessment procedures in response to these survey results.

This seems like a step in the right direction toward creating programs that reflect the needs, goals, and interests of the students. However, we would hope that these very broad and general goals are not used in some sweeping curriculum reform and then imposed on all ABE classes. Freire's description of the personal and culturally relevant knowledge needed by adult educators precludes such an approach. Further, it is motivated by the essential call for education that is empowering and liberating through critical reading of one's historical location and sociopolitical reality, essences missing in NIFL's EFF.

We would rather envision local explorations of ways to come to know our students as mutual subjects, that is, ways to become functioning members of the communities in which our students live, love, struggle, and survive to the greatest degrees possible, given individual teachers' specific life circumstances. We need to find a way to truly and meaningfully connect with our students so that we see ourselves as living and working for the same goals as they within the same world(s) and against the same elements of domination and control.

Is it possible, or practical, for the deep study of students' lives and cultures, called for by Freire, to become an inherent aspect of adult education? Most people think not. The days when teachers dedicated their entire lives and ways of living to their profession and to their students are long gone, and teachers rarely assume they will move into, and become part of, the communities where they teach. This is even more true for teachers who work with adults who live lives of poverty and struggle in communities of strife and deprivation. This truth is as undeniable as is our knowledge that doing so could better result in powerfully vital, empowering, and effective adult literacy programs and classes.

If we cannot reasonably expect all adult literacy teachers to learn about the communities and lives of their students to the depth that Robin did and does, then how can we begin to approach the Freirean ideal? There are no easy answers to this, but we firmly believe that adult educators must keep this issue before them and seek to find meaningful ways to learn about their students, their lives, and their realities, to truly become learners as well as teachers so that true dialogue can occur within a dialogical frame in their classrooms.

Teachers, Not Laissez Faire Facilitators

Freire and Macedo's (1995) point about the need for teachers not to interpret Freire's call for dialogue as a call for teachers to relinquish their authority in the classroom also bears examination in light of adult education practice. Macedo concluded that many North American educators have made such a misinterpretation and he called on Freire to clarify his thoughts. This misinterpretation, according to Macedo, results in teachers who do not, and will not teach but rather rely on the students to raise topics, pursue answers in their own ways, and to teach themselves and each other. We believe that Freire's response to this helps to clarify for teachers of adults the sometimes confusing ways in which Freirean theory does and does not overlap with non-Freirean student-centered learning theory, so in vogue in educational circles today.

Freire (Freire & Macedo, 1995) began with a statement of the relationship between teaching and facilitating. "… I consider myself a teacher and always a teacher. I have never pretended to be a facilitator. What I want to make clear is in being a teacher, I always teach to facilitate. I cannot accept the notion of a facilitator who facilitates so as not to teach." (p. 377)

Freire pointed out that teachers who fail to enter into dialogical relationships with their students deny themselves subject status in educational practice, fail to inform their students of what they think is just, and, thus, end up helping the power structure. By doing so, these teachers fail in the creation of a liberatory education, the core of Freirean-based pedagogy. We interpret Freire's "teach to facilitate" view as a call to facilitate students' critical readings of their realities. This focus is not present in progressive, student-centered pedagogy and, thus, does not act to preclude the type of teacher facilitation described by Macedo.

Again, the point must be made that dialogical practice with a teacher who exercises all of his or her authority does not mean that the teacher imposes, or insists on, his or her beliefs, values, and readings of the world. Rather, teachers must participate in a mutuality of power sharing with their students, contributing, informing, suggesting, and facilitating, all toward the goal of opening up the world to the critical analysis of their students so that the educational program of which the teacher is a part is truly liberatory and emancipatory.

As with topics discussed before, there is no one method, or way, of bringing about such a balance of leading and following, sharing and contributing. In this chapter we looked more closely at the ways in which Robin worked toward this within the context she was working. Each educational and classroom context will bring different conditions, participants, purposes, constraints, issues and concerns. It is the challenge of the individual teacher to instantiate dialogical practice within his or her own setting to meet the overall goal of liberatory education for adults.

ENDNOTES

1. Robin refers here to the fact that the stories used simpler vocabulary, drawings, and large print.
2. Robin worked as part of several teams of educators in the creation of new literacy materials. By the time she left El Salvador 3 years later, there were three major sets of new literacy materials that included a writing section within the presentation of each generative theme. This writing section asks that students write out their thoughts on the generative theme, in both an open-ended manner and in response to some general questions. These materials also include sections where students are asked to write out their thoughts regarding particular, relevant aspects of their life experience. As she participated in the writing of new literacy materials, however, Robin did not encourage that the dictation section be removed completely for literacy texts. She recognized the power of the familiar for the students and worked to incorporate it into the texts.
3. The Ministry stated that each of these levels had a grade-level equivalency, such as first grade, second grade, and so on.
4. "Highly Dialogic" programs, according to Purcell-Gates et al. (1998), are those where students work with teachers to create the course, choose the materials, activities, etc. Students are also involved in all aspects of the program, may serve on the board, make decisions regarding meeting times, class rules, class structure, and location, etc. Students may also work to publish newsletters and in recruiting students. These programs may mention Freire as a model. Sample

quotes from responses: "Specific readings/topics are determined by individual classes and are primarily generated from parents' suggestions" (from a Family Literacy Program). "Students are the primary decision makers" (from an ABE program). (p. 8)

"Somewhat Dialogic" programs were those

where student input is critical. Students work with teachers to create curriculum, to plan study, etc. There is total collaboration in choosing course content and activities. Students are in charge of their own learning. These programs may mention Freire as a model. Sample quotes from responses: "We have no specific textbooks. We draw from many sources and follow the lead of the participants' needs in planning curriculum" (from and ABE program). "At the end of each session, students evaluate the instructor, the materials, and class activities" (from an ABE program). (p. 8)

Somewhat Dialogic differs from Highly Dialogic in a matter of degree of student agency and activity in the co-construction of the course. Highly Dialogic programs described classes where student involvement in all aspects of the course and program was essential and these program aspects always included assessment procedures of student and program as well as participation in conceptualizing the principles and goals of the program. Somewhat Dialogic programs were essentially constructed by the teachers and program directors who invited and often used suggestions from the students. These programs did not include students on their boards of directors nor in program planning meetings.

5. *The Draft Summit Document, Version 3(A),* a collaboration of the Division of Adult Education and Literacy, the NIFL, and the NCSALL, concluded that ABE educators want the ABE system to be "learner-centered," which they define as directed by the needs of the ABE learners.

8

¿Quién fui, Quién soy, Quién puedo ser? Who Was I, Who Am I, Who Can I Be?

Before, because of our poverty, because of the war, there were many moments when we felt very oppressed, even in our hearts. We did not have a voice, to denounce anything, to explain how we were thinking and feeling. We could not explain this, and in some ways, we did not even understand why we felt so broken apart inside, so oppressed. But now, now that we are in the literacy class, learning to read and write, learning to reflect on the meaning of written word, now we are gaining the abilities and the courage to express ourselves, to express all that has happened to us in our lives. Yes, now we are slowly losing our fear of speaking, of expressing ourselves. In the literacy class, we have discovered many things, things that before we never knew. We are learning to read and write, we are learning about the value that we have. Too, we are learning new skills, so now we can contribute to the work in the community. This is important. Before we couldn't do this. Now we feel more important in the community.

—Comments made by several students during a class dialogue

Freire always stressed that reading the word and reading the world cannot be separated.

Progress, when considered within Freirean-inspired literacy programs, has always been viewed primarily as progress toward liberation, toward critical apprehension of one's reality and the praxis that accompanies this. Progress in literacy, alone and in the technical sense, is assumed within this larger context. But for our readers who are looking at this Freirean-based class through a literacy development lens, the questions remain. Did Deonicia learn to read print? To write print? How much progress with the technical aspects of reading and writing did each woman make?

In this chapter we look at the literacy progress made by the women in the Papaturro literacy class, looking at both reading and writing the word and the world but highlighting the print-based progress. This study, with its ethnographic design, cannot result in claims that the instruction instantiated by Robin "works" better than other approaches to teaching and learning. But we can look closely at what occurred within this class and speculate on factors that may have led to these outcomes.

THE PAPATURRO WOMEN'S SUCCESS

The eight women who began the Papaturro women's literacy class as virtually nonliterate, feeling blind and vulnerable, emerged after 18 months as literate, active members of their community, capable of incisive sociopolitical analyses of their lives and capable of expressing those analyses both orally and in writing. In addition, they could now read and write for their own purposes to meet their own relational and communicative needs. Members of the group had assumed leadership roles in their community that required the ability to read, write, and comment–reflect on text.

Not every woman achieved and grew equally in her literate abilities, but each one progressed to a remarkable degree. Their expressions of pride in their accomplishments and of their growing self-confidence became apparent after only a few months. By the end of 18 months, they each knew that they could read and write and expressed the belief that they owed this to the work they did in the women's literacy class.

The significance of this accomplishment to the ways in which they represented their lives, their lived realities, and their histories cannot be overstated. As Celia told Robin one day:

> We give thanks to God because we are learning to read and write. If we could have learned to read in that time that the war got started, we could have written a book—a book to write down everything that happened, everything they did (to us), and everything we saw with our eyes. We could give testimony to everything. Now in class, we do the activities of writing our stories. Remembering what we suffered, sharing it with the rest, telling them what we suffered.

We will look at the literacy development of each of the eight women profiled in chapter 4 and who comprised the core of the Papaturro Literacy Class.

Deonicia

The elderly, frail woman who could not write her name when the literacy class began, slowly but steadily learned to express her thoughts about love and justice and to read simple texts. Watching Deonicia struggle with the print–speech match was instructive from an emergent literacy perspective. This woman, who was almost 70 years old, had more trouble than the other women with such early literacy concepts as remembering to put spaces between words when writing. She found simply holding a pencil and making the letters to be a challenge. However, despite her previous experiences with failure to learn, she quickly became excited and engaged with the process of spelling and reading words. After only a few weeks of attending the literacy class, she attempted to write a word, *nena* (an affectionate term for referring to a young girl), on the board on her own initiative. Following this, she sat down and attempted to write a full sentence for the first time in her life:

meutecome
me gusta comer
(I like to eat)

Regular Attendance Despite Physical Difficulties. Deonicia had a history of suffering physical ailments that had interfered with the few opportunities she had to attend school. However, in the course of the women's literacy class she suffered no such difficulties. She attended every class, often being the first to arrive.

Although hesitant at first to attempt to write out words, she bloomed under the praise and overt support provided by Robin and the rest of the class and was soon making small but significant efforts to master the code of the language and to learn the conventions around writing out her thoughts. By the middle of the third month of the class, Deonicia was using invented spelling, achieving accuracy with some words and representing most of the sounds correctly with the others. And, Robin noted, "She was doing this without saying 'I can't!'" During this time, Deonicia often relied on Robin and Sylvia to transcribe her thoughts, which they did while explicitly teaching her many of the important concepts about written language, writing, and reading.

Working Out Basic Concepts of Print. Robin worked especially hard with Deonicia to sort out the concepts of *syllable*, *word*, and *sentence*. Her confusions around these concepts became apparent as she wrote, when she would sometimes produce a sentence with absolutely no spaces between the letters and at other times write with spaces between each syllable. Using her written sentences as reference points, since she could read them back as if they were divided into words, Robin explained the differences among syllables, words, and sentences. Deonicia slowly learned to make spaces between whole words, but for a long time had to think particularly hard about this, usually going back to correct her work after writing her thoughts.

Learning to Reflect on Themes.   Deonicia also progressed quite far in her ability to reflect on the themes being discussed in the class and to connect her writing to those thoughts. For example, during the first month of the class, she managed to formulate her own words in writing, but they were not at all related to the class sentence, which she had copied into her notebook before writing her own. For example, when the class sentence was "If there is any problem in the community, sit down together in order to dialogue about things", Deonicia wrote:

> *nidodepagaros*
> nido de pajaros
> (Nest of birds)

Eighteen months later, however, she reflected in her writing her increased capacity for sociopolitical analysis of the class topics, as well as her developing understanding of the written concepts of words, capital letters, spacing, punctuation and so on. For example, prompted by the class sentence, "Studying, for women is very important because it helps to awaken us", she wrote:

> *par saLide Laynorasi parsegy adelate parno se negnda*
> para salir de la ignorancia para seguir adelante para no estar engañada
> (In order to escape [leave] ignorance, in order to keep moving forward,
> in order to not be deceived.)

Peer Support Compensates for Slow Development.   Deonicia developed her reading and writing abilities more slowly than most of the other members of the class, and Robin often paired her with Tomasa, her daughter-in-law, for reading activities. This was helpful to Deonicia whose relational nature responded to this type of paired learning support. Over time, she needed less and less help with reading.

Indicators of Progress.   Near the end of January, about 4 months after the start of the class, Deonicia did quite well on a formal exam of spelling, which Robin had created using syllables that she and Sylvia had previously taught to the women. Deonicia missed only a few of the 20 words, a marked improvement over the first exam where she could spell only a few words correctly.

By March, Deonicia was able to read independently many of the words in the sentences of her student workbook—words of between one and six syllables. Robin noted:

> This is a clear sign to me of very significant improvement of Deonicia's reading skills. She herself was very pleased today and indicated that she is aware that her ability to read as she did is a sign that she is truly beginning to "be able to read."

At the end of the data collection period, Deonicia was reading and writing simple texts written in the popular style. Further, she was able to critically reflect both orally and through writing on the issues that impacted her life and the life of the community. She particularly enjoyed her hard-earned ability to read and reflect on Biblical text, treasuring her own copy of the Bible which she, and others in the community, received through a U.S. church donation made several months following the end of the study.

Tomasa

Tomasa, who had spent her childhood helping her mother about the home rather than attending school, flourished in the literacy class. Because she had sporadically participated in a literacy class for about 1 year while she lived in the refugee camp, she was able to write her own name and a few small words when she began. From this foundation, she quickly acquired reading and writing skills that made her among the most successful members of the group, particularly as fluency was concerned.

A Self-Directed Learner.   Throughout the course of the study, Tomasa stood out as firmly self-directed and clearly focused and determined to use the opportunity of this literacy class to learn to read and write. From the start, she appeared to soak up the instruction offered her.

Although Robin's practice of asking the women to provide their own words during syllable instruction and to write their own thoughts with invented spelling on the theme under discussion was new and uncomfortable at first, Tomasa quickly engaged with it, visibly pulling together what she knew about letters, syllables–sounds, and words to encode her thoughts and to read her own and others' writings on critical themes.

Engaging in Own Purposes for Literacy. Seeking out additional work, she asked Robin to give her homework—*un plan*—to hasten her growth and, perhaps, solidify some of the syllable-level skills she was learning in class. She initiated reading and writing events outside of class. She began to try to read greeting cards and community notices. She began regularly writing to her son in the United States following the lesson on personal letter writing. These literacy activities provided a beneficial practice effect that, along with her focus and determination, propelled her ahead as a reader and writer.

Major Conceptual Progress. The conceptual enormity of this accomplishment is not be underappreciated, though, even with such a motivated and industrious learner as Tomasa. As with her mother-in-law, Deonicia, Tomasa had many concepts to learn beside sound–symbol ones. Robin's description of a class in February of the first year reveals one of the effects of life as a nonreader and in an environment devoid of printed materials. Robin had just told the class that they could read the last of three stories in the *Three Stories of Jesus* booklet.

> As I indicated to Tomasa where the final story was in the book, she asked me which way she should read it—should she read back toward the front of the book, or should she read toward the back. I told her that she should read toward the back.

Early Move to Fluency. By the beginning of April, Tomasa was able to write out six full sentences, expressing her thoughts on the theme, during the time that it took everyone else, except Chunga, to write one sentence. Further, she was writing with very few spelling errors, and all of them except one involved the common error of confusing two letters that both have the same sound:

Theme: Heroes

(Class sentence) *Quedaron algunas personas del proceso revolucionario que todavía están trabajando para que se cumplan los acuerdos de paz.*

(Tomasa continued) ... *porque el gobierno se comprometio a cunpir los acuerdos de paz. Pero a esta fecha no se a visto nada. Por eso debemos luchar muy fuerte para que el gobierno cumpla y no se haga el olbidado. Porque al pueblo no se le ba a olvidar a Calderon. Se lea figura que el pueblo no se ba a quedar callado. Seguimos adelante con mas fuerza.*

Spelling errors: *cunpir* for *cumplir; a* for *ha; olbidado* for *olvidado; ba* for *va*

(Class sentence) There are some people from the revolutionary process who are still working so that the peace accords will be fulfilled.... because the government has committed to fulfill the peace accords. But up to today, we have not seen anything. For this reason, we must struggle very hard so that the government fulfills its word and not let it be forgotten. Because the people are not going to forget Calderon. One can see that the people are not going to forget. We move forward with more strength.

The season of Lent in late March of that first year of the class found Tomasa reading the Stations of the Cross aloud for the class as others listened, an authentic and familiar literacy event for the women of Papaturro. Tomasa joined other women from the class a year later in reading the Stations of the Cross for the community-wide celebrations and participating in the spoken reflections.

Moving Literacy Into Her Life.   Tomasa eventually was able to write with great fluency and expressiveness. She would regularly write one or two paragraphs expressing her thoughts on the day's generative theme. Her writing was always particularly insightful, reflecting both her critical thinking skills and the fact that she was not inhibited in her ability to write out almost every word that she desired to use. By the time Robin left El Salvador, Tomasa had become a regular correspondent with her son in the United States, writing to him and reading his replies. She also had begun reading to her children from the children's books Robin loaned out. In general, Tomasa was incorporating literacy into most aspects of her daily life.

Francisca

Francisca, who needed to hold her paper right in front of her nose to read, and whose extreme poverty and poor health prevented her from ever feeling fully vital, wrote three sentences of her own as part of her personal letter during the letter-writing lesson in January. Although she often failed to put any spaces between her words, she had only a few misspellings, attributable to dialect–sound confusions: *com* for *con*; and *Ruvina* for *Rubina* (this last was a common error for all of the students).

Slow But Steady Growth.   Despite her vision and health problems, Francisca faithfully attended the literacy class and contributed to the discussions around the generative themes. She always went on to write out her own thoughts relevant to the theme. She needed extra help with putting spaces between her words and usually worked slowly and carefully. By February, she was able to write the following sentence after a discussion of responses to poverty, following the reading of one of the stories in the *Three Stories of Jesus* book:

Zacceo se a repintio de las maldades que hizo con los pobres.
(Zaccheus repented the wrongdoing that he did to the poor.)

Her reading about this time was halting, but she was able to read with minimal support in the form of some assisted, or echo, reading. This support was noted only when she was reading text other than her own, such as a poem Robin provided or a letter written to her by Patty from the United States.

In just over a month, her sentences became longer and more complex. The following was written following a discussion of *El Bosque* (the forest).

No hay que quemar los bosques porque el aguase ba (va) apocando y es mejor que sembrmos (sembremos) mas arboles para que nosebolla (no se vaya) asecar hay que sembrar arboles.

(One should not burn the forests because there is less and less water, and it is better that we plant more trees so that things don't dry up. One should plant trees.)[1]

Real Commitment to Class.   Francisca appeared to feel that she was improving and learning to read and write. Her faithful attendance was highlighted in early April when she appeared at class following a traumatic incident during which she was knocked down and trammeled by a bull. Robin expressed surprise that she even came to class, given her overall weariness and weakness. She reflected:

I was amazed that Francisca even came to the class after what had happened to her. Given that the majority of the women in the class have become extremely faithful, I am inclined to believe that she came because of the commitment that she feels to the class. I believe that this is due in part to her sense that she is learning and improving, as well as the fact that she feels a sense of "community," a bondedness, with all of us who make up the class.

Feelings of Gratitude.   Francisca was grateful to be learning to write. "Now that I am learning to write, I can send a message to a family member or a friend, without bothering anyone (to ask them to read it for me). And now, I can write out my own thoughts. I can write a letter, or I can just write out what I am thinking. It is not the same when you cannot read or write for yourself."

Chunga

Although Chunga (Ana María Jesus) had to drop out of school after only a few weeks when she was a child, she quickly became one of the more able students in the literacy class. She had absorbed some literacy skills during her sporadic attendance at classes in the refugee camps, and by

December she was reading so well that Robin often paired Margarita with her for reading activities. At age 66, Chunga provided a dignified presence in the class, always attending to and participating in the dialogues with a quiet elegance and insight borne of many years living and surviving under trying and harsh conditions.

Growth in Skill and Fluency.   Chunga's writing in January, while growing in fluency, still reflected her acquisition of basic literacy concepts. During the letter-writing lesson, she wrote approximately one page to her son, single spaced, but failed to leave the conventional degree of spacing between her words. An analysis of her spelling errors in this draft revealed that she was encoding multisyllable words, representing all sounds with phonetically appropriate letters:

Chunga's Spelling	Conventional Spelling
debertidas	*divertidas*
clace	*clase*
grasas	*gracias*
atension	*atención*
Ruvina	*Robina*

A sample of her writing in February (without the focus—documentation of her spelling) reveals that she is now capable of writing complex sentences to fully express her reflections of the theme—Christian-inspired responses to poverty. After copying the class-dictated sentence into her notebook, Chunga wrote:

> *Pero Jesus querria que fueramos eriquezezadas en el amor (que) penetrara en el corazon de nosotras que sintieramos todo el dolor de todos.*
>
> (But Jesus would like that we would be enriched in love, that it would penetrate our hearts, that we would feel all the pain of everyone.)

Other writing episodes during this time period reflected growing fluency as reflected by the amount she was able to write in response to the generative theme. She and Tomasa regularly wrote at least twice as much on their own as did the others in the class, with the exception of Celia who occasionally wrote close to, but not quite, the same amount.

Using Print for Own Purposes.   Chunga's reading abilities were keeping pace with her writing and she was increasingly using print for purposes other than class-assigned activities. Robin noted an example of this in a report on the literacy class in mid-February:

Today during class, Chunga was reading a letter that had been written to her by one of her children. I did not have time to have her read it to me (she was "sneak"-reading it as we were doing other things!).

(Reflecting) I can at least say that this is an important example of improvement, as it is an example of her using print outside of class-assigned activities. She, as the others, have always had some relative (who can read) read them their mail. There may be many reasons why she brought it to class, but since I did not speak to her about it, I will not try and speculate.

A Fluent and Critical Reader/Writer. By March, Chunga's literacy skills reflected a marked increase in the ease with which she used them and the accompanying fluency and effectiveness with which she employed them as tools for critical thought and expression. With almost no spelling errors, Chunga wrote the following expressions on generative themes under discussion:

Theme: Organization

(Class sentence) Organization and the *asambleas* help the people to organize themselves so that they create the collective work. (Chunga's addition) The government wants to win the place (the favor). They need all of the poor, therefore they offered many things. When they felt with all of the power, they tried to deceive. For he that did not vote for the government, they fined him so that they could squeeze out a little sweat.

Theme: A second discussion of "Organization"

(Class sentence) We, as mothers, we recount to our children the way that life used to be. (Chunga's addition) We, in the past, we couldn't denounce anything because we did not have a voice. Everything was kept quiet. In the time of today, it is better because everything that we do not like is denounced so that we can resolve the problems.

Her writing and reading abilities continued to develop, and she remained one of the more fluent and expressive members of the class as they engaged in critical reflections and dialogue both oral and written.

Many Personal Motivations for Literacy. In addition to her abilities to use print for sociopolitical analysis, Chunga's other motivations for literacy became apparent as she increasingly engaged in the exchange of letters with her son who lives in the United States. She also became quite involved in pleasure reading, and can often be found reading her Bible and other books in the evening, by candlelight, when she has finally completed all of her daily tasks.

Celia

Celia's fervently held desire to learn to read as a child was finally fulfilled as a result of her participation in the literacy class. From the beginning Celia stood out as capable of complex and incisive sociopolitical analysis of the lives and histories of the *campesinos*, raising poverty, class, and gender issues during the class dialogues and in her writing. She combined this skill with her developing literacy abilities to move ahead quickly as a reader and a writer.

Acquisition of the Code.   Celia's literacy development proceeded normally, as one would expect of a beginning student. She worked hard to master the sound–symbol correspondences and to apply that knowledge to the work of sounding out words in print and to encoding her own words. Analysis of her spelling revealed her growing ability to match print with sound, with her spelling errors reflecting those difficult sound–letter matches involving different letters for the same sound or dialect differences between the *campesino* dialect and the standard printed form.

Internal Drive for Literacy.   Celia's internal drive to become literate for her own purposes was apparent in several ways. In class, while she was more often than not the leader in the oral dialogues, she would often pull herself away from the group to focus exclusively on the text she was attempting to read or write. At times, she would stay after all the other women had left for the day in order to finish a reading she had begun or a written analysis of the day's theme.

The following report from Robin in mid-January of the first year contained a typical description of this behavior (during this particular class the students had created a dialogue which ultimately focused on women's rights. After spending time individually writing about this theme, Robin had then instructed the students to read silently from one of their books):

> All the students stayed on past 4 p.m. as they were very engaged in their reading. When someone told them that it was almost 4:15, they started to get up and leave. Celia stayed behind and simply kept reading without stopping. I sat with her and, although she had always been reading aloud, she began to read more loudly and indicated that she was reading to me. After she finished the (Biblical) story, she put the booklet away. At this point, she began to discuss the theme of women's rights that she had been writing about.

High Level of Engagement.   This high level of engagement typified Celia's literacy learning. She would focus all of her energy on writing out her thoughts on issues about which she held complex and well-thought-out insights, incorporating reading and writing into the literacy events that mediated her sociopolitical analyses. In mid-February, Robin described Celia as engrossed in her writing and reading of text. The dialogue that followed a poem about the Salvadoran people particularly illustrates this point. The poem is contained in the literacy text used in the class. It is a strong poem, expressing that the Salvadoran people are "men and women of courage." It proceeds further, gaining momentum, speaking of the way that the Salvadoran people have struggled to attain justice, as well as "freedom with love" (as cited in Recinos, 1993). In this context, it ends with a strong statement of national pride.

Following the reading of the poem, Celia had started the discussion with, "In the time of the war, it wasn't just men who were working and struggling, it was the women as well. Everyone struggled together, struggling for justice. And no one was working for a salary. They were offering their lives up so that there would be justice, so that there would be less poverty, so that we would be able to study and learn, so that we would have opportunities to study."

Pointing to the aluminum storage bins for corn that the men in the community were working on in front of the open-air classroom, she said, "Yes, we struggled so that we would have things like those (the storage bins); we never had things like this before. We struggled together, both men and women so that we would have so much more than we had, so that there would be less poverty, so that there would be justice."

Following a class discussion of this poem, all of the students began writing out their thoughts on the central themes that arose. While most of the students remained in their seats, and occasionally spoke with each other about what they were writing, Celia chose to leave her seat and sit apart from the rest of the class in order to do her writing.

As was characteristic, she immediately became absorbed in her writing and, unlike the others, did not say a word to anyone while she was working. As she wrote, Celia referred back to the poem, rereading it at least three more times and reflecting to herself on its meaning and on her response. She continued to write until Robin asked her to stop.

Motivation Leads to Practice Outside of Class.   Outside of class, Celia's personal motivation for literacy was also apparent. Over time, she became a voracious reader. It was common for Robin to arrive to Celia's house and find her deeply engrossed in reading whatever was available for her to read, anything from a newspaper brought home by a neighbor who had been to Suchitoto, to the Bible or even a children's storybook borrowed from Robin's home.

Similarly, whenever Celia would visit Robin, she would quickly become distracted by anything that was written in Spanish. She would bring the book or pamphlet close to her face (due to her need for corrective lenses) and become engrossed in an effort to read what was written. At these times, Robin would abandon the previous subject of discussion and watch, encourage, and aid Celia as she read. Both women drew tremendous energy and happiness from Celia's progress. New worlds were opening up for Celia, and this increased her capacity to reflect on her past as well as her future.

Literacy Leads to More Community Involvement. Explaining to a visitor to the community one day how literacy development has helped her and the other students, Celia reflected on their increased ability to take on responsibilities in the community. "Studying is important for many things," she explained. "It helps us to be able to commit ourselves to whatever work is needed (in the community). All of us who are studying, learning to read and write and participate in discussion, can now accept any responsibility in the community. With this, we are important in the community, and we are collaborating as well." She added, "This is especially important for us women. Before we were more submissive, quieter. Before, women were expected to marry, care for the family and the house, and never do something like study. But now we are learning (in the class) to express our thoughts, to discover our opinions, through our dialogues. Now we feel more freedom to express ourselves."

Margarita

Margarita, although an equally dedicated student, was not able to achieve the same level of progress and success as Celia, Chunga, or most of the other students. It is unclear why she struggled as she did, but many aspects of her current situation, as well as her childhood, suggest what some of these factors affecting her literacy development may have been. Certainly poverty and the attendant malnutrition, fatigue, and sense of hopelessness had an effect. In addition, Margarita struggled during the time of our study with her caretaking responsibilities for her young children, as a single parent, and for her ailing mother. These sometimes resulted in extended absences from the literacy class, although, overall, Margarita was faithful in her attendance.

Possible Dyslexia. Another possibility that becomes apparent from studying her history of schooling and the nature of her struggles in the literacy class is that of dyslexia. The primitive conditions of the class make a diagnosis of learning disability, with its mainstream, developed-country context, impossible to make. However, Margarita's reported difficulty with learning in the refugee camp classes, in contrast to her siblings' relative success, and her memory of headaches and "severe eye strain" sound similar to phenomenological accounts from dyslexics in developed countries. Add to this the nature of her difficulties: problems remembering the shapes of letters, mastering a print or phonic concept one day only to forget it the next, obvious extreme difficulty hearing the separate sounds in words. It is possible that a neurologically based dyslexia, compounded by other environmental conditions, made learning to read and write unusually difficult for Margarita.

Extraordinary Effort and Peer Support Lead to Slow Development.
Within this, Margarita's unflagging effort and perseverance can be seen as key to her developing literacy abilities. When she attended class, she worked especially hard to unlock the words and to encode her thoughts, often taking up to 30 min to write a simple sentence. By the end of the study, Margarita, during the moments she seemed to have energy and capacity to focus, was able to write out one or two sentences of her thoughts on the day's theme.

As with Deonicia, Robin supported Margarita's learning by often pairing her with another class member for reading activities. During writing time, Robin, Sylvia, or both would sit with her and help her orally stretch out the words to hear the sounds in sequence and then to write those letters that encoded those sounds. With this support, Margarita was usually able to identify the letters needed to encode her thoughts, and her ability to work more independently grew throughout the course of the study.

Inconsistent Progress.   The sporadic nature of her development, though, is apparent when looking across selected reports of her achievement in the class:

12/15/94: Margarita attempts to write and read class sentence.

12/16/94: All women (including Margarita) read syllables with perfect accuracy independently.

Even Margarita successfully writes 3 new words with syllables.

12/19/94: Everyone (including Margarita) is able to write at least one sentence of their own thought and all relative to the theme.

1/16/95: Margarita is unable to write out thoughts but can read dictation of her thoughts. She then was able to write out a new sentence. She then was able to see where she made mistakes and to correct.

Everyone read their own lists of words (even Margarita) with 100% accuracy.

1/25/95: Margarita tried to write but could only write out a long series of letters in a row, with only a few of these letters representing the letters of the words she wanted to write.

Margarita could read back all of the words Robin wrote out for her and did not seem discouraged.

2/2/95: Margarita is able to read words of between one and three syllables, especially those they have studied.

2/15/95: Margarita, in spite of having missed class for 2 weeks, got 14 out of 20 words right on the exam.

2/22/95: All women, including Margarita, are able to read independently what Robin asked them to.

Margarita is able to echo read with Robin, often getting ahead of her.

2/24/95: Margarita finds word *excelente* in new student workbook and shows Robin in class, telling Robin that she had found it the day before when reading the text. Robin sees this as an indication of reading outside of class and a sign of her growing ability and desire to read. Robin believes she is losing her self-concept as a nonreader.

3/16/95: Margarita is showing some improvement in accuracy when writing.

4/5/95: Margarita is able to correctly write many words, forming a complete sentence. With help she could represent all sounds.

By the end of the study, Margarita was able to write several sentences on her own with some help. And, in turn, she was able to read back those sentences with just a small bit of support. So, while her progress was very slow, particularly in comparison to the others, she had clearly attained some of the foundational skills necessary for literacy development.

Progress in Critical Analysis. Moreover, Margarita had shown tremendous progress in her capacity to think critically and articulate her thoughts. Initially, she spoke out very rarely in the class. After 6 months, however, Margarita had become one of the most active participants in the class discussions. She also volunteered to participate in the community's pastoral team, helping to plan and guide the community's religious celebrations. Not only did Margarita participate actively in the planning meetings for these services, but she also began to speak out during the time of reflection and dialogue within these services, something unusual not just for Margarita, but for any woman in the community.

Satisfaction With Growth. Just before Robin left, Margarita told her, "I am happy now, very happy to be in the class and be able to learn a little. Studying is very important," she added. "This way, no one can deceive you. And another thing, if one desires to write a letter, she can. Or many other things, like read the Bible or the label on some medicine. When we can't read, it is as if we are blind, because we can see, but not understand—we do not know what it is that we are really seeing." Pausing, and then becoming a bit more animated, Margarita added, "And in the class, we have dialogue, and we are learning to express ourselves. We are learning to speak out, to know better what we think, know better how to understand things. Yes," she said with a smile, "studying is very important."

Carmelita

Lack of Critical Experience and Personality Related to Slower Growth. Carmelita also had more difficulty than many of the other women learning to read and write. As with Margarita, her attendance was not as regular as the others due to her own frequent illnesses as well as those of her many young children. Carmelita was also particularly shy and reticent in all class discussions, as well as in other community-wide gatherings.

While characteristic of most Salvadoran women, this reticence also seemed reflective of another aspect of Carmelita's formation, however. Because she was younger than most of the other students, Carmelita had not been exposed to the same degree of dialogue and reflection as the others in the class. Most of the other students were young adults in the time that the BCC movement began, a time when the *campesino* people were beginning to discuss the roots of their poverty and reflect on ways that they could work to overcome obstacles. Carmelita, not having had this experience, did not have the same insights and skills that would have helped her participate in discussions of sociopolitical topics in class. With much encouragement and prodding, however, Carmelita would contribute to a class discussion, but often with insights that were less complex and thought out than the others.

Within this, Carmelita also seemed to present the self-perception that she could not learn. She often spoke of, and tried to write about, the belief that it would be through prayer that she could possibly gain the skills necessary to learn to read and write. In this way, she conveyed her deep desire to learn, while simultaneously conveying that she did not seem to believe that she could actually attain it through her own efforts.

Hidden Development. Ultimately, however, Robin discovered that Carmelita's perceived inability to learn hid the degree to which she was developing not only her reading and writing skills, but accompanying analytical skills as well. During the third month of the class, Robin described Carmelita's emerging ability and self-concept as a learner:

I then passed on to Carmelita, and she had already begun to write out her own thoughts. She used invented spelling, sometimes using just one or two letters to write a four- or five-letter word. Most often she used a letter that is actually part of the word. Once, however, she read the word *traer* (to bring) where she had written some form of invented spelling for *comprar* (to buy). Both of these words make sense in the sentence, but when she was reading it, and I suggested the word *comprar*, she read it again, and again said the word *traer*.

After she read, Margarita (sitting next to her) asked her if she wrote that "alone," and Carmelita said, with a large smile on her face, "Yes, I did. It used to be that I couldn't even put four or five letters together, and now I am really writing, writing whole sentences."

Personal Attention Key to Development.   As with Margarita, Robin found that with sitting down next to Carmelita and helping her sound out each word slowly, Carmelita was soon capable of encoding her words with few mistakes. It was important, Robin felt, to help her write by herself rather than acquiesce to her seeming inability and scribe for her, as Sylvia was sometimes wont to do. Carmelita's willingness to try when prodded and ability to succeed, even though with "safe" words that she knew how to spell, confirmed this for Robin.

Her struggle with writing continued, however, for some time. In mid-February, Robin recorded the following event that captures Carmelita's difficulties as well as her easygoing personality:

Carmelita also had become absorbed in the student workbook, discovering pages that had simple words written in large, bold letters. Sylvia sat with her and helped her to read them. When I eventually sat with her, however, she had written one extra sentence beyond the copied sentence. I asked her to read it, and she was able to sound out the syllables she'd written, but the first two did not sound like any word that either of us could recognize. I drew our attention to the next words, though, and we were able to figure out what she had wanted to write—the invented spelling she used was close. But still, the words together did not really make up a complete sentence, although the words used reflected ideas relative to the theme. She laughed at the fact that we could not figure out what all the words were, nor the whole sentence, but did not express self-criticism or any discouragement. She had a smile on her face. I offered her words of praise and encouragement in every explicit way I could think of.

By April, Carmelita evidenced the ability to write two long sentences during the writing portion of the class with only one or two letters missing in each. Every word at this point contained many of the sounds needed.

Personal Uses of Literacy Become Evident.   Around this time, it also became apparent that Carmelita was engaging in reading for her own purposes outside of class, thus consolidating and building her skills. Francisco, her husband, told Robin that they had begun reading the Bible together every night. Carmelita further told Robin that she tried to read everyday at home from the "Jesus" book or from her student workbook, with her daughter's help. By the end of the study, Carmelita was engaging in a great deal of reading and writing at home. In addition to the above, print mediated her role as a mother of young children in many ways: she wrote in a journal and read children's books, medicine labels, notes from the health clinic; her children's homework, and other school-related print.

Esperanza

Esperanza had claimed, based on her experiences with three years of schooling as a child and many more in the refugee camps, that she was not "able to learn." However, she proved to be one of the more advanced students in the class. Drawing from some basic literacy skills acquired from her previous schooling experiences as well as adult-life experiences, Esperanza steadily improved in spite of her sporadic class attendance.

Keen Awareness of Functional Purposes for Print. With her involvement with the *tienda*, and her exposure to her husband's *directiva* responsibilities, Esperanza appeared to be particularly aware of the daily uses for basic literacy and math skills. Thus, she could more easily see the ways print could mediate her life, and she probably had more naturally occurring practice opportunities with authentic literacy events than the other women.

Difficulty With Critical Literacy. At the same time, though, Esperanza had difficulty determining what to write when asked to "write out her thoughts" on the generative theme of the day. Both Sylvia and Robin needed to spend significant time encouraging her, as well as reminding her of various aspects of her life that would be relevant to the topic. Once encouraged, and prodded, however, Esperanza was able to formulate at least one or two sentences, with few spelling errors. Robin saw it as a sign of progress that over time she could more easily write her thoughts—still with some prodding—but with much more skill and content than when she first began.

Esperanza, along with Carmelita, seemed relatively less engaged with the critical analysis aspects of the literacy class. Esperanza projected a much more utilitarian approach to life and literacy. She was very involved in day-to-day responsibilities within the community, and these seemed to be the focus of her interests. For example, at times special meetings would be called for the *artesania* workers, or for public health training, during the hours of the literacy class. Although Robin received permission for the members of the class to arrive late at these meetings, Esperanza always chose to attend the meetings, rather than remain in class with the other literacy class students.

Literacy Practices Move Into Her Life. By the end of the study, Esperanza had begun to employ literacy skills in many aspects of her daily life. She wrote letters to friends in the United States and independently read letters written to her; she began to read for pleasure at home; and she reported that she felt that her improved reading (and math) skills made a real difference in how she was able to manage the *tienda*.

She was very happy to be studying and learning, she told Robin. "It is important to learn to read and write," Esperanza related to Robin one day. "I am very happy in our class. Before, it was different. The teacher would put letters up on the board but not explain them.[2] Today, the teachers explain to us what the letters are and how they sound. And so now, I am learning to read and write ... just a little ... but I am learning."

The following two examples of her class writing in January and March of 1996 illustrate her literacy development over 15 months:

Topic: *Derechos* (Rights); Class Sentence: We have a right to land and a good house of adobe and tiles.

y tener una buena alimentación

(and to have good nutrition)

Queremos organisarnos mas para reclamar nuestros derechos que estudiemos mas para no cer engañado para salir de la ygnorancia

(We want to organize ourselves in order to reclaim our rights. We must study more so that we will not be deceived, and we can leave (escape from) ignorance)

Spelling errors: organi sarnos/organi zarnos; cer/ser; ygnorancia/ignorancia

Topic: Reflection on one of the Stations of the Cross; Class Sentence: We have carried this heavy cross when we left for Honduras.

Cuando nos fuimos para Hondura caminamos toda la noche co los niños en los brasos y otros en la nuca asta que yegamos al valle de los ernandes no yebabamos comida no yebabamos medicina

When we went to Honduras we walked all night with the children in our arms and others on our backs until we arrived in the Hernandez Valley. We had no food or medicine.

Spelling errors: Hondura/Honduras; co/con; asta/hasta; yegamos/llegamos; ernandes; Hernández

Note that her spelling errors reflect both the *campo* dialect as well as the effects of problematic sound–symbol relationships (e.g., different letters with the same sound, silent letters).

LITERACY PROGRESS INDICATORS

Many different lens and perspective points were used to draw the conclusion that the Papaturro women, as a whole and individually, made significant progress in their literacy development. We charted the *attendance and tardiness patterns* of the women and found that they regularly came to the class, relatively on time,[3] and maintained this behavior over time. Robin's sense was that they became even more committed to the class as time went on and as they experienced success and progress for themselves.

We also examined indicators of the women's *attitudes toward themselves as possible literacy learners*. Each woman changed her self-concept about herself as a learner over the course of the study. The move was from one of an assumption of hopelessness and self-denigration to one of excited realization that they were learning and, thus, it was possible that they could eventually read and write and realize their literacy-related goals.

Examination of the women's reading and writing over time revealed further important indicators of success. Each woman increased her *attempts to read and write* when asked to in class. The claims of "I can't" soon disappeared.

Reading and writing samples showed *increased accuracy* for all. This was also documented by the periodic exams Robin administered. These exams consisted of oral reading of single words, oral reading of short passages, answering questions in writing related to the passages, writing answers to simple personal questions, and writing words and sentences to dictation.

Related to this was the growing fluency, particularly marked for Chunga and Tomasa, but notable for most of the women. They wrote more and read more, with greater accuracy, automaticity, and ease as the class proceeded.

Documentation of class proceedings and Robin's on-going reflections on the activities of the women also revealed that they were each becoming much more independent in their reading and writing. As they gained in sound–symbol knowledge and acquired increased automaticity in their word recognition and spelling, they needed less help from Robin and Sylvia. With a few exceptions, most of the women eventually became capable of reading and writing on their own, capable of utilizing their own self-monitoring and self-correction strategies to make meaning from and with print.

The women, themselves, reported their *impressions that they were learning* and progressing. Often contrasting their experience in the Papaturro class with past attempts to learn to read and write, they would attribute this to both Robin's teaching and to their work together as a community of women learners. They each expressed repeatedly their excitement and joy with their growing literacy abilities.

Finally, the progress of the Papaturro women was indicated by the ways in which they began to *incorporate reading and writing into their lives* outside of the class. They each began to use print for communication, for community work, for daily tasks, for religious reflection, and for pleasure. To the degree that print mediated the lives of the people in the community, the women in the literacy class incorporated it into their own lives. They essentially joined the literate community of Papaturro as functioning participants.

PROGRESS TOWARD CRITICAL CONSCIOUSNESS AND VOICE

Previous Experience With Critique

Concomitantly, Robin noted progress over time in the women's abilities to critically analyze their realities and reflect on actions that they could take to transform these realities. In contrast to their literacy abilities, most of the women had some familiarity with the process of critical reflection resulting from their experiences with the BCCs before the war and the influence of Freire on the literacy classes that were offered in the refugee camps. Thus, this group of women did not totally reflect the fatalism ("What can I do? I'm only a peasant." [Freire, 1993, p. 43]) or alienation which Freire reported as typical of oppressed people before liberation.[4]

As survivors of a war intended to liberate them from centuries of hopelessness, they understood that their poverty and lack of life-sustaining essentials such as health care, food, and schooling were the products of a social, economic, and political system that relied upon them to be 'oppressed' so that others could dominate. Thus, they perceived aspects of their lives as that which were created by other people, and not as that which was the "Will of God." Their day-to-day struggles for survival, however, greatly influenced their capacity to believe that they would actually live to see any real change—either the fulfillment of those that were promised in the Peace Accords, or any others that they believed were necessary for an improved existence.[5]

Gender and Voice in Salvadoran Context

Within this, Salvadoran women exist within some particularly defined cultural attitudes toward females and their roles. These cultural ways appeared to be reflected in the very soft, both literally and metaphorically, voices that were first heard in the literacy class.

Generally and historically speaking, Salvadoran women are expected to be responsible for all domestic duties. This includes preparing all meals for the men and children in the family, washing all clothing, and cleaning the home and surrounding area at regular intervals. As mentioned in chapter 3, each of these tasks is labor intensive. For example, preparing meals involves such activities as collecting firewood, building a fire, and all aspects of preparing the corn for the tortillas such as boiling the corn, grinding it, and forming the tortillas. Washing clothing involves carrying heavy loads of clothing on one's head to the local stream and scrubbing each article against the rocks.

Within this setting, educating the Salvadoran females was not considered a priority; therefore, if educational opportunities were limited, the male members of the family were given the opportunity. Before the war, in particular, women were also often not considered skilled enough to hold particular political–social responsibilities within the community. Another aspect of attitudes toward Salvadoran women is the belief that women should simply stay at home and should not leave home to participate in any type of outside activity.

Modification of Gender Attitudes Since War.   All of these attitudes are generalizations, of course, and influenced the women in the literacy class to varying degrees. Further, it is important to note that these attitudes have been changing since the time of the war due to the increased reflection on many aspects of the sociocultural reality in El Salvador, including that of women. Robin observed that many literacy materials specifically focus on themes that affect attitudes toward women, potentially involving both men and women in the process of deconstructing attitudes. Regardless, it is important to acknowledge that all of the Papaturro literacy students were influenced, to some degree, by both historical and current attitudes toward females.

Salvadoran *campesinas* can be, therefore, traditionally deferent, soft spoken, and deprecatory about their abilities and strengths. Their voice is often not heard on the cultural and community level, and, on the individual level, it is often quite literally soft and quiet. In fact, one of the major drawbacks of the open-air classroom was the difficulty of hearing the women when they spoke or read orally. Their soft, hesitant voices were hard enough to hear within a small classroom; outdoors, these voices literally disappeared on the breeze.

Voice Develops Over Time.   Over time, as the women engaged in dialogue and wrote out their own thoughts about the generative themes which guided each class, they grew in their abilities to think critically and to shape those thoughts into language that they could express in oral and written form. While women like Celia and Tomasa quickly displayed their abilities to engage in complex sociopolitical analyses around the themes, those like Esperanza and Carmelita also grew in their abilities to formulate and then express in writing their thinking related to the issues raised in the class.[6]

At one point, Celia read a poem from the literacy workbook that had particular meaning for her. The poem, written by Eva Ortiz, began as a woman's cry, asking that there would be no more silence, that all forms of repression would come to an end. It invoked images of walls falling, all that has caused silence and suffering to fall and crumble. The poem then explodes with descriptions of women waking up, discovering their voice, placing their feet "firmly on the ground." The final line reinforces this new energy and freedom—"our hearts that seem to explode, have done just that." (as cited in Cartilla de Alfabetización para Neolecturas, 1995)

> *Para que se acabe el silencio que se acabe,*
> *que se caigan los muros de las casas, las carceles, las calles.*

After reading the poem aloud to Robin, in her home, Celia passionately shared the following reflection:

> What I think is that the walls they are talking about are the jails where we have all been, all of us who have been oppressed—principally those who have struggled for peace, those who have suffered, those who have been tortured. But when they talk about the walls of the kitchen, that refers to all of us women who never had the freedom to leave our homes when we were oppressed in this way. And where it talks about the blind women, these are the women who endured a silence that would have been for eternity except for the fact that the people of El Salvador became organized in the time of the war, organized in order to overcome all of the ignorance, the lack of education, that held us down. As it says in the poem, "waking up, we opened our eyes," this is when we recognized that some of these walls had fallen down! We saw that these were walls that were oppressing us women, that had kept us from waking up and realizing everything about our lives. Before, all we knew to do was care for children and cook, without ever being able to leave our homes. (Pausing to think before continuing with conviction) Now, the moment has arrived when the women have a strong voice. We are very firm in our struggle to be able to tear down the walls of silence and be able to be the protagonists, the heroes, of our own lives. Now

you will find us happy; you will find us clear and firm; and you will find us with a strong voice cutting through the silence. And this voice, we say, will continue, from now on, to be strong and clear! (New Year's Day, 1996)

Voices Heard Throughout Community.   In a similar manner, on the level of the entire community, the voices of all of the women in the literacy class grew more clear and strong as they increased their ability to respond to a generative theme and articulate related thoughts. One could now hear each student more clearly as they spoke out at the community-wide meetings, bringing their concerns about sanitary conditions or the accessibility of the clinic to the attention of the whole community.

One could also hear the voice of the students during the re-emerged BCC gatherings, as they took part as leaders as well as active participants. The women, consistently requesting to study the weekly Biblical text in class, now offered incisive insights about the relevancy of the text to the current social and political realities that affect the lives of the *campesinos*. They offered practical solutions as to how to put into practice the insights that they gleaned from reflection on the text, showing greater clarity than ever that they *could* be, and *need* to be, the central activists in bringing about any change that is necessary for an improved existence for their families and for the community as a whole.

And finally, even in the classroom, the students' voices became more distinct. The women now read and spoke more clearly and loudly, with greater confidence and ease.

PUTTING THE PAPATURRO CLASS IN CONTEXT

While progress was identifiable from the data collected for the Papaturro literacy class, the same indicators emerged from the data on the other literacy classes in *El Movimiento de Las Mujeres de Cuscatlán* program as indicators of relative lack of progress. It was this ability to look both within the Papaturro data and among the data sets for the other programs that strengthens the inference that the progress made by the Papaturro women was related to the particular instantiation of Freirean pedagogy in the Papaturro class.

Different Pictures of Progress

Teacher Training   A major part of Robin's assignment was that of teacher training and of supervision of the other 14 women's literacy classes in *El Movimiento de Las Mujeres de Cuscatlán*. She organized the training sessions to include training in the implementation of certain factors Robin deemed essential to the teaching of the literacy classes.

Facilitate Critique and Reading–Writing.   A regular component of these training sessions was a particular activity meant to facilitate critical analysis and discussion of the generative theme, with subsequent reading and writing activities that would flow directly from the discussion. Within this, the teachers were taught to start the class with a dialogue of a generative theme or word that resonates with the lives of their students; to extract a sentence from one of the students that could be considered a summary or key statement, and to write it (word-for-word, as the student says it) on the board; to read this sentence aloud and then read it together with the students two or three times; to have the students copy this sentence into their notebooks and have them read what they have copied aloud; to ask the students to try and write out more of their own thoughts on the generative theme, reminding them repeatedly that they should not be concerned with their spelling, but instead focus on expressing their own thoughts and opinions. This activity was underscored with the pedagogical beliefs, which Robin repeatedly expressed, that all aspects of adult education should engage the students, socially and politically, and that we learn to read by reading and to write by writing.

Teach Word Skills Using Students' Language.   Another factor included in the teacher training was ways to teach word recognition and spelling, including phonics lessons consonant with the syllabic approach used in the teaching of Spanish literacy, and the need to supplement this with sight word learning. For this aspect of literacy instruction, Robin stressed the need to use the women's own words/language as the basis of the syllabic instruction. She reiterated the value of having the students, themselves, identify exemplars of whatever graphophonic principle was being taught so that they could see and comprehend the link between print and language—between print and their language.

Incorporate Authentic Purposes for Literacy.   A third factor of each training related to ways of incorporating functional, "real life," uses of reading and writing into the class instruction. Robin instructed all *alfabetizadoras* to solicit input from all new students regarding their interests in learning to read and write. She explained that they, as *alfabetizadoras*, would need to facilitate this discussion, as many students would otherwise simply answer, "We want to learn to read and write everything!" Robin gave the *alfabetizadoras* ideas, suggesting that many students may desire such things as being able to read information regarding transportation, printed information in a clinic or a pharmacy, the Bible, or a religious songbook. Robin then explained that the *alfabetizadoras* needed to elicit this kind of information from the students and intentionally incorporate it into their instruction. She also instructed that, as *alfabetizadoras*, they also needed to be soliciting this information in an ongoing manner, as the students' awareness of such goals and desires would increase as they participate in the class.

Ongoing Evaluation. And finally, Robin instructed the *alfabetizadoras* regarding the implementation of ongoing methods of evaluation. She explained the need for ongoing evaluation as a way to ensure that the students were, in fact, learning and able to appropriate that which the *alfabetizadoras* were teaching. She discussed various activities that they could use to glean material for this type of assessment, and, together, she and the *alfabetizadoras* planned formal exams for determining if the students had passed onto another level of literacy, as measured by the Ministry of Education. Within this, Robin introduced the *alfabetizadoras* to a number of follow-up activities that they could implement when they discovered particular skills that they needed to review and reinforce.

Robin settled on this training format after having visited and observed each of the classes in the program over a period of several months. She also gleaned insight from her work of collaborating with other NGOs who work in the field of literacy and attending some of the meetings and trainings that they provided.

Obstacles to Teacher Learning

Low Educational Levels. Robin soon realized that the literacy–educational levels of the *alfabetizadoras* was so low (between second and sixth grade, with the average being closer to third grade) that they were unable to absorb much of what she initially attempted to present regarding the many ways literacy learning can be facilitated by different instructional activities. This inability to benefit from Robin's initial teacher training sessions was also significantly influenced by the degree to which this content was foreign to their schemas of teaching and learning. Thus, Robin chose to select only a few key elements of what she considered good teaching and to repeatedly present these through demonstration, discussion, and simulation (by the *alfabetizadoras*) each month.

Slow Teacher Change and Lack of Student Progress. However, at least a year passed before Robin began to report progress in the ability of the *alfabetizadoras* to implement the type of instruction she was focusing on in the trainings. And as Robin made her regular visits to the literacy classes in the communities participating in the program, she noted again and again the ways in which the classes were failing to serve the women.

In the following description of a class in a neighboring community, Robin conveyed a typical scenario that she often had to confront. This particular community is a rural repopulation community whose political and social makeup is very similar to that of Papaturro. This visit took place, after 6 months of training and community literacy class participation, on March 29, 1995:

(The class at this time had only four students left, two of whom did not come to class but received instruction from the teacher, CM, in their homes.)

The Notebooks: I asked to look at the student's notebooks. These notebooks contained only 12 pages of work, with the first being dated 22 February. Some of these pages contained *un plan*—a syllable written by CM at the top of the page, with the students having filled up the page with their copied version of this syllable. The other pages were filled with *un plan* of a sentence that the students had copied over enough to fill the page. These sentences were not anything that came from either the first student workbook nor the second one that the *alfabetizadoras* recently received. They were simple, short sentences about the characteristics of a local fruit, e.g. *Los guineos son bueno*. ("Bananas are good.") There were also a few pages that contained addition problems that the students had done. The only other thing that the students had in their notebooks were some drawings of objects with the names of these objects written below. Each of the two notebooks contained the same things.

The Class: (Following 45 min of work with a basic math workbook) CM began to look over the new student book (re-reading and writing) that I'd given her at the last training. (Because the people responsible for the printing of this book had not produced the copies for all of the students, as they had promised to do OVER 2 MONTHS AGO, at the last minute we made copies of the first section of the student book and the accompanying section of the teacher's guide and handed this out at the training.) CM studied this for several minutes before proceeding with the class. She did not have the teacher's guide with her.

CM then began to copy onto the board what was written on a particular page in the student book. She copied it exactly, copying numbers, the lines that followed, and the words that were written on the first line. What she was copying was the space where the students were to write (theoretically in their own copy of this student book) the words that they were able to form with the syllables that were listed, within a box, on the page before.

After CM copied all of this, I got up and went over to try and intervene, indicating that I understood the point of the exercise was for the students to form words of their own based on the syllables. I then had CM put her copy of the book in between the students, and I asked the students to begin to try and form words. CM asked them to write out the numbers 1 to 10 in their notebooks, as is written in the student book. After they did this, I again came over to where they were working, and I directed their attention to the example, explaining how it was a word that was formed by the syllables. I explained in great detail that we form words by uniting together syllables; that syllables united together create words that have meaning to us; they create the words that we speak, read, and write. I then asked each one of them to try and form words of their own and write them in their own notebooks.

At this point, CM also began to direct them to do the activity as it is supposed to be done according to the teacher's guide. I again sat down and observed.

The students were unable to do this activity independently. They were able to discover words only with a great deal of probing on the part of both CM and me. When I left, after observing until 3:45, the students had formulated three words on their own.

This observation took place during the same time period that the women in the Papaturro class were engaged in reading and writing around the Lenten observations, having long before reached the point where they could read text other than their own and write their own thoughts on a range of issues they considered relevant to their lives and sociopolitical context. Yet, in class after class in other communities, Robin observed a real failure to progress beyond rote copying of words that were unreadable to the students.

Retention Problems.   Other indicators of success for the Papaturro women, when applied to the other programs, documented their relative difficulties. Retention became a major issue in many of the other communities, with most classes losing over a quarter of their students. In fact, Robin observed that the problem of student attrition impacted all other literacy efforts throughout the zone, with several programs discontinuing services throughout Cuscatlán, based on their interpretation that the people of this region were not interested in literacy development.

Self-Attribution of Failure.   In the same manner, the students who dropped out of classes, as well as some who remained, attributed their failure to learn to their own inadequacies and "lack of motivation." They commonly expressed such beliefs as "I can't learn. Nothing sticks." "Because of all that I suffered in the war, I cannot remember anything that I am learning." "I can't learn ... I don't have the memory, I don't have the (necessary) intelligence." "I can't see well ... My vision fails me."

In the case of the latter, lack of access to vision exams and corrective lenses did have a tremendous impact on adult literacy students; some students simply could not see the board or their notebooks and did not have the money to remedy that problem. Apart from this explanation, however, students as well as Coordinators of other programs in the region were satisfied with explanations that Robin believed were misguided and limited. These explanations blamed the students for their "failure" and their "lack of motivation."

Fault Lies in Pedagogy.   Robin's observations led her to believe that issues of pedagogy and methodology resulting in educational experiences that were not particularly vital nor effective were more to the root of the problem. Her examination of the notebooks from all of the communities revealed none of the increased attempts to write, improved accuracy, or increased fluency and independence that marked the work of the Papaturro women. Further, there were no reported incidents of incorporating literacy into the lives of the students during the first year of the program for the women in the other communities. Rather, they (who continued with the classes) appeared "stuck" in the practice of copying print that came from sources other than their own minds and their own words. They remained estranged from literate activity, relegating it to *planes* and *dictados* assigned in class and directed by others.

FACTORS RELATED TO PROGRESS

Analysis of Robin's recorded reflections revealed numerous instructional factors to which we attribute the success of the Papaturro women: (a) a climate of relationship and respect among the students and between the students and the teachers, (b) the centering of the literacy activities around critical themes in the lives of the women, (c) teachers' assumptions of students' abilities and not disabilities or inabilities, (d) the incorporation of the students' own words and language into the texts used for learning to read and write, (e) teacher support and encouragement through affirmation and applause, (f) explicit explanations of the workings of the alphabetic nature of print, and (g) the intense engagement with which the women approached their reading and writing. In looking across all of the classes in the program, it was clear that while they all included the first two factors just listed, the remaining five were either absent at the other sites or were present to significantly lesser degrees.

Relationships of Mutuality

The use of community members as teachers, integral to the vision of community-based education held by the organizers of *El Moviemento de las Mujeres de Cuscatlán* [7] helped to ensure that the relationships between teachers and students were ones of mutuality, understanding, acceptance, and respect. Robin's presence as the exception to this—she came from outside the community and the culture—was mediated by the nature of the relationship she established with the women and the community. Assuming a dialogical stance, she too was able to establish genuine relationships of mutuality and respect with her students. By living among them and sharing their daily lives as a community member, she became one of them to the extent possible, given her history and her duties as their teacher as well as director of the larger program. The affective result of this relationship was to help the women feel comfortable and accepted and to create personal bonds of commitment to the class.

Focus on Generative Themes and Critique

In addition to the climate of genuine relationship, all of the classes in the program included the Freirean-influenced focus on generative themes and critical analysis. This focus was incorporated into the published materials made available to the teachers. It was also known to them. Through the training received by the *campesino* literacy educators during the war, and the *campesinos'* experiences with the BCCs and their critical analyses of texts and realities prior to the war, the Salvadorans were quite familiar with Freirean philosophy and perspective and the notion that we are protagonists of our own lives. The belief that it is necessary to analyze our own reality in order to transform it was familiar and easily accepted by all of the *alfabetizadoras* and their students. However, while our analysis pointed to the critical role this focus played in the engagement of the students in their literacy learning, it was clear that, alone, it was not enough to engender the type of progress made by the Papaturro women.

Assumption of Ability to Learn

The remaining success-related factors listed above were present to a much greater degree in the Papaturro class, and, therefore, must be regarded as crucial aspects when reflecting on the degree of progress made by Celia, Tomasa, and the other women of the class. In relation particularly to the progress made by students such as Deonicia, Margarita, and Carmelita, Robin noted the positive effect of a teacher's assumption of all students' ultimate ability to learn. By refusing to allow these students to "pass" when asked to write or think of their own words, and by insisting that they try with appropriate support, Robin believed that she could facilitate learning and overcome student's perceptions (learned from previous experiences of schooling) of themselves as unable to learn.

This factor was less likely to be operative in other classes in the program. Robin often documented cases where *alfabetizadoras* would not call on students who they felt could not do what they were asking, would write out words for students who claimed they could not write, would simply correct student writing with no explanation, and read for students who were reluctant to try.

Affective Encouragement

Another aspect of teacher support evident in the Papaturro class was that of overt, public affirmation and applause which Robin incorporated daily into the instruction. This was critically instrumental in encouraging the women—especially those who initially appeared to have a more difficult time and who progressed at a slower rate than the others—to try and try again. Further, by providing public and, at times, effusive praise of hard-won progress, Robin believed that the women were more likely to undergo transformations in their beliefs about their innate abilities to learn.

Again, this was much less apparent in the other classes, partly, Robin felt, because of the inherent shyness of Salvadoran women and reluctance to display effusive emotions. In comparison, Robin observed that the Salvadoran *alfabetizadoras* were often shy, sometimes even awkward, not yet feeling entirely comfortable with being a "teacher." Therefore, it was clear that Robin's "brazenness" in praising through such expressions as frequent applause and showing affection by hugging students was too far removed from the cultural norms of the *alfabetizadoras* for them to spontaneously engage in such behavior.

As Robin spoke to them in the monthly trainings about the importance of affirmation and praise, however, she observed that they began to incorporate some understanding of this into their classes. Over time, Robin observed that the *alfabetizadoras* learned to recognize specific measures of student improvement and verbally point those out to their students, doing so in an enthusiastic, celebratory tone. Ultimately, it was clear that learning to recognize every aspect of student progress, both personal and academic, and explicitly naming that, was a vital part of motivating students and furthering their progress. Therefore, Robin, along with the Salvadoran women who worked with her in giving the teacher training, continually discovered ways to incorporate this belief into their training in ways that would fit with cultural norms.

Using the Language of the Students

Another element missing from the other classes was the emphasis placed, and the importance assigned to, the reading and writing of the women's own words. As discussed in the preceding chapters, this practice was completely foreign to the Salvadoran conception of how one learns to read and write. In the Papaturro class, all of the words read and written by the women were self-generated[8] until they were fluent and skilled enough to read the words of others. This allowed them to make real conceptual links between what they knew and the way print works to encode meaning. It also made it easier for them to begin to incorporate reading and writing into their lives outside of the classroom sooner since what they were reading and writing in class was virtually the same as that which they wanted to read and write outside of class and they could see that they already possessed the language needed to do this.

Explicit Explanations of Print–Speech Relationships

Robin's repeated inclusion of explicit explanations of the ways that sounds, when encoded, relate to letters and represent one's personal words and meanings was also instrumental to student progress. Students often contrasted this with previous experiences of literacy instruction in which teachers would simply put syllables and words on the board to be copied and 'learned' but would fail to explain how the letters represented 'sounds' of words. Thus, the women were never allowed access to the system and systematicity of an alphabetic language such as Spanish and were unable to generalize to new words as the need arose. This reliance on rote copying without explanation of the underlying system of phonemic representation was obvious in the teaching by the *alfabetizadoras* in the other classes. It was quite a while before Robin's attempts to shift them into a more conceptual approach began to take effect and become apparent in their actual daily teaching.

Engagement

Finally, the quality of high engagement among the women students that was so apparent in the Papaturro class was almost totally absent in the other classes whenever Robin observed. As we discuss earlier, this engagement appeared to result from a confluence of several factors that we have identified as indicators of progress, specifically the focus on generative themes relevant to the lives of the women, facilitating a dialogue that leads the women to reflect on the theme, giving them a forum to discuss previous insights with others, as well as helping them to discover new insights; the inclusion of their own words and ways of expressing themselves; and the very visible progress itself. Success begets success, and the high engagement of the Papaturro women in their reading and writing was fed by these factors, and itself led to further success. Thus, a loop of engagement/success was created, the presence of which accounted for the continuing progress of the women in the Papaturro class.

The absence of these same factors also helped explain the lack of, or slower rate of, progress of the students in other classes in the program. As was evident in almost all of Robin's field notes reporting her observations of these other classes, most of the *alfabetizadoras* were not able to facilitate an engaging dialogue on the generative theme. More important, most *alfabetizadoras* also lacked an understanding of how to link the dialogue with related writing and reading activities. These classes were dominated by rote copying, which did not intellectually engage the students in any way that would further their literacy acquisition. Robin often reported that for a class lasting 90 min, the students were engaged in less that 15 or 30 min (maximum) of that which engaged them toward actual literacy development.

INSIGHTS FOR ADULT EDUCATION

This chapter focused on describing and documenting the progress made by the women of the Papaturro literacy class. Thus, it raises the issues—so problematic in the field of adult education—of assessment and evaluation. Within this, our description of the different women and their differing routes to literacy identifies several broadly recognized types of learners that are relevant to any discussion of adult literacy program evaluation. We discuss this latter implication first.

Types of Adult Learners and Implications for Evaluation

Margarita's hypothesized dyslexia raises the significant issue of the reported high incidence of adults with learning disabilities (LDs) within the ABE population. Teachers of adult literacy anecdotally report across programs that many of their students exhibit clear signs of neurologically based learning difficulties, with dyslexia being the most frequent[9]. Unfortunately, very little empirical evidence has been gathered to reliably estimate the size of this reported subgroup of adult literacy students.

A NCSALL-sponsored study (1996) showed early promise of attempting to gather such data. Led by researcher John Strucker, this project is designed to describe the reading strengths and weaknesses of the ABE population (pp. 36–42). Included in the intent of this study was to document the degree of adult dyslexics attending adult literacy classes. However, the difficulty of documenting a neurologically based disorder (which needs to be done with neurologically based tests and procedures and not only tests of reading abilities) on such a large scale proved too daunting, and any focus on dyslexia has been dropped.

The need for such documentation continues, however, due to the instructional implications of the presence of learning disabilities in a student's profile. By definition, students with documented neurologically based LDs do not benefit from the type of instruction that facilitates learning with their non-LD peers. Students with neurologically based LDs process information differently and thus learn differently. Teachers of such students need special training, and the students need individually designed accommodations and targeted instruction designed to circumvent their processing difficulties in informed ways. Finally, assessments of programs with a mix of LD and non-LD students must take this mix into account—a process that no one seems to know how to do at the present time.

The training, or lack of, of adult literacy teachers in general is a problematic issue for the field. More calls are being made to increase the teacher preparation of adult educators, and serious moves are being made to require credentialing of adult teachers across the United States. Similar concerns are being raised in other countries (Draft Summit Document, 1997; NCAL, 1995). In addition, there is no serious attempt to look at the required specialized training that is required for work with LD adults, much less design and provide such courses for adult educators. Given the obvious presence of adults with diagnosed and undiagnosed learning disabilities in adult literacy classes, this is a pressing issue that deserves immediate attention. An even greater challenge to the field is the design of training courses for teachers, which synthesize and integrate ways of teaching adults with specific learning disabilities with a community-based, Freirean-based focus.

Another typical adult literacy class scenario that presents challenges for program evaluation emerged in the Papaturro class: the presence of a range of ages, abilities, life experiences, and attendance patterns. Adult educators often report the same for their classes in the United States, Britain, and elsewhere (Finlay & Harrison, 1994; Padak, Davidson, & Padak, 1994; Padak & Padak, 1994). Although individual progress can be measured with a thoughtful evaluation scheme, evaluation of the overall program is more challenging under such circumstances. This difficulty is merely an indicator, though, for the challenges for instruction with such a mix of students. Attempts are made for general leveling of students in ABE classes regarding their reading–writing abilities when they enter, but all adult education teachers know that even within basic, intermediate, or GED classes, the range of proficiencies, strengths, and weaknesses can be overwhelming. Add to this the significant impact of differing life experiences, including experiences with (or without) schooling, and age and maturity. Clearly these present challenges that never face K–12 teachers.

The insights gained in this study suggest that programs that focus on issues of importance to the students beyond the mere technicality of reading and writing can be successful in developing the depth of engagement and commitment from the students that can override many of the complications that arise from differing abilities, ages, and life experiences. Students are reading and writing—at whatever levels they are capable—about events and issues that are critical to their lives at that moment in that place. They have authentic reasons and purposes to decode and encode print, and their literacy skills develop as they acquire and use them to accomplish their needs as developing critical analysts and protagonists of their own lives.

The Challenge of Adult Literacy Program Evaluation

Overall, it appears that the biggest challenge and controversy facing the issue of adult literacy program evaluation is that of the nature of the assessment. Most educators, and virtually all funders, agree that appropriate and interpretable evaluation needs to be a key component of any program (Bear, Ferry, Templeton, 1987; Knudson-Fields, 1989; NCAL, 1995; Padak & Padak, 1994; Steele, 1989). It provides feedback about the efficacy of the instruction, recognizes individual and programmatic achievement, and allows for the examination of goals (Finlay & Harrison, 1994). But how to assess program and individual achievement is the point of contention. For the most part, teachers and program directors have agreed that the evaluation needs to reflect the life-contexts and personal goals of the students. This tends to preclude standardized, norm-referenced tests, often favored and demanded by policy makers and large funders.

Many reasons are cited for the undesirability of standardized, norm-referenced tests with adult learners. Many claim that these assessments are inappropriate to use with people who have had negative experiences with them when they were previously in school (Finlay & Harrison, 1994; Taylor, 1997); standardized tests assume an autonomous view of literacy instead of recognizing that reading and comprehending always reflect the context of the reading and background knowledge of the reader (Street, 1984); standardized, norm-referenced tests are not normed on the population of adults represented in adult literacy classes (Johnston, 1997); scores by adult students on norm-referenced tests often inordinately reflect their anxiety, underpreparedness for taking such tests, and regression to the mean effects (Sticht, 1990); standardized, norm-referenced tests are inherently culturally biased and the cultures of the adults of marginalized groups who predominate in adult literacy classes are unfairly penalized because of this (Taylor, 1997); and the short, isolated passages on standardized, norm-referenced tests are unlike real-life reading materials that the adult students need to learn to read, but the pressure of impending tests results in teachers "teaching to the test" and thus wasting valuable instructional time.

In place of such tests, most adult educators prefer measures that reflect the literacy contexts and needs of their students. Robin's procedures for documenting progress are reflective of such types of measures. Noting the retention patterns of the students can give valuable insight into the students' feelings of progress and personal engagement. With their busy lives, adults will not continue to make the sacrifices needed to attend literacy classes unless they believe that they are benefitting in meaningful ways. Keeping track of individual student's growth in decoding, spelling, fluency, and comprehension, as well as growth in the ability to critically analyze their realities, also provides teachers with student-specific information on progress, or lack of same. Further, this type of "student-watching"[10] provides immediate feedback to the teacher on the impact of her instruction, allowing for appropriate modifications to better fit the needs of the individual students. Noting the ways in which students are incorporating the uses of reading and writing in their out-of-classroom lives is also an excellent measure of program impact and may be the most ecologically valid of all assessment measures[11]. Listening to the students' own evaluations of their progress, which may include explicitly checking against and updating student-generated goals lists, also allows teachers to measure program and student success.

All of these informal, yet systematic, assessment measures allow adult educators to show program impact and success. They also provide crucial feedback to teachers and students in a timely and meaningful way, unlike the more distanced and problematic standardized, norm-referenced tests. Providing adult teachers with the tools and means to carry out such assessments needs to be an essential component of teacher training.

Teacher Training and Materials: Need to Change Undercommitments of Policy Makers

The final issue raised by this chapter is that of the state of the adult education field world-wide. The degree to which policy makers and funders have failed to take seriously the need to educate adults with little formal education has resulted in the dismal picture we have documented in El Salvador and in other nations of the world. Teachers, many of whom are themselves lacking in experience with any kind of formal education, struggle to help their students learn without the training in literacy development and literacy instruction that they so desperately need to effectively work with adults who have little or no literacy abilities. Students and teachers continue to meet in dismal and, in many cases, completely inappropriate physical conditions, making do to the best of their abilities. Materials are seriously deficient both in quantity and quality. In many countries, they are almost totally nonexistent. When they are available, they are often inappropriate for the students for a variety of reasons: (a) They are cast-off materials originally written for children. (b) They are written in languages that are different from those of the students. (c) They reflect cultures foreign to the students, and these cultures are often those of the dominating or colonializing cultures.

Robin's relative success with the Papaturro class demonstrates some possibilities for adult education. Given appropriate education and training, commitment to the lives of the students, and a minimal level of support for materials, the outcome of adult literacy classes could be vastly improved around the world. By upgrading the physical conditions of adult classes and the materials, this outcome would become even more impressive. But before any of this can occur, politicians and taxpayers need to come to grips with the ways in which the education of all people, children and adults, is inherent to the futures of everyone. Serious policy changes must be made and committed to before we can begin to expect results from adult literacy classes.

ENDNOTES

1. Historically, it has been customary to burn large fields in an effort to prepare this land for future planting. There is currently a movement in El Salvador to provoke discussion and environmental consciousness regarding this practice. The ultimate hope is that farmers will not choose to burn forests, but instead make on-going efforts to plant more trees as a way to help replenish the country's natural water supply.

2. Hammond (1998), in describing the workings of the popular education movement in El Salvador before and during the war, claimed that it was a principle of popular education that dedication and motivation were the most important characteristics of popular teachers. Thus, there was no, or very little, teacher training that focused on pedagogy beyond the basic processes of using generative words and facilitating discussions. It was believed, according to Hammond, that if the teachers were dedicated and motivated to "share what little I know" so that others could learn, they would figure out on their own how to teach. In Barndt's (1993) description of the popular education movement in post-revolution Nicaragua, she documented the difficulties of training (a) experienced teachers in a pedagogy that differs so significantly from that learned under the old oligarchic regime, and (b) inexperienced popular teachers (who numbered in the thousands) for whom limited funds and limited time existed for teacher preparation.

3. Most of the literacy students arrived, consistently, 30 min late to class. Robin observed, and the students explicitly stated, that this is reflective of a relaxed atti-

tude toward time that exists in certain subcultures in El Salvador. It is jokingly referred to as *la hora Salvadoreña* (Salvadoran time), translating to mean approximately 30 min after the stated hour of a meeting or a class.

4. Freire (1993) named several characteristics of oppressed peoples as they take on the beliefs of those who are oppressing them. One is an almost irresistible attraction toward the oppressors and their way of life. They want to be like them, to follow them. Another is that of self-depreciation, which comes from internalizing the opinion that the oppressors hold of them. Another is emotional dependence, which can lead to destructive behavior toward themselves and their fellow oppressed.

5. The Peace Accords are a political agreement that was signed by the FMLN and the government in January 1992. General areas of reform included agrarian, security forces, human rights, judicial, and electoral.

6. A logical question here is how the men in Papaturro responded to the growing empowerment of the women's voices. For the most part, the response was positive. This appeared to be the result of several interlocking factors. Recall that Papaturro was an intentionally created unit, with all of the families belonging to the same political party associated with the FMLN and who shared the same prewar, war, and refugee experiences. The FMLN and many of the member political parties worked throughout the struggle for social justice to change the social and cultural attitudes toward women and to increase both their educational opportunities and their ways of participating in the governance of the community. The president of Papaturro's *directivo* wanted very much for the women to participate more in the community at all levels and responded to their growing voices with community praise and assignment of responsibilities. Robin reported, however, that this attitude toward women was not uniform throughout El Salvador at that time. She noted mixed reactions to women's participation in educational opportunities in some communities and outright opposition in others.

7. Most social service programs created after the signing of the Peace Accords (during "Reconstruction") reflected the general values of Popular Education. (As described in chapter 3, these values are significantly influenced by interpretations of Freirean philosophy.) One significant aspect of this set of values is that education is central to all aspects of social and political development. Inextricably related to this value is the belief that it would be particularly valuable if those in any type of educator role were actually from the communities being served. Coming close to realizing this ideal (but not quite reaching it), it was common, therefore, for the people who functioned in such roles as teachers, health care workers, agricultural educators, or women's advocates to be from the communities where they worked, and for those who trained and supervised these people to be familiar with, and supportive of, the life and aspirations of these communities.

8. This is true with the exception of the generative words, which are chosen and incorporated into the curriculum because they are assumed to be of the culture of those who are students in the program.

9. *Dyslexia* is defined as a neurological disorder related to visual and/or auditory processing that results in extreme difficulty in recognizing letters and words and in

interpreting information (letters, words, and/or numbers) that is presented visually or auditorily. Lerner (1993) asserted that, although various explanations for its nature and cause exist, there is general agreement on four points: (a) It is probably due to a congenital neurological condition. (b) The resultant problems persist into adolescence and adulthood. (c) Dyslexia has perceptual, cognitive, and language dimensions that create subtypes of dyslexia. (d) It leads to deficits in many skill areas as the individual matures.

10. This is a variation of Y. Goodman's (1978) term "kid watching," which has become a classic method of assessing children.

11. Purcell-Gates (1996a) is using this method to explore the relationships between the dimensions of (a) dialogic practice and (b) life-contextualized activities and materials in adult literacy classes and change in type or frequency of out-of-school literacy practices. This study is being sponsored by NCSALL and is being conducted in adult literacy programs across the United States.

PART III
INSIGHTS FOR
ADULT LITERACY
EDUCATION

9

Literacy Development and Freirean-Based Pedagogy

I could not tell North American educators what to do, even if I wanted to. I do not know the contexts and material conditions in which North American educators must work. It is not that I do not know how to say what they should do. Rather, I do not know what to say precisely because my own viewpoints have been formed by my own contexts.
—Freire & Macedo (1987, pp. 134–135)

We have closely examined one Freirean-based adult literacy class to gain deeper insight into, and understanding of, literacy development as it occurs within such a theoretical context. Our primary lens has been that of adult basic literacy development, a lens that has not previously been applied to the study of Freirean pedagogy, at least to the depth and extent to which we have taken it. In applying this lens, we have sought to understand how the principles, processes, and procedures inherent to Freire's beliefs about education, and its purpose and role in society, transact with the acquisition and development of reading and writing skills by adults. The findings presented in this book represent our analysis and interpretation of data collected over 18 months, triangulated to provide varied perspectives on the phenomenon of interest: the women's literacy class in Papaturro.

The challenges of adult education in conjunction with an evolving world economy and the subsequent increased and related literacy needs argue for attempts, such as this, to strive for more meaningful insights into the relationships between theory, curriculum, and literacy development. Although Freire evolved his theories of education, literacy, and sociopolitical change almost half a century ago, and although adult education programs based on his beliefs have been in operation around the world since the 1970s, very little empirical research has been conducted to explore this theory and the resulting educational praxis. This we have attempted to do, and we believe our close description of one such class and our interpretation of the processes of literacy development that took place within this class will provide valuable information to the literacy field.

In this chapter, we summarize our findings and the implications we believe they hold for practice and for future research. We do not present our analysis as a how-to manual for designing and running a Freirean-based adult literacy program. The literacy class Robin and her students developed is just one instantiation, or manifestation, of such a program. It was the result of one teacher, with specific prior experiences, beliefs, goals, and values, who found herself within a specific sociocultural context with its own history, belief system, goals, and values and with particular women whose beliefs, goals, and values were shaped by their own experiences within this context. It cannot, nor should it, be duplicated in a rote manner. Freire (Freire & Macedo, 1987) explicated this foundational principle regarding his work: "Experiences and practices can be neither exported nor imported. It follows that it is impossible to fulfill someone's request to import practices from other contexts" (p. 132).

Rather, Freire stated, it is the principles of his theory that one can study and come to understand in such a way that they, if found valid, can be reinvented in other contexts and adapted to fit those contexts. It is our hope that adult educators, researchers, theorists, and, ultimately, students will find ways to take from this ethnography instructional ideas, insights, and questions. We hope that those who work with oppressed and marginalized learners will glean from this analysis that which connects with their own work in varied, yet situationally specific, ways. Finally, we hope that this analysis will contribute to the growing body of knowledge about the ways that adults learn to read and write within different sociocultural contexts.

FREIREAN OR PROGRESSIVIST?

Freirean Focus on Transactive Nature of Education and Quest for Social Justice

Before focusing more exclusively on the processes of literacy development within Freirean-based programs, it is helpful to reiterate what qualifies a program as Freirean-based and to distinguish it from what can be called "progressive" education. Freire made it very clear that education is a political process and act. Education is the act of becoming aware, through critical apprehension involving reading the word and the world, of one's reality—a reality that has been formed by human historical forces. Literacy development within this view is the development of the ability to read the sociopolitical world of the students and the written words that contain the meaning of that world—those words that are "pregnant with the meaning of the world," as Freire (Freire & Macedo, 1987, p. 35) said. Decoding words within this view is not only decoding on a graphophonic level, but also deconstructing the intricacies of the sociopolitical and sociocultural meanings of these words in order to better understand how one's reality has been, and continues to be, shaped and formed. In turn, "writing the word and the world" (Freire & Macedo, 1987, p. 35) involves both encoding on a graphophonic level as well as re-constructing one's sociopolitical and sociocultural world through such things as participating in community-based projects aimed at achieving goals arrived at during class dialogues. Education is not complete, within this theoretical system, without the learning and acceptance of the necessity of praxis to follow on the critical apprehension of one's reality. *Praxis*, "the relationship between theoretical understanding and critique of society ... and action that seeks to transform individuals and their environment" (Lysteina, et al., 1996, p. 342), goes back and forth, dialectically, between reflection and action, according to Freire. Thus, education and the quest for social justice are transactive and synergistically related in a Freirean-based program.

Condemning a banking concept of education, where information that is selected and shaped by the dominant levels of society is "poured into the heads" of empty (of knowledge), unquestioning, and obedient students, Freire adopted a problem-posing approach to teaching and learning where students and teacher work together to learn about and come to critically understand issues of relevance.

Critical Education Not the Same as Progressive

Centering classroom learning and teaching around themes, or problems, and emphasizing discovery over rote learning are also central tenets of much progressive education, and, thus, it is possible to conflate Freirean and progressive theories to the point where one no longer sees the differences (Freire & Macedo, 1995; Shor, 1993). Freirean scholars, as well as Freire, have protested and cautioned against this, pointing out that, whereas much of what counts as 'progressive' education can be found in Freire's vision, his central themes of social justice and social change through empowerment are usually not found in programs identified as progressive.[1]

For those adult educators who wish to implement Freirean-based programs, the inherent conflicts between Freire's conception of education and that of the dominant society is all too clear. Funding for adult programs often comes from governmental agencies controlled by the power elites. This group has its own agenda for adult education, and it undoubtedly does not include social change and restructuring of the sociopolitical order. Rather than focusing on helping adult students recognize the power that they already have (albeit at times unrecognized and undeveloped) and efforts toward social change, most adult education policy is based on a market ethic: Increased literacy achievement will translate into increased workplace productivity and to maintenance of the status quo (Davis, 1994). As a result, community-based programs that focus on helping adult students recognize and utilize their power toward social change can have real problems sustaining themselves. According to Heaney (1989), for example, "most emancipatory or liberatory literacy programs have been sustained by governments for only a brief time following either a revolution or a declaration of independence" (as cited in Davis, 1994, p. 21).

We present this admittedly brief discussion of these issues to clarify for the reader what we have been examining: a Freirean-based literacy program and some of the attendant concerns and issues inherent in establishing such a program in contexts different from the one reported here. Although some of the insights we came to regarding literacy development (e.g., engagement and motivation) can be thought about and explored in the contexts of non-Freirean, progressive theories of education, we remind the reader that our insights are constrained by the fact that our research was undertaken within the context of a Freirean-based program and that this is a significant parameter.

Further, when thinking about implications for future Freirean-inspired programs, many issues of power and ethics are inherently involved, and we caution against a simplistic, naive application of our findings. We do aspire, though, to future dialogue and consideration of the insights we raise from our analysis of the Papaturro literacy program.

VITAL ENGAGEMENT WITH TEXT
LEADS TO LITERACY DEVELOPMENT

Oral and Written Engagement Needed

What accounts for literacy development within a Freirean-based adult literacy class? Our central insight regarding this question is that it is the energy and engagement that is aroused in the students by the processes involved in dialoguing—through verbal interchanges and in print—about the issues central to their critical reading of their realities. Oral dialogue, alone, cannot be the key. Nor can reading and writing one's thoughts, in the absence of the oral dialogues.

Rather, we conclude that it is the powerful combination of and transactions (Rosenblatt, 1989) between oral dialogues centered around critical themes and the literacy knowledge gained through encoding and decoding print that holds the meanings that the learners are making of these themes. This transactive dynamic engages the learners at such a level that they are able to work through the difficulties inherent for all in the beginning phases of acquiring reading and writing knowledge and skills. In doing this, students overcome their learned negative beliefs about their inherent abilities to learn. Ultimately, they have increased motivation and desire to regularly attend class despite their pressing daily responsibilities.

Engagement Theory

Engagement theory (Guthrie & Wigfield, 1997) explains this dynamic, predicting that high levels of learner engagement will result in high motivation, which in turn will activate the cognitive strategies needed for successful reading. These strategies are deliberate, conscious, and effortful and thus are dependent on motivation for maintenance. Engagement research in the field of reading has linked motivation to personally meaningful reading. We conclude that the most personally meaningful reading for adults of marginalized and oppressed groups is that which engages with critiques of their marginalized status, critiques of the power relationships inherent in situations that keep them marginalized, critiques that lead to political praxis and social change, critiques that quest for social justice.

Engaged with print, that is, reading and writing about powerfully meaningful ideas, adult learners learn written language by using it for genuine communicative functions. They learn both by discovering the underlying principles of the print–speech connections and by working with a teacher who explicitly points out and explains to them many of these key principles, gives them critical feedback on their attempts, and acts as a communicative partner in the on-going dialogue.

Measuring Progress as Program Evaluation

Progress, or development, can be visible and concrete when teachers and program administrators regularly observe their students across time as they engage with text in critical ways. Fluency and automaticity develop in both their reading and writing. Their ability to critically read the language of others grows after they master that of their own mouths and minds. Students who are developing critical literacy abilities will make every effort to attend class regularly, and retention problems will be less prevalent and not the cause of program failure. The students, themselves, will express their feelings of accomplishment and growth.

Based on this central insight into the process of literacy development within a Freirean-based program, we suggest that teachers critically examine their programs if any of these indicators of progress are missing. If students who started the class with high expectations and motivations begin to drop off and out, if students are not gaining in fluency and skill, if students are expressing feelings of failure and low self-esteem as learners, then perhaps some element of this transactive unit of critique-engagement-process is missing or relatively weak. As did Robin, teachers can reflect daily on how the class seemed to go and to make adjustments to their pedagogy. Robin's focus on the energy of the class was particularly informative. When she observed, for example, that the students were less engaged in oral dialogue and wrote only a little and with great frustration and difficulty during the lessons that began with skill work, she concluded that all classes should begin with oral dialogue around a critical theme. This was necessary, she concluded, to raise the energy level—the engagement level—to the point that it could work in the ways we have identified.

COMPONENTS OF AN ENGAGING FREIREAN-BASED LITERACY CLASS

A Freirean-based adult literacy class that engages the students in highly motivated oral and written dialogues is made possible through the synergistic presence of several key components, according to our analysis. The literacy instruction must be of a type that allows for growth and development, the teacher must possess certain characteristics and predispositions, and the program itself must reflect community goals and purposes.

Instruction for Engagement

Instruction that seems to best allow for literacy development is that which is (a) dialogic; (b) accepts, validates, and incorporates the language(s) of the students; and (c) involves the learners in reading and writing for authentic purposes with explicit explanations of print-speech principles and conventions, as well as of different written discourse conventions as needed.[2]

Dialogic Student–Teacher Relationships. Students with recovered or recognized self-power and agency are present in a classroom gestalt that recognizes the essential subjectivity of the students. Teacher and student power relationships need to reflect a mutuality that is genuine and that is incorporated into an on-going process of teaching and learning for all participants, both teachers and students. This is the basic principle that allows for dialogue or problem-posing instruction. Anything else, according to Freire, is misleading, unauthentic, and manipulative and, rather than leading to increased student agency, results in reinforcing the marginalized and oppressed position of the learners. Subjugated students, who believe they are less worthy than the teacher and who persist in blindly and passively accepting information spoon-fed to them, cannot, by definition, be engaged learners, readers, and writers.

Instruction Based on Students' Language. Within this, a genuine appreciation for and acceptance of the language of the students is inherent to a dialogic relationship between teachers and students. The very essential meanings we make of our worlds are tied up in and made possible by our language, and to deny this to students attempting to learn to read and write is not only oppressive and thus not dialogic, but ill-informed and ultimately ineffective. We have demonstrated the ways in which Robin incorporated her students' language, their *campo* dialect, into her literacy instruction, using it to make visible the connections between speech and print and to facilitate the expression of critical meaning-making during oral dialogues and while reading and writing.

Learners who are engaged and who recognize the knowledge and power that they have understand the ways in which their language knowledge allows them access to the world of ideas. They do not deny their own knowledge; they use it for their own purposes.

Authentic Literacy With Explicit Explanation. Finally, engaged readers and writers develop their skills and their fluency by engaging in reading and writing of authentic texts for authentic purposes. They are helped to do this by timely and explicit explanations of principles and conventions of written language that are new and unfamiliar to them. They are neither turned loose in a sea of printed words and expected to figure it out on their own, nor are they constrained to endless, out-of-context, skill drills without access to actual written discourse. Rather, they are allowed to maintain their engagement and motivation, focusing on the meanings they are creating with print, by a teacher who helps them understand how to decode and encode in order to make meaning. Further, as a component of a dialogic instructional model, the students' own preferences and ways of learning are recognized and incorporated into the processes and procedures of the classroom as part of dialogic, collaborative relationships between students and teacher.

Teachers of Engaged Readers and Writers

Commitment to Social Change.   Several key characteristics of teachers of engaged readers and writers within Freirean-based programs suggest themselves from our analysis. Primary is that teachers must believe that education is always political and must possess political knowledge and insight and a belief in praxis.[3] As described above, for a program to be considered Freirean, it must have this commitment to social change and justice, and the teacher needs to be clear as to how he or she can play a key role in helping to bring this about. Freire (Freire & Macedo, 1987) described this requirement: "We need political clarity before we can understand the political action of eradicating illiteracy in the United States or any other place. Educators who do not have political clarity can, at best, help students read the word, but they are incapable of helping them read the world. A literacy campaign that enables students to read the world requires political clarity" (p. 132).

Pedagogical Knowledge.   From this base of political insight and commitment to social change, Freirean-inspired teachers of engaged readers and writers bring to the classroom a solid base of pedagogical knowledge about literacy development, language development, and the balance between exploration and explicit explanation that is required for maximum progress in reading and writing. Knowing what is involved in learning to read and write and then knowing what to do as a teacher to foster this learning in students is critical to the development of engaged readers and writers.[4]

Cultural Knowledge.   As part of this, the effective teacher must have a broad and deep knowledge of the community from which her students come. She needs to know the functions for literacy within this community, the language forms used by the people in the community, the pragmatics of language use in the community, the social structures, the history and sociocultural location of the community, the beliefs and values of the community, the patterns of life within the community, the gender roles accepted within the community. Freire (1993) described this cultural knowledge required of teachers, explaining the need to understand the totality of the community by decoding it into its partial dimensions for study and reassembling these parts into a whole which is now known, understood, and accepted as a legitimate social entity.

As we have suggested, the optimum scenario is one with teachers who are of the community. The next best scenario would be one similar to that described in this study, where the teacher moves into the community and lives within it as a member, learning about it over time.[5] At the very least, however, teachers who come into the community to teach, returning to their own communities each day, must take serious measures to learn all of the above about the communities from which their students come.

Teachers Not Facilitators.   Finally, within the classroom, teachers of engaged readers and writers must always retain their roles as teachers and bring to the learning event their knowledge and beliefs as an essential part of the dialogical relationship between students and teachers. They must be clear that to leave the learning solely to the student is not indicative of an ultimate belief in the inherent power and abilities of the students. Rather, such laissez-faire facilitating is actually an abdication of their responsibilities as teachers and essentially and ultimately oppressive, manipulative, and dishonest (Freire & Macedo, 1995).

COMMUNITY-BASED PROGRAMS FOR ENGAGED READERS AND WRITERS

The final insights to come from our analysis of the Papaturro literacy class speak to policy and program planning. The ultimate desirability of community-based adult literacy programs seems clear within this discussion of high engagement with the learning process and with text.

Transitoriness of Adult Literacy Programs

The history of adult literacy programs is one of temporariness: programs come and go. If they manage to get started at all, they often end up closed for lack of participation. Adult students have all kinds of legitimate reasons for failure to attend or to continue with literacy programs. They have responsibilities to jobs, to children and spouses, and, often, to extended families. They are usually struggling with financial difficulties that make the breakdown of a car or a raise in the price of subway tokens insurmountable obstacles in the way of attending literacy class. Their poverty is also related to serious, chronic health problems that often interfere with regular attendance.

Many potential adult literacy students never attend classes. The adult literacy programs in community colleges, universities, and high schools have been described as serving only the cream of the adult nonreading population (Davis, 1994; Hunter & Harman, 1979; Kozol, 1985; Mezirow, Darkenwald, & Knox, 1975).

Why do these programs have such difficulty attracting and keeping the bulk of adults in need of literacy help? Beder and Quigley (1990) noted several factors that could be involved in this "resistance phenomenon": (a) Resistance can be either overt or subtle as resisters respond to values imposed on them in different ways. (b) Resisters may find the program values, not the content, to be unacceptable. (c) Resisters may find the content of the program to be irrelevant to their lives. (d) Resisters are aware of the consequences of their resistance and nonresistance (e.g., learning to read may isolate them from their social networks).

Promise of Community-Based Programs

The most promising alternative to programs that emanate from mainstream institutions with their inherent mainstream values and goals are community-based programs (Anorve, 1989; Davis, 1994; Fingeret, 1983, 1984, 1989; Heaney, 1989; Hunter & Harman, 1979; Isley, 1985a, 1985a, 1989; Jurmo, 1989; Kozol, 1985; Zachariadis, 1986). Such programs are based in the community, staffed by community members, and serve an identifiable constituency. They are autonomous and thus do not rely on mainstream institutions for instructional or managerial guidelines. They serve groups who typically do not attend mainstream programs. They link individual achievement to community achievement, group solidarity, and social change. And they provide learner-centered instruction based on learner's objectives rather than prescribed activities and subjects (Barndt, 1993; Zachariadis, 1986).

In this study, we saw the power of the community in sponsoring and supporting the Papaturro literacy class. With the impetus and the direction coming from within, rather than being imposed from without, the students in the class could fully engage in a program that was completely congruent with their lives, histories, values, and goals. This is surely a key component of a program for engaged readers and writers.

FINAL OFFERINGS

We hope that this close analysis and interpretation of literacy development within the Freirean-based women's literacy class in rural El Salvador contributes to the discourse on adult education, adult literacy development, and the roles that power, social and political marginalization, and economic and social justice play in our continuing struggle to provide equal access to education and opportunity for all people. We have tried to tell the stories of the Papaturro women and to let those stories teach us all about literacy, freedom, dignity, and equality. As Celia responded when asked for permission to write about her:

> It gives us pleasure, and great meaning, to share our stories. We want the people of the United States, and everywhere, to know of our struggle. We want them to know all that we have been through and all that we are learning now as we study together here in the literacy class. Here, we are discovering our voice, we are learning to express ourselves, we are learning how to read and write so that we can participate in our community, and so that we can no longer be deceived. As we are learning, we hope, too, that others can learn from us. We know that all of us have something to share; all of us can learn from one another. This gives us great pleasure ... and is a comfort.

ENDNOTES

1. Note also Freire's objection to the progressive notion of facilitator as teacher to the extent that the teacher abdicates his or her role in the educative process. (See discussion in chapter 7.)
2. With this study, we were dealing with beginning readers and writers and thus the explicit explanations given by Robin were more focused on speech-print principles and conventions rather than those of more broadly based genre discourse principles and conventions. However, we believe that the principle of explicit explanation for acquisition of new language forms is valid at the discourse level as well.
3. By political, we mean that education always reflects and impacts the social, cultural, and political realities of students' lives.
4. In the light of the success of other Freirean-inspired popular literacy campaigns, such as that among the *campesinos* in El Salvador and described by Lino in chapter 3, this statement may appear to be extreme. We make it based on the data we collected for this study, but we acknowledge that many marginalized people have learned to read and write with teachers who had little or no training in teaching reading and writing. Because no similar research exists on these programs, we can only speculate on their effectiveness. Drawing from insights gleaned from our data, together with information about the historical contexts of such programs, we suggest that students in such programs drew motivation and drive from their

collective quest for social justice. (Many of these programs took place in the context of social upheaval and revolution.) Simultaneously, these students drew from their desire to attain literacy skills, always aware of a possible, inextricable link between literacy acquisition and social transformation. Because of the tremendous energy and motivation generated by both internal and political forces, therefore, we believe that these students were able to overcome the inherent limitations of learning to read and write with teachers who, while equally committed to political and social action, knew relatively little about the learning and teaching of reading and writing.

5. See Barndt (1993) for a description of the Literacy Crusade in Nicaragua during which thousands of volunteer literacy teachers, *brigadistas*, moved into the rural communities and impoverished urban neighborhoods for a period of time to both learn about the lives of the people and to help them learn to read and write.

Appendix A

Researchers' Histories and Stances

V ictoria Purcell-Gates

I came to this study ready to explore Freire's precepts in greater depth. I had just finished writing the book *Other People's Words*, and my analysis had led me independently to Freire, albeit too late for substantive inclusion in that work. One of my final conclusions from that data was that while Jenny and her family were excluded from attainment of full literacy[1] by their own stances and inexperiences with written discourse, equally compelling were the ways in which the mainstream powerholders shut door after door in Jenny's face when she dared to demand a real response to her son's inability to learn to read. I was encountering the overwhelming amount of data that demonstrated this before I had ever seriously read Freire. Thus, I feel that I "discovered" for myself, working as an ethnographer within a culture and seeking the informants' perspective, the oppression that Freire wrote so eloquently about many years ago.

However, I was uncomfortable with the Marxist tone of Freire's discourse: "peasant," "oppressors," "revolutionary change," "liberation." It seemed somewhat irrelevant to the U.S. context with which I was concerned and unnecessarily inflammatory and offputting. At the end of this current project, though, I am much more attuned with this prose. I am now considering myself to a greater degree than before I began this journey a political worker as much as a literacy teacher.

Before I reached this point, I viewed myself, and largely still do, as primarily a teacher of persons—children and adults—who want to learn to read and write. It is true that I now spend much of my time in teacher training and in research into literacy issues, but all of this is driven by the primary intent to teach people to read. Each academic position I had held up to the point of the completion of this study included the directorship and daily involvement in an on-site practicum where real children come to learn to read and write with the help of my university-level students. This kept me grounded, I believe, in the actual world of literacy learning and teaching.

During my full-time teaching days, I taught learning-disabled children, most of whom could not read past a beginning primer level. After several years of this, I moved to teaching "remedial reading" to a wider spectrum of learners, although many of the issues (and some of the students!) were the same. During this time, I found myself intellectually driven to discover both the processes of efficient reading and then the beginnings of disability.

I encountered the early work of the Goodmans (1970, 1986, 1987), and their data on process was fascinating to me. I restructured my classes so that my students were encouraged to read whole texts, self-chosen, while I worked with them on the parts of the process that seemed to present stumbling blocks. This was the beginning of my whole–part–whole approach that drove my teaching in university-based clinics (Purcell-Gates, 1996b). I immediately saw impressive results! My seventh and eighth graders became readers: They liked to read, they believed they were readers, they did read, and they scored significantly higher on standardized tests of reading comprehension, even on subtests of isolated skills that I did not directly teach. When I returned to graduate school, my quest for an explanation of this drove my studies.

My research in graduate school began to focus on the role of linguistic context on rapid, accurate word recognition. Building on the work of cognitive psychologists (Becker, 1982; Biederman, 1972; Caplan, 1972; Meyer, Schvaneveldt, & Ruddy, 1979; Neisser, 1976; Stanovich & West, 1979; and many others), I built a case for the hypothesis that one reason for the positive correlation between level of oral-language development and success at learning to read is the "expectancy effect" on perception. Specifically, I concluded that semantic and syntactic expectations by the reader will facilitate word recognition during the process of learning to read (Gates, 1984). I later modified this to conclude that semantic and syntactic expectations of *written language* will result in this facilitation of word recognition after studying with Wallace Chafe and becoming familiar with his work on oral–written language differences (Chafe & Danielewicz, 1986).

I integrated this emerging picture of efficient reading into my interest in the very beginnings of the learning to read process and situated my doctoral studies within the relatively new field of emergent literacy. I was no longer looking for the beginning of disability. Rather, I decided that before this could be done, I needed to really understand the beginning of ability. Thus, I narrowed my lens to intensively study children who learned to read easily and successfully.

My doctoral research on the linguistic knowledge of written register held by well-read-to kindergartners and second graders embodied this focus. Through this study, I demonstrated that children who experience years of listening to written stories implicitly learn the linguistic differences between oral discourse and written storybook discourse, particularly the literate vocabulary, complex grammatical constructions, and the decontextualized nature of written language (Purcell-Gates, 1988). This knowledge, I postulated, provided an important context for these beginning readers as they took on the task of learning to decode and process print for meaning.

My first research as an employed academic extended this interest in the types of written-language concepts that are brought to school by young children and looked at a different population and at the actual effects on their success at learning to read and write in school. While my well-read-to study did not consider socioeconomic status as a control variable, rather experience with being read to (the participants in that study came from all SES strata), Karin Dahl and I intentionally nested this next study (Purcell-Gates & Dahl, 1991) within the low-SES population of the midwestern city in which we worked. This was done to look for variation within this group, which continuously scored lower nationally on all tests of reading achievement as compared to their economically more advantaged peers.

Following this group of entering kindergartners for 2 years, closely observing focal children learn in classroom contexts, we were able to analyze their progress in light of the emergent literacy concepts we measured at the beginning of the study (assumed to have been acquired in their home–community lives during their preschool years). In addition to our conclusions that children with the Big Picture (knowledge that print "means" linguistically and that it serves many purposes in people's lives) of literacy functions take more intentionally and successfully from instruction, I walked away from this study with a dawning appreciation of literacy as a cultural practice as well as a set of skills.

From this, I went into the nonliterate family study (Purcell-Gates, 1995) where I could focus more closely on the cultural minority group, urban Appalachians, who had scored so significantly lower on all tests of emergent literacy knowledge as well as school-based achievement tests in the previous study. My study of Jenny and her family completed the process of my move to viewing literacy as cultural practice, and I would never again be able to think about literacy development and literacy achievement without nesting it in specific sociocultural contexts.

I am still primarily interested in the teaching–learning of reading and writing. In other words, while I acknowledge the sociocultural, sociopolitical nature of these activities, my primary focus is, taking this into account, how can we best facilitate, insure that, ALL persons who so desire achieve full literacy and the self-determination that can accompany full literacy. From this interest, focus, and knowledge base came the sociopsycholinguistic lens applied to this current study. This is not to say that I do not care about social justice and liberation of peoples from oppressive sociopolitical–cultural systems. I do. But I believe that my talents and my heart lie primarily in the arena of teaching for full literacy. As this is contextualized by sociopolitical factors, then those factors, conditions, and consequences must be accounted for in all instructional decisions and assessments.

My central concern is how to erase the unconscionable gap in literacy achievement between the social classes and to assure that ALL children can achieve to their full potentials as literate beings. I now strongly suspect, though, that the only way to do this is to change the power relationships current in the world, working for social justice and sociopolitical change.

Related to these personal intentions is my commitment to empirical research. I define empirical research as data-based and I do not confine it to experimental research. While I have a healthy respect for experimentation and the scientific method for those research questions that allow for such a design, I also appreciate and employ more qualitative studies that allow for intensive study of intact phenomena. Within the qualitative and ethnographic paradigms, I strive to adhere to rigorous methodology, following prescribed procedures for systematic data collection, analysis informed by all of the data, member and informant checks, and an openness to emerging theories and interpretations never before considered.

I object to qualitative studies that appear to serve only to advance preconceived beliefs and agendas because I believe they ultimately destroy credibility in research and reduce us all to isolated self-serving political communities while the subjects of our research—children and adults working to become literate—continue to flounder and fail. I truly believe that the educational researcher should forever strive to keep ego and personal gain out of the research event and to maintain a strict and clear focus on the purported goal of the inquiry, that is, learners and their struggles to achieve. As such, I acknowledge an ambivalent stance that straddles both positivist and postmodern perspectives. So be it—for now.

I went into this present study with this goal in mind: To gain an in-depth understanding, using a literacy development lens, of a Freirean-based literacy class. I wanted to see if in fact it was effective in helping adults learn to read and write and if so, why. I had read some critiques of the Freirean "method" from literacy professionals in this country, lamenting its focus on phonics and drill. It seemed as if we U.S. literacy researchers had access to only scant and surface descriptions of the pedagogy and on the basis of that it appeared to be in serious conflict with the holistic, process-driven pedagogy enjoying growing popularity in the United States and being increasingly advocated for those low-SES populations for whom Freire wrote, albeit in a different national and cultural context. So when this opportunity presented itself to me, I immediately saw the significance of and need for such a study. In addition, the pragmatic challenges of conducting this study were irresistible!

R obin A. Waterman

Before Vicki and I began the study, my life and work had involved a combination of undergraduate studies in anthropology, educational work with the marginalized poor in the United States as well as Mexico, and an opportunity to study Freire in-depth as I worked toward my Master's at Harvard Graduate School of Education (HGSE). As I was about to begin literacy development work in El Salvador, Vicki proposed the idea of the study. I immediately knew that it would be a valuable opportunity to develop my understanding of Freire and its implications for education, both locally and globally. I agreed to collaborate.

I have felt drawn to the writing and ideas of Paulo Freire ever since I first encountered them in my work in Denver, Colorado. At that time, I was working as the Director of a community-based Family Literacy Program in a multiracial, inner-city neighborhood. Freire was not well known, nor was his thinking sought out among the adult education population in this somewhat conservative Western city. Yet, when I first heard Freirean concepts articulated, they felt potent and compelling to me. I began to seek opportunities to study Freire, as well as ways to incorporate his ideas into the adult literacy component of my program. Although I was only minimally successful at integrating and synthesizing them at the time, I grasped a sense of Freire's main philosophies and values: Oppression and inequality exist, societal systems are some of the root causes of that; developing critical thinking should be a central component to all education; education should involve discussion of social and political issues, with educators looking to generate a "spark" that will bring the students, and the learning process, alive; all learning, and all personal and social transformation, will take place through the vehicle of this dialogue and the passion, heightened consciousness, and interest that it inspires.

Over time, I have continued to identify strongly with the role of educator, with a particular focus on a Freirean understanding of education. I see literacy acquisition and development as much more than learning to read and write. In fact, I believe that there are particular methods of teaching reading and writing that contribute to perpetuating dulled thinking, and ultimately, inertia, oppression, and inequality.

I am committed to a form of education that leads all people to be able to "read and write the word and the world" (Freire & Macedo, 1987), a form of education that inspires critical thinking, allowing all people to recognize that "words are pregnant with the meaning of the world"; words are full of social and political meanings that shape and re-shape the world around them. Students need to be able to "deconstruct," that is, critically analyze, words and the reality they encompass and then "reconstruct" both the meaning of these words and their world around them. In doing this, they come to better understand (read) their world and ultimately transform (write) it as they would like it to be. Literacy instruction, as well as other kinds of adult education, can be a vital way for adults to develop critical thinking skills and necessary political and personal awareness, while at the same time enabling them to acquire the necessary decoding and encoding skills to be able to (simply) read and write.

I have also been increasingly influenced by the Liberation Theology movement and the subsequent Base Christian Communities (BCCs; politically and socially motivated Biblical reflection groups) that have come out of Latin America. Liberation Theology emphasizes a social justice reading of religious faith, based on a critical look at current reality. I have found this faith perspective profoundly compelling, particularly when I was living in Mexico and Central America. My own experiences of Liberation Theology, as well as my exposure to others who have lived lives inspired by this faith perspective, have touched my mind, heart, and soul, engendering tremendous vitality and commitment. For these reasons, I have experienced a renewed desire and capacity to contribute to the struggle toward social transformation.

Within this, Liberation Theology, as it overlaps with Freirean philosophy, has greatly influenced my role as an educator. In the BCCs, for example, the three component steps are *ver* (look, at your reality), *pensar* (think, analyze that reality) and *actuar* (put into action that which is inspired by your reflection and analysis). In a similar manner, Freirean philosophy requires that the entire educational process draw from dialogue and reflection, and that the ultimate focus be practical implications, for example, how the students could act on their newfound insights. Consequently, it became important to me that all forms of education that I participate in have the objective of critical reflection and social transformation, co-created with the students. Moreover, I have developed an understanding of my role as educator as an expression of a larger commitment toward helping co-create a society where all have equal access to resources and awareness and experience of their own dignity.

My undergraduate and graduate studies in anthropology, and my subsequent identification as an anthropologist in my work, have also had a significant influence in my choice to be an educator and my understanding of how to best perform that role. Primarily, anthropology has guided the way that I live and work with people of different cultures. It has guided various frameworks and skills. I always try to be cognizant of aspects of my own culture that I would bring to any relationship, for example, and consciously work to diminish the impact this would have on how I think and behave. I have also focused on developing skills for being critically aware of the distinct characters of the culture of those with whom I'm relating.

For both ethical and professional reasons, therefore, I was always clear that it was vital that I try and be sharp and disciplined about maintaining this kind of critical awareness in all aspects of my work and life among the Salvadoran women who were a part of our study. For example, my own experience of Liberation Theology would have had no relevance or influence if it had not been a central part of the history and cultural–political development of the women of the literacy class. But, because Liberation Theology (in the form of the BCC Biblical reflection groups) played a vital role, my understanding of this aspect of Central American history and culture allowed me to better draw out this aspect of class dialogue and reflection.

Another central aspect of my educational career has been recognizing the value of personal relationship with the students of the program. In my work in Denver, for example, identifying as an anthropologist, a person with particular theological and political convictions, and as a committed educator, I decided that it was central that I live in the same neighborhood where I worked. I recognized that this allowed me greater understanding of, and greater compassion for, my students. And in direct relation to this, being a neighbor allowed for a connection with the students in my program which was based on trust and affirmation. This, I came to see, facilitated many aspects of success in the learning process and the program as a whole. Much of this way of thinking resonates with Freirean philosophy. Freire, for example, speaks of the importance of knowing the subculture of your students. All educators, Freire believes, need to draw from some understanding of the history and culture of their students.

My role as an anthropologist as well as my evolving role as an educator are also influenced by my understanding of socially defined ways of describing the students with whom I work. Early on in my career, I knew that I needed to always have contact with the "base," with those that the program meant to be "serving." I knew enough to know that I was still influenced by a lack of true understanding of the roots of inequality and poverty. (I was very influenced by Malcolm X's statement, "Don't ever trust a white man who can't admit he's a racist." Whether we are "good" people doing "good" things or not, I believe, we absorb racism, elitism, etc. by osmosis in our U.S. culture. We must be vigilant about thinking critically, deconstructing and reconstructing the values and language of the dominant culture.) I knew, therefore, that, in spite of my "good intentions" and "politically correct" attitudes, I had not had sufficient exposure to the real lives of the populations that I was working with such that I had developed the ability to critically analyze many of the dominant culture's attitudes toward those people; for example, why some have money, power, and formal educational degrees, and others don't.

Therefore, in spite of the many administrative tasks that characterized my work of coordinating the Family Literacy program in Denver, I was intentional about having personal interviews with every new student, as well as always working as a teacher. It was at that time that I began to understand why it is that some are marginalized, kept away from even the possibility of developing their skills and their thinking. I recognized the way that one's self-image becomes affected by early experiences of marginalization, failure, or both. I made a commitment to myself to truly look for all of the skills that poor, marginalized people have, skills that are not recognized, named, or valued by mainstream, dominant cultures.

At first, this was a concerted effort, requiring discipline and focus. Now, years later, it is more of an instinct, a natural response, and I can more clearly recognize the labels placed by the dominant culture and the values and potentials that go unrecognized. Regardless, I believe that thinking critically and living intentionally should be a life-long commitment for all. This way of thinking, living, and working has further inspired and guided me to an even greater commitment to share my time and skills with those who are poor and marginalized. I have come to see, for example, my own skills and power as a result of privilege and opportunity. I believe, therefore, that my efforts to help develop the skills of others (who would not otherwise have the chance) is an important step toward creating more equality and more dignity in our world.

My studies in graduate school were an attempt to gain further understanding and skills in my work as an educator. While pursuing my Masters degree in Education at HGSE, I studied literacy theory and practice, with an emphasis on Freire, as well as related studies in Liberation Theology and Anthropology. I studied under Victoria Purcell-Gates and worked as her research assistant on an ethnographic study of low-income families, focusing on use of print in the home.

I learned a great deal from Vicki that was relevant throughout my literacy work in El Salvador. I was particularly influenced by the idea of incorporating into instruction the students' own words, student writing on relevant topics, and exercises involving real-life uses of print.

After graduate school, I began literacy development work in Latin America. I worked in this field for 3 1/2 years, working in Mexico, El Salvador, and Guatemala. The focus of this study is on the 2 years I lived and worked in El Salvador. By the time I arrived in El Salvador, I was fluent in written and spoken Spanish, and I conducted all of my work in Spanish, the language of the people with whom I worked.

In El Salvador, I lived in a small, rural repopulation village. This is a community of 75 families, all of whom have settled back in El Salvador after having fled to Honduran refugee camps during the civil war. These families live in extreme poverty. I lived in standards similar to all of the families, living in a one-room mud house, without electricity or water.

My work consisted of training the literacy teacher who lived and worked in this village, as well as training 14 other teachers who lived in the geographical region, each living in a similar type of repopulation village. I also spent a significant amount of time collaborating with several Salvadoran nongovernmental organizations (NGOs) in the writing of new literacy materials.

As with my previous work in the United States, I found it compelling and vital to be living among those who represent the student population, while simultaneously making connections with others at the national level who write materials and administrate literacy programs. I particularly valued bringing the voice of the base, that is, the students and teachers, to those who are otherwise detached from that reality (yet still making decisions "for" them).

It was clear from the outset that my participation in this research project would be completely congruent with the goals of my work and the values and theoretical frame that I brought to the work. As the research work unfolded, it proved to be more fruitful than I originally imagined. As Freire and many others recommend, it is tremendously valuable to be reflective about our work. Reflecting on aspects of our work allows us to gain insight that can guide our subsequent work. It is most often the case, however, that we do not have the necessary time to be able to do this.

Living alone in an isolated rural village allowed me the time and space for reflection on my life and work as never before. The structure of my data collection facilitated this as well, in that twice a week I recorded my observations of the classes I taught, accompanied by subsequent reflections and recommendations. My reflections gave rise to decisions and behaviors that I would never have discovered had I not taken the time to write out what had happened in the class and make attempts to analyze it. As a result, I found that I was much more prepared and insightful as I conducted my work in El Salvador than I had previously been in the United States.

The research project also proved valuable as it allowed me a sense of hope and meaning when the immediate circumstance seemed discouraging. When observing certain teachers, for example, women with very few literacy skills themselves who were unable to easily understand and appropriate new methodological points, I would often feel discouraged at the multiple levels of poverty within the culture and the related ramifications. In these moments, I consciously shifted my focus from my more immediate teacher-training goals to the long-term goals of the study. In this way, I again found reward and hope in my work, remembering that research can provide guidance toward new thought and behavior, which potentially can allow for long-term change.

I also found particular inspiration and value in one of our stated project goals: "What insights can we glean from this inquiry for literacy programs in the United States working with low-literate adults and children?" As Vicki established in an initial research proposal:

> In the United States, the historical gap in literacy achievement between people from low-SES, mainly minority populations, and those from the mainstream, is a shameful and frustrating fact for education practitioners, researchers and theorists (Kaestle et al., 1991). Despite years of compensatory education funding, years of researching and theorizing, and years of "special" curriculum and programs, children who are born into low-SES homes and communities continue to exhibit significantly lower levels of literacy skills at the end of their years of schooling as compared to children of the middle-SES groups. The price we pay at personal and societal levels for this failure by the schools is incalculable.

Both Vicki and I believe that Freirean philosophy can provide insight into how to better address this gap in literacy achievement. It has become clear that an increasing number of U.S. educators are also looking to Freire for insight. The most significant obstacle is that Freire presents his ideas as a philosophy, and not a methodology, thus requiring that all educators determine appropriate methodological applications according to the particular student population with whom they are working. As stated in our study proposal, the problem has been that many researchers and practitioners who struggle to find effective ways to teach children and adults to read and write have little familiarity with Freire's philosophy or pedagogy. Moreover, most have even less of an understanding of possible ways to apply Freirean philosophy and pedagogy in their own classrooms. Many wonder, for example, how they could incorporate Freire into their daily lesson plans and the curricular expectations of school administrators.

At the same time, many of the critical theorists who advocate such radical educational change have little real knowledge of the complex cognitive and linguistic processes involved in literacy acquisition and how different methods of teaching reading and writing adhere to, violate, or interact with these processes. Thus, the goal of this study is to attempt to inform educational practices in the United States through our description and analysis of my experience of applying Freirean philosophy in a literacy class in rural El Salvador.

ROBIN'S JOB DESCRIPTION AND RESPONSIBILITIES

As is common in most development work, my job description and responsibilities evolved as I began the work, came to know the Salvadoran people and their reality, and conducted on-going evaluation. Initially, several Franciscan nuns, who had been working in the Suchitoto region for almost 8 years, asked that I collaborate in the work of adult literacy. Through their work in the region, and their collaboration with several Salvadoran NGOs, they had evaluated that there was a great need for an adult literacy program.

There was a shortage, however, of people with the skills, time, and/or necessary financial backing to participate. The prevailing poverty, for example, prevented local Salvadorans from being able to take time away from their daily survival tasks. This same poverty was also the reason that many local Salvadorans did not have the necessary training and experience to be able to fulfill the job.

I began, therefore, working alongside one of these nuns, Patricia Farrell, helping to coordinate a literacy program for women. This program was one of two programs initiated by *El Movimiento de Mujeres de Cuscatlán*, a local group of *campesina* women who had met and decided that literacy was one of the primary needs of the *campesina* women in the zone.

Eventually, when Pat Farrell determined that she should focus her time in other areas of work, I took over complete responsibility for the literacy program. At this point, the program involved 14 different rural communities, with 14 *alfabetizadoras* (literacy teachers) and three zonal coordinators.

The *alfabetizadoras* were *campesina* women who lived in the communities where they were teaching the class. The coordinators were also *campesina* women, living in rural communities in the area. The *alfabetizadoras* were responsible for teaching class 2 hours a day, 5 days a week, and were asked to submit, once a month, an attendance list, with comments about the students' thoughts and feelings about the class. The coordinators were responsible for three to five classes in their geographical zone, and were required to visit each of these classes twice a month, writing reports of their observations which they would submit to me at a monthly meeting.

These written reports from the *alfabetizadoras* and the coordinators gave me input regarding such things as the methodology employed by the *alfabetizadoras*, the factors that facilitate or block student learning, the effectiveness of the materials, and the effectiveness of the monthly trainings.

Throughout the month, I, too, made visits to the communities and observed the classes. As this involved the hour-long journey of walking out of Papaturro, and then time spent on the bus, with another 30 to 90 min more of walking to reach the other community, I was not able to visit the literacy classes nearly as often as I wanted. For this reason, the written reports given me by the *alfabetizadoras* and the coordinators were essential.

Once a month, I conducted a training for the *alfabetizadoras* and the coordinators. The prime focus of these trainings was introducing some basic educational philosophy, such as the practice of learning reading and writing by engaging in the process of reading and writing. I stressed the importance of incorporating reading and writing activities that would be meaningful to the students. I also instructed that the *alfabetizadoras* encourage invented spelling as a step toward gaining writing skills. (Otherwise, the *alfabetizadoras* believed that their students could do nothing other than copy until they had "perfect" writing–encoding skills.) Together, we would then discuss these new ideas. Finally, I would ask that they role-play some instructional situations in order to develop their understanding of the new concepts as well as allow me to identify what I needed to explain and teach further. Twice a month, I would also meet with the coordinators in order to evaluate these trainings as well as give one another input about our work. My primary goal going into literacy development work in El Salvador was to "work myself out of a job," that is, to leave behind a program that was completely coordinated by the Salvadoran people. Therefore, a year into the work, I began to train the coordinators to be able to participate in all aspects of the administration of the program: planning and conducting teacher training, conducting on-going evaluation, obtaining materials, and obtaining on-going funding.

It was quickly obvious that the coordinators were tremendously capable, flourishing with just a small bit of guidance when given new responsibilities. When I left El Salvador in May 1996 to take a job in Guatemala, the coordinators took over complete responsibility of the program. When I left Central America in December 1996, returning to the United States, the program was as successful and strong as it had ever been.

Throughout my time in El Salvador, my primary home was in a rural, repopulation community called Papaturro. For many reasons, I also wanted to work on this local level, collaborating in the work of education in Papaturro, and not work exclusively on the regional–national level. It was fortuitous that in September of 1994, the same month that I arrived, the community was initiating two new literacy classes, one for basic literacy and the other for those with (approximately) a second- or third-grade reading level. Initially, these classes were funded by a NGO called *Fundación 16 de Enero* (F-16). Six months later, when the funding from F-16 ran out, I incorporated the classes in Papaturro into the literacy program of *El Movimiento de Mujeres de Cuscatlán*.

Throughout this time I was a volunteer, raising my own financial support–salary. My supporters were all personal friends who responded to and believed in the work I was doing. I was also supported by Capital Heights Presbyterian Church in Denver, Colorado. They provided institutional support by acting as my sponsor, thus receiving and managing all donations.

Because I was an independent volunteer, I had the freedom to choose my organizational affiliations and to create my own job description. Consequently, I chose to collaborate with F-16 as part of my work, helping to teach the classes in Papaturro as a way to provide on-going training to the local *alfabetizadoras*, gain insight into the materials that we were using, and provide input regarding future *alfabetizador* trainings.

I also collaborated with various staff members at F-16, helping to develop new literacy materials for students at a level beyond basic literacy. At that time in El Salvador, there were no materials available for this student population. The students in the second-level group in Papaturro, for example, were using the same materials being used in the beginning literacy class.

I found my coworkers at F-16 very insightful about Freirean theory and content, but with little exposure to some basic methodological practices that were well known in the United States, such as the use of actual student writing (and not simply copying) in teaching writing and the use of invented spelling as a step toward developing encoding skills. Our work together, therefore, felt dynamic and valuable as we seemed to complement one another, ultimately creating materials that were more effective than those currently available.

Throughout my time in El Salvador, I also collaborated with two other NGOs in the work of creating new literacy materials (e.g., student books, facilitator–teacher guidebooks) and designing trainings for coordinators and *alfabetizadores*. As with my previous work in the United States, I found it compelling and vital to be living among those who represent the student population, while simultaneously making connections with others at the national level who write materials and administrate literacy programs. I also appreciated that I was learning valuable educational insights from my Salvadoran peers that could complement and enhance educational theory and practice in the United States.

Appendix B

Methodology

INCEPTION OF STUDY AND DESIGN

This study was not designed a priori; rather, the idea for conducting the study came in response to an existing situation that appeared to lend itself to such a study. Thus, many of our early research decisions were bounded by preexisting conditions.

Robin dropped into Vicki's office for a quick visit during the summer of 1994. She was about to leave for El Salvador where she had agreed to accept the position of Director of a regional literacy program entitled *El Movimiento de Mujeres de Cuscatlán* (The Cuscatlán Women's Movement), in a rural zone north of San Salvador. We discussed her plans for the position and she explained that the materials and methodology currently used in teacher training and individual classes were supposedly heavily influenced by Freirean thought.

It was during the course of this discussion, and our mutual delight that she would have the chance to actually work on the inside of a Freirean-based program, that the inspiration for a close study of the program came to Vicki. She advanced this notion to Robin who, after some reflection, agreed to its feasibility and certainly to its significance for U.S. populations. She was leaving the country in a few days so we quickly settled on some research procedures, tentative plans for communication, and the fact that Vicki's immediate role would be to obtain some funding to purchase a laptop computer for Robin to record field notes on.

Then, after several excited good-bye/good-luck hugs, Robin was off! Vicki did not see her again for 13 months and it was 8 months before they actually spoke directly to each other via phone. Within a month, however, Vicki had received a thick pile of field notes from Robin, written on an old typewriter, single-spaced to save paper, and sent via a friend–courier who was traveling from El Salvador to the United States. The study had begun.

It should be noted that Robin and Vicki began with a solid year of shared research experience and procedures behind them. Two particular experiences contributed to this. First, during Robin's year at Harvard, she had worked under Vicki's supervision in the Harvard Literacy Lab, tutoring a student as part of a class requirement. One of the procedures she learned in that class was that of writing up "Session Reports" following each meeting with her student. These reports had two main sections: (1) report of what happened during the session, including activities, materials used, teacher and student behaviors; (2) reflections on what happened during the session, including on-going diagnosis of student strengths and weaknesses, meanings of behaviors in light of future instruction, insights into her own teaching, and so on. Samples of student's work were attached.

Robin also gained research experience with Vicki by working as one of six research assistants in a study of literacy practices in the homes of 20 low-SES families. The data collection required for this study involved noting down all literacy activities during participant–observation in the homes, while keeping researcher reactions, comments, questions separate in another section of the field notes. The field notes also included contexts, participants, and samples of reading and writing that occurred in the home.

Both of these activities resulted in Robin's feeling of ease and familiarity with the data collection procedures she and Vicki had agreed on for the El Salvador study. They had worked together in like circumstances and knew what to expect from each other. Thus, their seemingly hasty research decisions before Robin left for Central America were not as poorly defined as one might think for others with such little preparation time.

DATA COLLECTION

We followed the same procedures for data collection throughout the bulk of the study period, which spanned 20 months, from September, 1994 through May, 1996. For the first 12 months, Robin made detailed notes, each week, of the events of two of the daily literacy classes, classes she

was teaching/co-teaching in the community of Papaturro. These field notes consisted of the following sections: (a) Contextualizing information, (b) Attendance, (c) Observations, (d) Reflections of the events of the class, and (e) Samples of work done. A shortened version of a typical daily field note follows to give a flavor of each of these sections:
From Field Note October, 27, 1994

Contextualizing Information: Once again, the people of Papaturro left to go and harvest the coffee today. They arose at 5:00 a.m. and began their daily work of milking the cows and making the tortillas. At 7:00 a.m., they left to begin the harvesting, and returned between 3:30 and 4:00 p.m. At this time, they began the job of cleaning out the pile of berries (which contain the coffee beans), picking out the green berries and all the twigs. I passed a few women as I was walking into the community, and they said that they had to go back to their homes (which are located 1/4 to ½ mile from the school) in order to prepare dinner—meaning that they had to grind the corn, start a fire, and make and cook the tortillas and beans. They said that they would come to the class, but never did show up.

Attendance: Class started late again because of the coffee harvesting, but we had a surprisingly good attendance: Celia, Esperanza, Domingo, Mariano, Simona, Elsa, Deonicia, Sonia, Carmela.

Observations: I started the class with some review. I wrote the words *comunidad* and *chilate* on the board, along with the accompanying syllables that were taught: *ma, me, mo, mi, mu; na, ne, no, ni, nu; cha, che, cho, chi, chu....* I then began the next theme in the book, *chilate*, which Sylvia (the *alfabetizadora* [literacy teacher] apprenticing under Robin for this class) had introduced the day before. I presented the new topic–theme with a code as I always do. I put up a large drawing of a pot cooking over a wood fire. Beneath the pot was written the word *chilate*. I asked the students what they saw in the drawing, and they began by saying, " a pot." I probed, asking what might be in the pot, and they answered "coffee" and others said, "milk." I probed further, and some eventually said *"atole"* and *"chilate."*.... I was able to create conversation but it did not strike me as one that inspired people.... therefore I diverged from the suggested questions, and began to speak to them about traditions from the perspective of how they felt when they were in a *guinda* (the word Salvadorans use to describe the time period that they lived in the mountains during the war, constantly fleeing the Salvadoran army).... I had to cut the conversation a bit short because we had started late, and I knew that the sun would go down such that we would not be able to see after 5:30.... At this point I asked that someone give me a sentence that captured some of what we were saying, and Simona gave me *"Yo me sentía triste y desesperada cuando no tenía tortillas y frijoles."* ("I felt sad and desperate when I did not have tortillas and beans.") I wrote it on the board. We read it together, and then I had the students read it alone (with some quiet help from me) a second time, and then they read it completely alone a third time. At this point, I asked that they copy it in their notebooks.... Sylvia and I began to go around and observe their work. With Simona, for example, Sylvia observed that she was unable to correctly make the letter *s*, and the letters *r* and *e*, so Sylvia asked that she try and practice making the letter *s*.... I wrote out a few examples and took her hand in mine and made the letter with her a few times ... I instructed that the rest of the students continue to try and write more of their own thoughts re: how they felt during this time of the *guinda* and in Honduras (in the refugee camps). Once again, everyone attempted this, and did not stop until I had to ask them to (in order to proceed to the next activity). Some even continued to write after I had moved on to the next activity.... Because people did not use each of the syllables in the words they wrote (another activity aimed at hearing/writing the sounds), I erased their words, and wrote out five different words.... At this point, many said that they could not see very well. With a few of these students, I wrote out the words for them in their notebooks, and then we stood where the light was better. I held the book close to their faces and had them read it aloud....

Reflections: In the experience I've had here in Papaturro, as well as the other communities, coffee and milk are the most common drinks. Because of the peace accords, many people have had access to loans that were specifically aimed at buying cows, so many people now have access to milk, and it is customary to cook it in a large pot with a bit of cinnamon and sugar and drink it in the morning (which is the time that they milk the cows). Most communities also grow coffee, and even if they don't, it is easily accessible. Coffee, therefore, is also a very common drink, with breakfast and again with the evening meal. Because of this observation–understanding of their reality, and because of the way the students interpreted the "code," I was not sure how much *chilate* is a part of the daily lives of the students. (*Chilate* is a warm drink made of corn.) Therefore, at this point early in our discussion, I began to ask them if they drank *chilate* very often, and I began to ask them to tell me more of what it is. They essentially told me that it is a corn drink, and they said that it is common in some areas. *Atole* is a similar type of drink, more common in Papaturro (I have never seen *chilate* here, only *atole*) yet it is made of cinnamon and milk and flour. They were somewhat animated as they tried to explain to me what it was, and I interpret this as characteristic of the students' desire to educate me, to give something back to me, and in general to please me (as it was obvious that I did not know much about *chilate*). I encouraged this discussion and reinforced for them the Freirean idea that "no one knows nothing, and no one knows everything; we are all learning together," something I have said to them ever since the first class. But it is also my assessment that *chilate* is not a very common drink, at least not nearly as common as coffee and milk.... And thus, I feel it was a good decision to divert from the theme of *chilate* and talk about something that is much more loaded with historical and present significance—the concept of daily rituals–customs and the time in their lives when the students were refugees on the run and had to live without these. (I believe that, in part, I was guided toward the insight to use this perspective by my own experience of being without my daily rituals and my efforts to recreate some here in my life in Papaturro.)

In addition to these observational field notes, Robin also wrote personal letters to Vicki in which she commented on the process of conducting the research, provided additional contextualizing details about her life in El Salvador, her assignment, the life of the country in general (e.g., life in the *campo* [countryside] or the general climate in the country of El Salvador), and some personal news. Parts of these letters were also treated as data. Further, Robin regularly (about once a month) wrote a general letter to the group of people and organizations who were contributing money to support her work. In these letters, Robin described the rural area where she lived and worked, various aspects of her own experience of living out in the rural area, the people she was coming to know, and the current political and personal issues, particularly those that most affect the *campesino* people. These letters also became data. Robin also sent Vicki some xeroxed copies of the literacy materials she was using, which were also added to the data. As the study progressed, Robin obtained demographic data, census data, as well as other documents, such as the recently signed Peace Accords, filling out our contextual knowledge of the literacy class and its participants. Another source of data was the e-mail communication between us in which we reflected on the data, refocused the observations, and discussed procedural details. These were printed and added to our data. We initially established e-mail communication in March of 1995. Before this, we communicated by mail.

According to the agreed on procedures, Vicki read and reflected on all material sent by Robin. She then wrote out reflective memos that she sent back to Robin, including specific questions for her to either answer or investigate, and suggestions for focusing–refocusing the research over time. For example, early on Vicki suggested, and Robin agreed, that we focus the research on the Papaturro class since this was where Robin was spending the bulk of her time, both in the literacy class and as a community resident.

While she was responsible for 14 classes in other communities in the region, her actual access to them was limited by her lack of transportation, as each of the other communities was equally isolated, and she had no means of transportation other than walking. Robin was also limited because of her other administrative responsibilities in the program: (a) planning and conducting teacher training in a centrally located small town in the zone, and (b) working with several different NGOs, as well as the Salvadoran Ministry of Education, on writing adult literacy materials (a job which took her into the capital city, San Salvador, every 2 weeks).

We decided, therefore, for many reasons, that our research questions could best be answered by close observation of the Papaturro class and community. At another time, Robin made a note of all uses of print in the community in general, and in the lives of the women in the class, in response to Vicki's sense from her field notes that there were few uses for print in the community, something that theoretically would significantly affect the outcomes of any literacy class.

Robin recorded several interviews with the women in the literacy class. Initially, she focused her interviews around their motivations for learning to read and write. At another time, she structured the interviews in order to obtain what we termed "literacy histories," each woman's personal experience with schooling from childhood up to the present. Robin transcribed the first set of interviews and included the data in her field notes. Tapes of the literacy history interviews were sent to Vicki for transcription. Two Spanish-speaking graduate students, working with Vicki as research assistants, transcribed and translated these in field-note form for coding.

After 6 months of observational descriptions of the literacy class, we agreed to focus more exclusively on the classwork–behaviors of specific individuals during the class, assuming that the overall procedures of the class would continue as in the past. Thus, the field notes changed somewhat because of this refocus, with Robin noting when there were procedural changes or other "new" events that Vicki could not assume from the pattern that had been established by the field notes during the first 6 months.

We discussed (via our memos) which individuals to focus on; Vicki initially thought of choosing types, such as two high progress and two low progress. Robin objected to this as she felt it did not reflect the reality of the class; she reported that all of the students who attended regularly were progressing well, that those who were not progressing as well had been affected by their low attendance, which was itself a result of such things as attending to a sick family member, childcare needs, or having to work in the fields. Consequently, we ended up collecting close observational data on the eight women who regularly attended the class, adopting more subtle ways of distinguishing between their literacy progress–behaviors.

September of 1995, approximately 1 year into the study, Vicki traveled to El Salvador for a site visit. We spent several days in San Salvador where Vicki accompanied Robin to the Ministry of Education where Robin picked up materials and met with some of the regional staff with whom she occasionally collaborated. While in the capital, we also spent about 10 hours total discussing our evolving interpretations of the data and some evolving theories. During this time, Vicki questioned Robin directly about details and background information that had confused her as she had read and coded the field notes. Vicki recorded on audiotape a 3-hour question-answer/discussion session between them that she later transcribed and treated as data. Other observational and informational data Vicki recorded in field-note form that she later prepared for coding.

We also spent one half day in Suchitoto, the town where Robin held teacher trainings.

The rest of Vicki's visit was spent in Papaturro, travelling via bus and on foot, carrying all of our belongings on our backs, just as Robin did regularly. In Papaturro, Vicki observed the literacy class for 2 days, noting all events in field-note form. Vicki also met the members of the literacy class, eating meals with several of them, and, with Robin translating, conversing with them at odd moments about their lives and their responses to learning to read and write in the class.

One memorable night, with the small flame from a *candil* illuminating our faces, Vicki sat with Robin in her small, one-room hut recording the voices of Celia, José, and Lino as they took turns individually relating their stories of what life was like for the *campesinos* before the civil war, the beginnings of protest and nonviolent demands for social justice, the ways in which the Jesuit-driven theology of liberation contextualized this movement and the accompanying push for literacy, and the horrors of the armed combat that soon followed. Vicki later transcribed this discussion and added the transcript to the data.

Another day, Vicki observed Robin observe a new literacy class that had just begun. This class consisted of beginning literacy students, as the students of the other class had reached a more advanced level. Irma, the *alfabetizadora* of this class, was a young woman from Papaturro, who worked as a teacher of kindergarten children and had received a small amount of training in adult literacy methodology. Before the class, Robin spent time explaining the class materials with Irma, helping her to prepare her lesson plan for the day. During this class, Robin observed Irma teach for about 10 min, and then stepped in and conducted the class so that the Irma could observe certain instructional principles. Thus, Vicki was able to observe first hand Robin's method with very beginning students, something she had only previously read about from her field notes.

Vicki also accompanied Robin during her other activities in the community, such as visiting individuals in order to encourage their participation in the class, discussing problems and solutions with one of the zonal coordinators of the *Movimiento de Mujeres program* (who happened to also live in Papaturro), and aiding other literacy teachers in the community as they prepared their lesson plans. She met several members of the *directiva*, the local governing body of the community. One day, she also accompanied a stream of people from Papaturro, mainly women and children, as they walked to the next community to participate in a Catholic Mass being held by a visiting priest.

Vicki observed and participated in Robin's activities with the children in the community, which included gathering them inside her hut one evening to listen to her read from one of the children's books that a number of people had sent to her from the United States. Another late afternoon, Robin made popcorn for the children and then let them look at, and read if they were able, her entire collection of children's books. During this session, several of the older children sat with Vicki and read to her from several picture books, attempting to teach her Spanish. They were very patient and encouraging, and she made some progress!

Finally, Vicki made continuous notes of community life: the homes, the clinic (where she slept at night), the two children's schools, the small store, the latrines, the water supply, and the daily routines of the people.

Following this visit, we agreed that Robin's efforts should mainly focus on documenting the following: (a) teacher trainings; (b) observations of other classes, from the *Movimiento de Mujeres* program; (c) collection of writing notebooks from other communities as well as from Papaturro, as a way to show progress over time; (d) collection of census data concerning literacy in the country and specific data concerning the rural communities; (e) background on the influence of Freire on the different literacy campaigns in the country. Robin continued to note the progress of the women in the Papaturro class as well, although not as frequently as before. All data collection ended in May of 1996 when Robin left for Guatemala to begin a new job of training development workers who would later work in El Salvador.

WRITING UP OF FIELD NOTES

Robin initially noted her observations in scribbled notes to herself during class or while observing others. As noted previously, she also audiotaped periodic interviews. She transformed these notes into field-note form later in the day, using either a manual typewriter or a laptop computer. These field notes took the form described above, with real attempts made to place her interpretations, evolving insights, and reflections in a section apart from her observations of student behavior.

Once or twice at the start of the study, before Vicki had sent her a laptop with long-lasting batteries, Robin sent handwritten field notes. These, however, were "cooked" in that she had constructed them into the agreed-on form from notes taken earlier.

ANALYSIS

Preparation of Field Notes for Coding

Immediately after receiving the field notes, letters, and e-mail messages from Robin, Vicki transformed them into a form amenable to coding. This consisted of a page, the top one third of which was left blank for indexing and for noting (a) place and (b) date. The index on each page captured the contents of the field notes on that page, for example, on page 1 of FN 10/23/94: "coffee harvesting" "literacy class." The text of the field notes was triple spaced and the right margin was 3 inches wide for coding and analytic notes. The transcriptions of interviews were similarly transformed for coding.

Coding

Vicki began first-level coding of the field notes in January, 1994. These codes categorized the data as it reflected sociocultural context and literacy learning factors. She also made every attempt to sort out and flag Robin's personal theories of practice, stance, and influence on the data being reported. Of course, her notes on the Papaturro literacy class were in actuality notes on herself as the teacher and creator–director of the activities, including the topics of the discussions.

One of our early research decisions was to accept the fact that the study could not be one of a Freirean "method" but a close analysis of ourselves, in particular of Robin, as we instantiated a Freirean-based literacy class in this particular context. Thus, from early on in the study we were always quite conscious of the complexity of reporting on oneself and tried to handle this as best we could through the field-note form, the coding, and the analysis. First of all, Robin separated what happened in the class from her reflections and thoughts on what it meant or what she thought about it. Secondly, Vicki used codes to mark instances of Robin's implicit and conscious theories and beliefs about instruction, learners, Freire, and so on throughout the field notes. These beliefs and theories could be identified in both the "what happened" section of the field notes and in the "reflections" section.

Examples of first-level codes include ASN (Robin's assignment and job duties); CHL (children's literacy); FEL (learners' feelings about illiteracy); FRE (Freirean theory); LVN (literacy environment); MOT (motivations of learners for learning to read and write); and PLC (Papaturro literacy class). Several of these codes had subcodes. For example, the Motivation code had among its subcodes BIB (Biblical reading); COM (communication with other people); and SFE (self esteem). The Papaturro Literacy Class had the most subcodes as it was the center and focus of the study. These included the codes ATN (attendance); EXP (explicit explanation by teacher); RDG (reading); SWO (sight words); and WRT (writing) with a subcode of CPY (copying). In total, we had 140 first-level codes and subcodes by the end of the study. In addition, we had 21 codes for individuals, including Robin.

Codes Management.   A research assistant began inputting these first-level codes into a data management system, Excel, in September, 1995. Entered into the program were (a) code, (b) date, and (c) field-note page number. This served as a form of indexing that was easy to use as analysis and writing proceeded.

Coding Insights Record.   As Vicki coded the field notes, she kept a record of her evolving reactions to the data, questions she had to ask Robin, inferences she was making of the data, and emerging themes as they occurred to her. She noted these in a separate notebook, each with the date and page number of the field note she was coding as the thought occurred to her.

Second-Level Coding.   In October of 1995, Vicki reviewed her Coding Insights, reread all of the coded data, and arrived at seven macrocategories that seemed to capture all of the data and data codes and that remained relevant to the focus of the study as we were analyzing/interpreting it as it proceeded. She assigned these second-level codes (a) WPW (whole-part-whole basic structure of the literacy teaching in the class and integral to Robin's theory of practice that she tried to teach to the literacy teachers in the other communities); (b) SIG (quality of significance/ authenticity to the texts that the women in the Papaturro literacy class read, mainly through their own requests); (c) LAN (the ways in which considerations of the language of the people played out in Robin's teaching decisions, the learners' writings and spellings, and their ability to read other texts than their own); (d) PED (issues related to the imbalance of knowledge/experience held by educational personnel in the country. Their knowledge of sociopolitical factors integral to education and of Freirean beliefs and precepts far outweighed their knowledge of effective pedagogical practices for the teaching of literacy to this population); (e) CON (daily life conditions for the study participants and the surrounding rural communities); (f) SPH (sociopolitical history and present sociopolitical context); and (g) STU (study methodology and Robin's theories of practice and of sociopolitical change as they impacted on the study).

Analysis

While analysis began with the first reading and response to Robin about her field notes, and continued as coding proceeded, Robin and Vicki first began to focus on final themes when we worked together in the fall of the second year. In November of 1995, Robin returned to the United States for a month. During this time, we worked together on analysis for 2 weeks. Vicki shared her coding and Robin took time to review all of the coded field notes to see if she agreed with the first-level codes and to see if she could think of any other codes that could mark relevant data. Robin agreed with these first-level codes, and did not think that any had been left out.

Secondly, we discussed each second-level code, elaborating on them, as well as sharpening our definitions of them. Robin then went through all of the field notes to see if she agreed with these second-level codes and to see if she felt any were left out. She agreed with all of these second-level codes.

Vicki also gave Robin a copy of her Coding Insights and she went over each one, referring to the field notes noted. She then responded to each one in writing. We discussed her responses, added new insights to the original record, and created an expanded record of insights on, and responses to, the data. We then individually wrote reflective memos on each of the second-level codes, referring to the field notes as needed. Robin returned to El Salvador before she finished this but completed the memos on site and e-mailed her responses. Vicki also shared hers with Robin.

This began a 6-month series of correspondences wherein we discussed, via e-mail, our evolving interpretations of the data and identified and refined the relevant themes as they related to our purpose and goal for the study, which was to describe a Freirean-based literacy program through a literacy development lens, with insights for U.S. populations. Soon after Robin returned to El Salvador, Vicki had clean copies of all of the prepared field notes and all of the transcribed–translated interviews sent to her for her use in the ensuing analysis.

The months of January through May, 1996 were devoted to a stream of e-mail messages between us as we both continued to reflect on the data we held. At this time, we had arrived at commonly held interpretations of the meanings of the findings and had tentatively agreed on which aspects of the study held significance for populations outside of the immediate context of El Salvador. We continually held the U.S. adult education audience in our focus, and at times extended this to both the U.S. K–12 education audience and to a world-wide educational audience, particularly that concerned with educating the world's marginalized populations.

During this time, Robin began a series of memos in which she speculated on the Freirean connection to the events of her teaching and observations. In service of this, she reviewed Freirean writings as well as the field notes. She then would write her reflections on this connection and send them to Vicki.

Additionally during this time period, a Harvard-based research assistant began the task of combing the field notes and interview transcripts to construct literacy histories of the women we had identified as key players in the story we had to tell. All data related to schooling, including contextual information, were synthesized into a narrative relating each woman's experiences with learning to read and write. This included the literacy development patterns observed in the classes taught by Robin as well as samples of their work, including their performances on the examinations administered during the course of the study.

In the summer of 1996, Vicki conducted a final review of the reflective memos sent during the January-to-May period and constructed a tentative final-level of themes. She sent these to Robin in the form of a draft outline of the book. She responded to these with suggestions and further insights.

THE WRITING PROCESS

Vicki began drafting chapters of the book while Robin was in Guatemala. We continued to communicate via e-mail and Vicki sent her chapters as she finished them. In December, 1996, Robin returned permanently to the United States. She spent 2 months in Cambridge where we worked together on revisions and elaborations on the chapters, as well as outlining those not yet written. When Robin left for Denver in March, we had settled on a division of writing responsibilities: Robin would do the first draft of the chapters dealing with the establishment of the class (chapter 4) and the examples of the oral and written dialogues engaged in by the students (chapter 5) and send it to Vicki for revisions; Vicki would do the first draft of the remaining chapters and send them to Robin to fill in blanks, add text, and make revisions. During the months that followed, we communicated through e-mail, over the phone, and on the "traveling disk," which went back and forth between us with drafts and subsequent revisions. We also met for face-to-face discussions at the 1997 National Reading Conference in Phoenix, Arizona, where we presented a piece of the study.

Although distracted by competing responsibilities, we both committed to a final "push" to finish the manuscript over the summer of 1998. During this time, the final chapters were written and revised, the footnotes inserted, and the "applications to adult education" sections written for the separate chapters. The first draft of the manuscript was sent to potential publishers in September, 1998, 2 years after Robin had left El Salvador.

ENDNOTE

1. By "full literacy" I mean the ability to read and write for the purposes and to the degree to which individuals feel the need given their individual life contexts and aspirations. This is a sociocultural definition and, thus, one that is relative to individuals within their sociocultural contexts. This definition precludes one standard or measure for what counts as full or fully literate.

References

Adams, J. (1971). Our Appalachian children face special problems in school. Reprint from the *Cincinnati Post* and *Times Star* on file at UAC Library, Cincinnati, OH: Urban Appalachian Council.

Anorve, R. (1989). Community-based literacy educators: Experts and catalysts for change. In A. Fingeret & P. Jurmo (Eds.), *Participatory literacy education: New directions for continuing education* (Vol. 42, pp. 35–42). San Francisco: Jossey-Bass.

Archer, D., & Costello, P. (1990). *Literacy and power: The Latin American battleground.* London: Earthscan Publications.

Auerbach, E. (1995). Deconstructing the discourse of strengths in family literacy. *Journal of Reading Behavior, 27,* 643–660.

Auerbach, E. (1996). *From the community to the community: A guidebook for participatory literacy training.* Mahwah, NJ: Lawrence Erlbaum Associates.

Baker, L., Afflerbach, P., & Reinking, D. (Eds.). (1996). *Developing engaged readers in school and home communities.* Mahwah, NJ: Lawrence Erlbaum Associates.

Barndt, D. (1993). *To change this house: Popular education under the Sandinistas.* Toronto, Canada: Between the Lines; Jesuit Centre for Social Faith and Justice; Doris Marshall Institute.

Bear, D. R., Ferry, C., & Templeton, S. (1987). *Project TACL: A team approach to community literacy, needs assessment.* (ED 291 057).

Becker, C. (1982). The development of semantic context effects: Two processes or two strategies. *Reading Research Quarterly, 17,* 482–502.

Beder, H., & Quigley, B. A. (1990). Beyond the classroom. *Adult Learning, 1,* 19–21, 30.

Benjamin, R., Graham, M., & Phillips, M. (1978). Color them children. Series appearing in the *Cincinnati Post,* beginning July 22. Cincinnati, OH.

Berryman, P. (1987). *Liberation theology.* New York: Pantheon Books.

La Biblia Latinoamerica (1972). Madrid, Spain: Editorial Jerbo Divino.

Biederman, I. (1972). Perceiving real world scenes. *Science, 177,* 77–80.

Boff, L., & Boff, C. (1987). *Introducing liberation theology.* Maryknoll, NY: Orbis Books.

Borman, K. M. (1991). *Overwhelmed in Cincinnati: Urban Appalachian children and youth.* Report to U.S. Department of Education.

Borman, K. M., & P. J. Obermiller (Eds.). (1993). *From mountain to metropolis: Appalachian migrants in the American city.* New York: Greenwood Press.

Briton, D. (1996). *The modern practice of adult education: A post-modern critique.* Albany, NY: State University of New York Press.

Brizius, J., & Foster, S. (1987). *Enhancing adult literacy: A policy guide.* Washington, D.C.: The Council of State Policy and Planning Agencies.

Caplan, D. (1972). Clause boundaries and recognition latencies for words in sentences. *Perception and Psychophysics, 12,* 73–76.

Cartilla de Alfabetización para Neolecturas [Literacy Workbook for New Readers]. (1995). San Salvador, El Salvador: Las Dignas, 122.

Chafe, W., and Danielewicz, J. (1986). Properties of spoken and written language. In R. Horowitz & S. J. Samuels (Eds.), *Comprehending oral and written language.* New York: Academic Press.

Clay, M. M. (1975). *What did I write?* Auckland, New Zealand: Heinemann.

Clay, M. M. (1991). *Becoming literate: The construction of inner control.* Auckland, New Zealand: Heinemann.

Cunningham, P. (1991). *Phonics they use: Words for reading and writing.* New York: HarperCollins.

Danner, M. (1994). *The massacre at El Mozote.* New York: Vintage Books.

Darkenwal, G. G., & Merriam, S. B. (1982). *Adult education: Foundations of practice.* New York: Harper & Row.

Davis, D. M. (1994). Adult literacy programs: Toward equality or maintaining the status quo? In M. C. Radencich (Ed.), *Adult literacy: A compendium of articles from the Journal of Reading* (pp. 17–21). Newark, DE: International Reading Association.

Deci, E. L. (1992). The relation of interest to the motivation of behavior: A self-determination theory perspective. In K. A. Renninger, S. Hidi, & A. Drapp (Eds.), *The role of interest in learning and development* (pp. 43–70). Hillsdale, NJ: Lawrence Erlbaum Associates.

Delpit, L. D. (1990). Language diversity and learning. In S. Hynds & D. L Rubin (Eds.), *Perspectives on talk and learning* (pp. 247–266). Urbana, IL: National Council of Teachers of English.

Draft Summit Document: Version 3(A). (Dec, 1997). Washington, DC: The Division of Adult Education and Literacy; The National Institute for Literacy; and The National Center for the Study of Adult Learning and Literacy.

Dweck, C. S., & Leggett, E. L. (1988). A social-cognitive approach to motivation and personality. *Psychological Review, 95,* 256–273.

Dyson, A. (1982). Reading, writing, and language: Young children solving the written language puzzle. *Language Arts, 59,* 204–214.

Ellsworth, E. (1989). Why doesn't this feel empowering? Working through the repressive myths of critical pedagogy. *Harvard Educational Review, 59,* 297–394.

Fingeret, A. (1983). Social network: A new perspective on independence and illiterate adults. *Adult Education Quarterly, 33,* 133–146.

Fingeret, A. (1984). *Adult literacy education: Current and future directions* (Contract No. 400- 81-0035). Columbus, OH: National Center Publications, National Center for Research in Vocational Education. (ED 246 308).

Fingeret, A. (1989). The social and historical context of participatory literacy education. In A. Fingeret & P. Jurmo (Eds.), *Participatory literacy education: New directions for continuing education* (Vol. 42, pp. 5–16). San Francisco: Jossey-Bass.

Finlay, A., & Harrison, C. (1994). Measuring "success" in reading in adult basic education: A United Kingdom perspective. In M.C. Radencich (Ed.), *Adult literacy: A compendium of articles from the Journal of Reading* (pp. 61–69). Newark, DE: International Reading Association.

Flecha, R. (1997). *Compartiendo palabras: El aprendizaje e la personal adultas a traves del diálogo.* Barcelona: Paidos.

Freire, P. (1985). *The politics of education.* South Hadley, MA: Bergin & Garvey.

Freire, P. (1993). *Pedagogy of the oppressed* (New Rev. 20th-Anniversary Ed.). New York: Continuum.

Freire, P., & Macedo, D. (1987). *Literacy: Reading the word and the world.* Westport, CN: Begin & Garvey.

Freire, P., & Macedo, D. (1995). A dialogue: Culture, language, and race. *Harvard Education Review, 65,* 377–402.

Gates, V. (1984) *The expectancy effect of a language schema on word recognition: Advantages for beginning readers.* Unpublished Position Paper. Berkeley: University of California at Berkeley.

Gee, J. P. (1989). Literacy, discourse, and linguistics: Introduction. *Journal of Education, 171,* 5–17.

Giroux, H. (1985). Introduction. In P. Freire (Ed.), *The politics of education* (pp. xi–xxv). South Hadley, MA: Bergin & Garvey.

Goetz, J. P., & LeCompte, M. D. (1984). *Ethnography and Qualitative Design in Educational Research.* San Diego, CA: Academic Press.

Goodman, K. (1994). Reading: Transactional-sociolinguistic model. In R. B. Ruddell, M. R. Ruddell & H. Singer (Eds.), *Theoretical models and processes of reading.* 4th Ed. (pp. 1093–1130). Newark, DE: International Reading Association.

Goodman, K. (1986). *What's whole in whole language.* Portsmouth, NH: Heinemann.

Goodman, K., Smith, E. B., Meredith, R., & Goodman, Y. M. (1987). *Language and thinking in school.* New York: Richard C. Owen.

Goodman, Y. M. (1978). Kidwatching: An alternative to testing. *National Elementary Principals, 57,* 41–45.

Gutierrez, G. (1985). *We drink from our own wells.* Maryknoll, NY: Orbis Books.

Gutierrez, G. (1994). Epilogue: Destination Unknown. In P. Casaldaliga & J. M. Vigil (Eds.), *Political holiness* (pp. 208–218). Maryknoll, NY: Orbis Books.

Guthrie, J. T., Schafer, W. D., Wang, Y. Y., & Afflerbach, P. (1995). Relationships of instruction to amount of reading: An exploration of social, cognitive, and instructional connections. *Reading Research Quarterly, 30,* 8–25.

Guthrie, J., & Wigfield, A. (1997). Reading engagement: A rationale for theory and teaching. In J. Guthrie & A. Wigfield (Eds.), *Reading engagement: Motivating readers through integrated instruction* (pp. 14–33). Newark, DE: International Reading Association.

Harste, J., Woodward, V., & Burke, C. (1984). *Language stories and literacy lessons.* Exeter, NH: Heinemann.

Hammond, J. L. (1998). *Fighting to learn: Popular education and guerrilla war in El Salvador.* New Brunswick, NJ: Rutgers University Press.

Heaney, T. (1989). Freirean literacy in North America: The community-based education movement. *Thresholds in Education. Adult Literacy: Global Perspectives, 15,* 21–26.

Heath, S. B. (1983). *Ways with words.* New York: Cambridge University Press.

Heckelman, R. G. (1966). Using the neurological impress remedial technique. *Academic Therapy Quarterly, 1,* 235–239.

Heckelman, R. G. (1969). Neurological impress method of remedial reading instruction. *Academic Therapy Quarterly, 4,* 277–282.

Heller, C. E. (1997). *Until we are strong together: Women writers in the tenderloin.* New York: Teachers College Press.

Horowitz, R., & Samuels, S. J. (Eds.) (1986). *Comprehending oral and written language.* New York: Academic Press.

Hunter, C. S. J., & Harman, D. (1979). *Adult literacy in the United States.* New York: McGraw-Hill.

Isley, P. (1985a). *Adult literacy volunteers: Issues and ideas* (Information Series No. 301). Columbus, OH: ERIC Clearinghouse on Adult, Career and Vocational Education. (ED 260 303).

Isley, P. (1985b). Including educationally deprived adults in the planning of literacy programs. In S. H. Rosenblum (Ed.), *Involving adults in the educational process: New directions for continuing education* (Vol. 26, pp. 33–42). San Francisco: Jossey-Bass.

Isley, P. (1989). The language of literacy. *Thresholds in Education. Adult Literacy: Global Perspectives, 15,* 6–10.

Jenkins, C. (1995). Reflective practice: Blurring the boundaries between child and adult literacy. *Adult Basic Education, 5,* 63–81.

Johnston, P. (1997). Standardized tests in family literacy programs. In D. Taylor (Eds.), *Many families, many literacies: A declaration of international principles* (pp. 142–148). Portsmouth, NH: Heinemann.

Jurmo, P. (1989). The case for participatory literacy education. In A. Fingeret & P. Jurmo (Eds.), *Participatory literacy education: New directions for continuing education* (Vol. 42, pp. 17–28). San Francisco: Jossey-Bass.

Kaestle, C. F., Damon-Moore, H., Stedman, L. C., Tinsley, K., & Trollinger, Jr., W. V. (1991). *Literacy in the United States.* New Haven, CT: Yale University Press.

Kirkwood, G., & Kirkwood, C. (1989). *Living adult education: Freire in Scotland.* Philadelphia: Open University Press.

Kirsch, I., & Jungeblut, A. (1986). *Literacy: Profiles of America's young adults*. Final report of the National Assessment of Educational Progress. Princeton, NJ: Educational Testing Service.

Kirsch, I. S., Jungeblut, A., Jenkins, L., & Kolstad, A. (1993). *Adult literacy in America: A first look at the results of the National Adult Literacy Survey*. Washington, DC: National Center for Educational Statistics, U.S. Department of Education.

Knudson-Fields, B. (1989). A study of adult literacy service providers in the state of Idaho. *Dissertation Abstracts International, 49,* 10.

Kozol, J. (1985). *Illiterate America*. New York: Anchor/Doubleday.

Lankshear, C. (1993). Functional literacy from a Freirean point of view. In P. McLaren & P. Leonard (Eds.), *Paulo Freire: A critical encounter* (pp. 90–118). London: Routledge.

Leistyna, P., Woodrum, A., & Sherblom, S. A. (Eds.) (1996). *Breaking free: The transformative power of critical pedagogy*. Harvard Educational Review, Reprint Series No. 27. Cambridge, MA: Harvard Graduate School of Education.

Lerner, J. (1993). *Learning disabilities: Theories, diagnosis & teaching strategies* (6th ed.). Boston, MA: Houghton Mifflin.

Lipson, M. Y., & Wixson, K. K. (1991). *Assessment and instruction of reading disability: An interactive approach*. New York: HarperCollins.

McAfee Brown, R. (1984). *Unexpected news: Reading the Bible with third world eyes*. Philadelphia: Westminster Press.

McIntyre, E. (1996). Strategies and skills in whole language: An introduction to balanced teaching. In E. McIntyre & M. Pressley (Eds.), *Balanced instruction: Strategies and skills in whole language*. Norwood, MA: Christopher-Gordon.

McIntyre, E., & Pressley, M. (Eds.) (1996). *Balanced instruction: Strategies and skills in whole language* (pp. 1–20). Norwood, MA: Christopher-Gordon.

McLaren & Leonard (1993). *Paulo Freire: A critical encounter*. London: Routledge.

Meyer, D., Schvaneveldt, R., & Ruddy, M. (1979). Loci of contextual effects on visual word recognition. In P. M. A. Rabbit & S. Dornic (Eds.), *Attention and performance, Vol. 5* (pp. 98–117). New York: Academic Press.

Mezirow, J., Darkenwald, G. G., & Knox, A.B. (1975). *Last gamble on education*. Washington, DC: Adult Education Association.

Morrow, L. (1993). *Literacy development in the early years: Helping children read and write* (2nd ed.). Boston: Allyn & Bacon.

Murray, K. (with Barry, T.) (1995). *Inside El Salvador*. Albuquerque, NM: Resource Center Press.

National Center for the Study of Adult Learning and Literacy (NCSALL). (1996). *The national research and development center for improving adult learning and literacy: A proposal to the Office of Educational Research and Improvement*. (CFDA No. 84-309B). Cambridge, MA: Harvard University.

National Center on Adult Literacy. (1995, May). *Adult literacy: The next generation*. (NCAL Tech. Rep. No. 95-01). Philadelphia: University of Pennsylvania.

National Institute for Literacy. (1995). *National Literacy Grants Program, 1992–1993, Final Report*. Washington, DC: National Institute for Literacy.

Neisser, U. (1976). *Cognition and reality*. San Francisco: Freeman.

Neuman, S., & Roskos, K. (1993) Access to print for children of poverty: Differential effects of adult mediation and literacy-enriched play settings on environmental and functional print tasks. *American Educational Research Journal, 30,* 95–122.

Ogbu, J. (1974). *The next generation: An ethnography of education in an urban neighborhood.* New York: Academic Press.

Padak, N. D., Davidson, J. L., & Padak, G. M. (1994). Exploring reading with adult beginning readers. In M. C. Radencich (Ed.), *Adult literacy: A compendium of articles from the Journal of Reading* (pp. 56–60). Newark, DE: International Reading Association.

Padak, N. D., & Padak, G. M. (1994). What works: Adult literacy program evaluation. In M.C. Radencich (Ed.), *Adult literacy: A compendium of articles from the Journal of Reading* (pp. 86–93). Newark, DE: International Reading Association.

Peirce, C. S. (1998). *The essential Peirce: Selected philosophical writings, Vol. 2.* Bloomington, IN: Indiana University Press.

Pintrich, P. R., & Schrauben, B. (1992). Students' motivational beliefs and their cognitive engagement in classroom academic tasks. In D. H. Schunk & J. L. Meese (Eds.), *Student perceptions in the classroom* (pp. 149–184). Hillsdale, NJ: Lawrence Erlbaum Associates.

Purcell-Gates, V. (1988). Lexical and syntactic expectations held by well-read-to kindergartners and second graders. *Research in the Teaching of English, 22,* 128–160.

Purcell-Gates, V. (1995). *Other people's words: The cycle of low literacy.* Cambridge, MA: Harvard University Press.

Purcell-Gates, V. (1996a). Literacy practices of adult learners. In National Research and Development Center for Improving Adult Learning and Literacy, *A proposal to the Office of Educational Research and Improvement, CFDA No. 84-309B* (pp. 105–110). Cambridge, MA: Harvard University & World Education.

Purcell-Gates, V. (1996b). Process teaching with direct instruction and feedback in a university-based clinic. In E. McIntyre & M. Pressley (Eds.), *Balanced instruction: Strategies and skills in whole language* (pp. 107–127). Norwood, MA: Christopher-Gordon.

Purcell-Gates, V. (1996c). Stories, coupons, and the *TV Guide*: Relationships between home literacy experience and emergent literacy knowledge. *Reading Research Quarterly, 31,* 406–428.

Purcell-Gates, V., & Dahl, K. (1991). Low-SES children's success and failure at early literacy learning in skills-based classrooms. *JRB: A Journal of Literacy, 23,* 1–34.

Purcell-Gates, V., Degener, S., & Jacobson, E. (1998). *U.S. adult literacy program practice: A typology across dimensions of life-contextualized/decontextualized and dialogic/monologic* (NCSALL Reports No. 2). Boston: The National Center for the Study of Adult Learning and Literacy.

Quigley, B. A. (1987). *The resisters: An analysis of non-participation in adult basic education.* Unpublished doctoral dissertation, Northern Illinois University, DeKalb.

Recinos, A. H. (1993). *Sembramos La Semilla* [We Cultivate the Seed]. San Salvador, El Salvador: Alfalit.

Rosenblatt, L. M. (1989). Writing and reading: The transactional theory. In J. Mason (Ed.), *Reading and writing connections* (pp. 153–176). Boston: Allyn & Bacon.

Shraw, G., Bruning, R., & Svoboda, C. (1995). Sources of situational interest. *Journal of Reading Behavior, 27,* 1–17.

Shaull, F. (1993) Foreword. In Freire, P., *Pedagogy of the oppressed* (pp.11–16). New York: Continuum.

Shor, I. (1993). Education is politics: Paulo Freire's critical pedagogy. In P. McLaren & P. Leonard (Eds.), *Paulo Freire: A critical encounter* (pp. 25–35). New York: Routledge.

Sobrino, J. (1988). *Spirituality of liberation.* Maryknoll, NY: Orbis Books.

Spradley, J. P., & McMurdy, D. W. (Eds). (1972). *The cultural experience: Ethnography in Complex Society.* Chicago: Science Research Association.

Stanovich, K. E., & Cunningham, A. E. (1991). Studying the consequences of literacy within a literate society: The cognitive correlates of print exposure. *Memory & Cognition, 20,* 51–68.

Stanovich, K. F., & West, R. (1979). Mechanisms of sentence context effects in reading: Automatic activation and conscious attention. *Memory & Cognition, 7,* 77–85.

Steele, H. (1989). Illiteracy then and now: North Carolina and Wake County, 1900–1980. *Dissertation Abstracts International, 49, 7.*

Sticht, T. (1988). Adult literacy education. *Review of Research in Education, 15,* 59–96.

Street, B. (1984). *Literacy in theory and practice.* Cambridge: Cambridge University Press.

Sticht, T. (1990). *Testing and assessment in adult basic education and English as a second language programs.* San Diego, CA: Applied Behavioral & Cognitive Sciences. (ED 317–867).

Taylor, D. (1983). *Family literacy: Young children learning to read and write.* Portsmouth, NH: Heinemann.

Taylor, D., & Dorsey-Gaines, C. (1988). *Growing up literate: Learning from inner-city families.* Portsmouth, NH: Heinemann.

Teale, W., & Sulzby, E. (1986). *Emergent literacy: Writing and reading.* Norwood, NJ: Ablex.

Todorov, T. (1984). *Mikhail Bakhtin: The dialogical principle.* Minneapolis, MN: University of Minnesota Press.

UNESCO. (1997). *UNESCO Statistical Yearbook 1997.* Paris: UNESCO.

Venezky, R. L., & Wagner, D. A. (1994). *Supply and demand for literacy instruction in the United States.* NCAL Report TR94-10. Philadelphia: University of Pennsylvania, National Center on Adult Literacy.

Wagner, D. A. (1992). *Literacy: Developing the future.* International Yearbook of Education, Vol. XLIII-1991. Paris: UNESCO.

Werner, D. (1992). *Where there is no doctor,* 226. Palo Alto, CA: Herperian Foundation.

Wigfield, A., & Eccles, J. S. (1992). The development of achievement task values: A theoretical analysis. *Developmental Review, 12,* 265–310.

Wigfield, A., & Guthrie, J. T. (1995). *Dimensions of children's motivations for reading: An initial study* (Reading Research Report No. 34). Athens, GA: National Reading Research Center.

Zachariadis, C. P. (1986). *Adult literacy: A study of community-based literacy programs* (Vol. 1, study findings and recommendations). Washington, DC: Association for Community Based Education.

Author Index

Subject Index

Note: Page numbers in *italic* refer to photographs or illustrations. Members of Papaturro community are indexed by first names.